Arab Women's Activism and Socio-Political Transformation

"This is a much-needed scholarly contribution to the literature on Arab women, activism and feminism. The outstanding collection of chapters critically addresses what contemporary transformations and activism mean for women's lived realities, identities and ongoing struggles, complicating assumptions about gender roles and gendered identities and offering a nuanced approach to addressing Arab feminism(s) as a dynamic ongoing phenomenon. Its meticulous scholarship and breadth make it invaluable to students and scholars interested in issues of media, gender, activism and feminism in the region."
—Dr. Dina Matar, *SOAS, UK*

"This collection of essays is a must-read for students and academics analyzing gender issues in the aftermath of the Arab Spring. The contributions, penned by experts on the Arab region, provide an invaluable insight into the impact of the social revolution, as manifested in different Arab countries, which paralleled the political uprisings since 2011. The book includes a wealth of empirically rich cases that can guide future investigations of gendered activism in the Arab world and beyond."
—Professor Noha Mellor, *University of Bedfordshire, UK*

"The essays contained in this edited volume document and confirm the constant acts of heroism of Arab women, as they actively contribute to contemporary social and political movements in the Arab region. The volume's contributors present original research on female engagement with multiple forms of activism, therefore challenging and disavowing Western stereotypical notions of Arab women's disempowerment. The volume's essays also offer commentary on the important shifts in how Arab women articulate and perform their subjectivities as agents of change in our globalized era. This volume is a must-read for scholars and students interested in the evolving transitions taking place in the Arab world with respect to women's empowerment."
—Professor Valérie K. Orlando, *University of Maryland, USA*

Sahar Khamis • Amel Mili
Editors

Arab Women's Activism and Socio-Political Transformation

Unfinished Gendered Revolutions

palgrave
macmillan

Editors
Sahar Khamis
University of Maryland
College Park, Maryland, USA

Amel Mili
University of Pennsylvania
Philadelphia, Pennsylvania, USA

ISBN 978-3-319-60734-4   ISBN 978-3-319-60735-1 (eBook)
DOI 10.1007/978-3-319-60735-1

Library of Congress Control Number: 2017960199

© The Editor(s) (if applicable) and The Author(s) 2018
This work is subject to copyright. All rights are solely and exclusively licensed by the Publisher, whether the whole or part of the material is concerned, specifically the rights of translation, reprinting, reuse of illustrations, recitation, broadcasting, reproduction on microfilms or in any other physical way, and transmission or information storage and retrieval, electronic adaptation, computer software, or by similar or dissimilar methodology now known or hereafter developed.
The use of general descriptive names, registered names, trademarks, service marks, etc. in this publication does not imply, even in the absence of a specific statement, that such names are exempt from the relevant protective laws and regulations and therefore free for general use.
The publisher, the authors and the editors are safe to assume that the advice and information in this book are believed to be true and accurate at the date of publication. Neither the publisher nor the authors or the editors give a warranty, express or implied, with respect to the material contained herein or for any errors or omissions that may have been made. The publisher remains neutral with regard to jurisdictional claims in published maps and institutional affiliations.

Cover illustration: Andrey Nekrasov / Alamy Stock Photo

Printed on acid-free paper

This Palgrave Macmillan imprint is published by Springer Nature
The registered company is Springer International Publishing AG
The registered company address is: Gewerbestrasse 11, 6330 Cham, Switzerland

*To ALL the strong and brave Arab women who are STILL fighting
for their rights
To the strong women in my life: My mom, Dawlat, and my sisters
Samah, Eman, and Heba
Sahar Khamis*

*To my beloved Serena, Farah, and Noor
Amel Mili*

Preface: Why This Book?

For a long time, stereotypical images of Arab women have captured the imagination of global audiences across different genres, such as classical literature, drama, movies, and soap operas. However, many of these images, as depicted in most colonialist, orientalist representations, were far from flattering because they mostly confined Arab women to the realm of either domestication or sexuality. In other words, they projected an image of either a mostly subdued, oppressed, and helpless Arab woman who is confined to the domestic sphere, subjected to male domination, and victimized by societal repression and cultural discrimination, or a highly sexualized Arab woman who is confined to the harem, as strictly an object of male pleasure, or is simply shown as an exotic, oriental figure, such as a belly dancer.

In every case, we can argue that these faulty (mis)representations and distorted stereotypical images subjected Arab women to multiple layers of invisibility, whether in real life, through mediated images, or in academic literature (Khamis 2004), which subsequently obscured their complex, rich, and diverse realities as professionals, leaders, activists, or even rebels.

This volume is a serious attempt to cut through these multiple layers of invisibility which have clouded Arab women's multiple realities, identities, images, and struggles for many decades by enabling their genuine, alternative voices to be heard, and their authentic, alternative stories to be told, either through their own words, as in the case of some of the empirically based case studies, or by theoretically analyzing their lived realities and unpacking the complex cultural, social, political, and legal aspects underlying them. This is especially important since "women have historically been underrepresented in the public sphere, where male voices and perspectives dominated" (Radsch and Khamis 2013, p. 881).

To achieve its goal, this volume includes the work of an array of scholars from different disciplines, and from both inside and outside the Arab region, to reflect on the meanings, manifestations, and implications of the ongoing political, social, and legal realities and transitions in the Arab region in the realm of gender equity. The purpose is to understand the broader and shifting context in which women's rights are articulated and negotiated within their specific localities and through their multifaceted realities.

Specifically, we attempt to explore the intertwined evolutions of gendered struggles and sociopolitical transformations in Arab countries before, during, and after the democratic transitions known as the Arab Spring movements, in the political, social, and legal domains simultaneously.

In doing so, we avoid faulty assumptions of causality between gendered activisms and resistances, on the one hand, and the shift towards sociopolitical transformation and democratic reform, on the other hand. In other words, we do not naively assume that one is directly caused by the other, or that one necessarily leads to the other. Rather, we deal with both phenomena and depict them as simply correlated and associated with each other, with a possible "catalyzing" effect whereby each could possibly boost and speed up the other rather than create it. In other words, we agree with Verta Taylor (1999) that the relationship between gender activism and social activism is bidirectional in the sense that gender agendas affect the course of social movements and that social movements affect the social definition of gender relations. We contend that this bidirectional relationship is therefore cyclical, ongoing, and dynamic, rather than linear, straightforward, and static.

Similarly, we do not assume a straightforward, direct relationship between causality and the phenomenon of "cyberactivism" (Howard 2011) whereby new media tools and technologies are deployed to enact sociopolitical change, which is difficult to achieve offline, and the shift towards democratization and sociopolitical transformation. Here again, we deal with this phenomenon as a possible "catalyst," which can aid in triggering and speeding up mass mobilization and giving the initial impetus to get the ball of sociopolitical activism rolling, rather than a be-all and end-all "magical tool" which is capable of bringing transformation all by itself.

The theoretical and empirical investigation of these complex phenomena in this volume extends temporally across different historical phases, specifically before, during, and after the so-called Arab Spring or Arab Awakening movements, and extends spatially across different Arab countries, including countries which witnessed the Arab Spring uprisings, such as Egypt, Tunisia, and Bahrain, and those that were not part of this particular wave of uprisings but continue to have their own set of gendered struggles, albeit in different forms and with varying degrees, such as Lebanon, Morocco, and Saudi Arabia.

Although the scope of this book extends temporally before, during, and after the Arab Spring uprisings, and it extends spatially to cover both countries which were part of this wave of upheaval and those which were not, it still pays special attention to the Arab Spring as a particularly important turning point in contemporary Arab history, and as a central, focal point which had numerous implications for Arab women's ongoing political, social, and legal struggles, which are equally acknowledged and addressed in this volume.

This is especially important for the purpose of this book, since one of the most shining aspects that sparkled and glowed in this wave of revolt, which took the whole world by surprise and turned its attention to this vibrant and dynamic region, was Arab women's heroism, activism, leadership, and resistance (Al-Malki et al. 2012; Heideman and Youssef 2012; Khamis 2011, 2013; Radsch 2011, 2012; Radsch and Khamis 2013). Here it is worth noting that this leadership and activism, which took many forms and expressed itself in numerous ways, was not exclusively confined to the political domain; rather, it extended to create the necessary link between the political, social, and legal domains simultaneously.

In other words, we can argue that although Arab women fought alongside men to overcome dictatorship and autocracy, "unlike men, women face two battles: the first for political change and the second to obtain a real change of their societal status to become fully equal to their male counterparts" (Heideman and Youssef 2012, p. 14). Needless to say, the fight for gender equality cuts across the legal realm of seeking constitutional reform; the social realm of overcoming negative cultural practices, stagnant mindsets, and obsolete traditions; and the political realm of seeking representation and fighting against dictatorship and authoritarianism.

In analyzing the effects and implications of the Arab Spring movements on Arab women's activisms and resistances, as well as their gendered gains, we are well aware of not just the potentials and opportunities which have been made possible for Arab women, but also some of the challenges, limitations, and setbacks as well. For example, while the removal of authoritarian rulers may have initially improved satisfaction with public institutions or decreased perceived corruption, for some Arab women the uprisings may have resulted in greater perceived or reported crime, including rape, sexual assault, and other forms of violence, deeper material hardships, or even a regression in their political and/or legal gains (Salem 2015; Dawoud 2012).

In recognition of these potentials and opportunities, as well as these constraints and backlashes, this book complicates the concepts of multiple gendered identities, resistances, and struggles as they take different forms and exist through various sites if resistance. In fleshing out these multiple sites of resistance and struggle, we acknowledge that they do not just exist in the physical world, or in physical spaces, such as Tahrir Square in Egypt or Pearl Square in Bahrain. Rather, we recognize that these sites could be metaphorical, as in the case of drafting new laws and constitutions to fight gender inequity; or virtual, as in the case of deploying new tools of communication, such as social media to aid women in their political struggles, as in the case of young women activists in Bahrain who used it in their struggle against the regime in power, or to aid them in their social struggles, as in the case of young women activists in Egypt, who used their activism on social media to fight epidemic sexual harassment in the streets of Cairo.

Moreover, we acknowledge how a woman's body could oftentimes be perceived as a site of resistance and struggle, as in the case of women who fell victim to rape or other sexual violence in the context of the ongoing political conflicts in the region, or those who were subjected to severe invasions of their bodies and their privacy, as in the case of virginity testing, which was conducted on young women activists in Tahrir Square in Egypt after the 2011 revolution, for example.

In every case, we remain loyal to the diversity, fluidity, dynamism, and complexity of Arab women's gendered struggles, and the multiple physical, metaphorical, and virtual sites of resistance through which they reveal themselves, across different countries, contexts, phases, and domains. In unpacking these significant and intertwined issues, the valuable intellectual contributions in this volume cut across both theoretical and empirical terrains. We can, indeed, argue that "The interactions in the real world between intellectual work and gender activism are reproduced in this volume via the textual interactions between scholarly and activist discourses" (Khalil 2014, p. 132).

The main theoretical underpinning on which this book rests is the exploration and investigation of the complex notion of gender, as it reveals itself through the equally complex phenomena of gendered activism(s) and gendered resistance(s), which exhibit themselves in multiple forms and across different contexts, platforms, settings, and nations within the Arab world. We argue that the complexity of gendered identities and resistances defies categorization or fixation because it constantly evolves and reveals itself in a dynamic, cyclical, and ongoing process, across different spatial, temporal, and historical contexts, and with serious political, legal, and social manifestations and implications.

In exploring the complex notions of gendered identities and resistances in this volume, we move away from a monolithic, uniform, or fixed notion of feminism as a narrowly defined concept from a purely Western, Eurocentric and ethnocentric perspective to a more robust, comprehensive, and diverse conceptualization of multiple feminism(s), activism(s), and resistance(s), which can only be fully grasped and genuinely appreciated when contextualized within their respective historical, social, political, and legal contexts.

Here it is worth noting that while some scholars have introduced the concept of "Islamic feminism" (Khamis 2010) as a viable alternative to Western feminism, we argue here for a unique and distinct concept of "Arab feminism(s)," which uniquely distinguishes itself from both the commonly held notion of "Western Feminism" and its alternative newly introduced notion of "Islamic feminism" as it cuts across broader categories of women, including those with secular and liberal, as well as religious and conservative, affiliations and orientations.

We argue that this phenomenon of Arab feminism(s), which evolved over subsequent historical phases and through different political, social, and legal contexts, is still very much an ongoing phenomenon in the making rather than a completed effort or a finalized mission. This volume illustrates how this complex phenomenon continues to evolve dynamically and to take different shapes, forms, and meanings at the hands of women activists, who share the common national identity of being "Arab" and the common gendered identity of being "women," but who still exhibit distinct differences because they come from different countries; cut across the categories of being secular or religious; use multiple resistance tools and techniques, whether on the ground, online, or both; and focus on political, social, or legal issues, or all three simultaneously.

In attempting to understand the evolution of Arab women's gendered activisms and resistances across different phases, ranging from nationalist discourses to top-down state feminism, and finally bottom-up grassroots movements, we claim that Arab women's multifaceted roles and realities, as initiators and active agents of change, have to be fully appreciated and respected in their totality, and with all their complexities and variations, across the legal, social, and political domains which are tackled in this book. We also argue that they cannot be fully grasped or totally appreciated except when accurately contextualized within their unique historical, political, and social contexts.

In revisiting the concept of gendered activisms and resistances, and their evolution in this volume, an array of topics are covered, ranging from the so-called "Jasmine revolution" in Tunisia, the so-called "Cedar revolution" in Lebanon, and women's rights in Saudi Arabia, and we revisit gender gains in some post-Arab Spring countries, including Egypt.

The other topics include the role of "cyberactivism" (Howard 2011), and more specifically "cyberfeminism," which is defined as "the innovative ways women are using digital technologies to reengineer their lives" (Daniels 2009, p. 103) to raise awareness of women's issues and to overcome the challenges confronting them (Daniels 2009; Fernandez et al. 2003; Gajjala 2003; Khamis 2013), whether in terms of achieving political goals in some Arab countries, such as Bahrain, or in terms of achieving social goals, such as fighting sexual harassment in Egypt.

Another topic is the continuous effort to achieve gender equity through constitutional reform in a number of Arab countries, such as Egypt, Tunisia, and Morocco, and the various victories and shortcomings in this regard.

This multifaceted sociopolitical struggle asserts these women's position as members of a "subaltern counterpublic" (Fraser 1992) who are forming their own "resistance communities" in political and social domains, both online and offline. By doing so, they are establishing the missing link between private spheres, (traditionally (mis)perceived as the feminine domain) and public spheres (traditionally (mis)perceived as the masculine domain) by increasing the visibility of women's issues and cultivating support for them in the reordering of their transitioning societies (Khamis 2013).

In covering these topics, it is fair to say that "The scope of the contributions ranges from theoretical considerations on how the female body has been a site of governmental and state power to more empirical case studies of the struggles for gender-sensitive legislation waged in the transitional period" (Khalil 2014, p. 132). We believe strongly that it is only through this unique combination of theoretical insight and empirical evidence that the complexity and nuance of the topics tackled in this volume can be unpacked and captured.

By providing this panoramic view of a wide umbrella of gendered activisms, ranging from calling for constitutional rights and legal reform as a way of reshaping the cultural understanding of the concept of gender and securing significant gains for Arab women, to the deployment of new tools of communication to fight autocratic regimes, stagnant cultural norms, obsolete traditions, and sexual harassment, this intellectual effort contributes to shattering many of the long-held myths about Arab women, by unpacking their complex identities, multifaceted realities, ongoing struggles, and unfinished revolutions.

University of Maryland, College Park, MD, USA Sahar Khamis
University of Pennsylvania, Philadelphia, PA, USA Amel Mili

BIBLIOGRAPHY

Al-Malki, A., D. Kaufner, S. Ishizaki, and K. Dreher. 2012. *Arab Women in Arab News: Old Stereotypes and New Media*. Doha: Bloomsbury Qatar Foundation Publishing.
Daniels, J. 2009. Rethinking Cyberfeminism(s): Race, Gender and Embodiment. *Women's Studies Quarterly* 37 (1–2): 101–124.
Dawoud, A. 2012. Why Women are Losing Rights in Post-Revolutionary Egypt. *Journal of International Women's Studies* 13 (5): 160–169.
Fernandez, M., F. Wilding, and M. Wright. eds. 2003. *Domain Errors! Cyberfeminist Practices*. Brooklyn: Autonomedia.
Fraser, N. 1992. Rethinking the Public Sphere. In *Habermas and the Public Sphere*, ed. C. Calhoun, 109–142. Cambridge, MA: MIT Press.
Gajjala, R. 2003. South Asian Digital Diasporas and Cyberfeminist Webs: Negotiating Globalization, Nation, Gender, and Information Technology Design. *Contemporary South Asia* 12(1):41–56.
Heideman, K., and M. Youssef. eds. 2012. *Reflections on Women in the Arab Spring*. Washington, DC: Women's Voices from Around the World, Woodrow Wilson International Center for Scholars.
Howard, P.N. 2011. *The Digital Origins of Dictatorship and Democracy: Information Technology and Political Islam* New York: Oxford University Press.
Khalil, A. 2014. Gender Paradoxes of the Arab Spring. *The Journal of North African Studies*, 19 (2): 131–136.

Khamis, S. 2004. Multiple Literacies, Multiple Identities: Egyptian Rural Women's Readings of Televised Literacy Campaigns. In *Women and Media in the Middle East: Power Through Self Expression*, ed. N. Sakr, 89–108. London: I. B. Tauris.

———. 2010. Islamic Feminism in New Arab Media: Platforms for Self-Expression and Sites for Multiple Resistances. *Journal of Arab and Muslim Media Research*, 3 (3): 237–255.

———. 2011. The Arab "Feminist" Spring? *Feminist Studies*, 37 (3): 692–695.

———. 2013. Gendering the Arab Spring: Arab Women Journalists/Activists, 'Cyberfeminism,' and the Socio-political Revolution. In *The Routledge Companion to Media and Gender*, ed. C. Carter, L. Steiner, and L. McLaughlin, 565–575. London: Routledge.

Radsch, C. 2011. Re-Imagining Cleopatra: Gendering Cyberactivism in Egypt. Paper Presented at the Middle East Studies Association (MESA) Annual Conference, Washington DC, Dec. 1–4, 2011.

———. 2012. Unveiling the Revolutionaries: Cyberactivism and the Role of Women in the Arab Uprisings. James A. Baker III Institute for Public Policy of Rice University. http://bakerinstitute.org/publications/ITP-pub-CyberactivismAndWomen-051712.pdf

Radsch, C.C., and S. Khamis. 2013. In Their Own Voice: Technologically Mediated Empowerment and Transformation Among Young Arab Women. *Feminist Media Studies*, 13 (5): 881–890.

Salem, R. 2015. Gendering the Costs and Benefits of the Arab Uprisings in Tunisia and Egypt Using the Gallup Surveys, Working Paper 913, May 2015. Giza: The Economic Research Forum (ERF).

Taylor, V. 1999. Gender and Social Movements: Gender Processes in Women's Self Help Movements. *Gender and Society*, 13 (1): 8–33, Special Issue: Gender and Social Movements, Part 2.

ACKNOWLEDGMENTS

Every production process of a book is a journey. We would like to thank the different partners who accompanied us along this long, exciting, and rewarding journey, without whom this book would not have been possible. First and foremost, we would like to express our most sincere appreciation to the unique, special, and diverse pool of contributors to this volume for their valuable intellectual contributions and rich, insightful perspectives that made this volume what it is. We especially would like to thank them for their patience and support, when the book's journey witnessed unexpected turns and unanticipated detours. We would also like to thank the expert pool of reviewers who anonymously reviewed our volume and gave us valuable feedback and productive comments, which helped improve the final outcome. We highly appreciate the excellent endorsements this volume received from a number of distinguished scholars, namely Prof. Hamid Dabashi, Columbia University; Prof. Dina Matar, School of Oriental and African Studies (SOAS), University of London; Prof. Valerie Orlando, University of Maryland, College Park; and Prof. Noha Mellor, University of Bedfordshire. We would like to express genuine gratitude to the Palgrave Macmillan editorial team for their tireless help, especially Ms. Ambra Finotello and Ms. Imogen Gordon Clark for their continuous support, accommodation, and professionalism. We are very thankful to the production staff of Palgrave Macmillan/Springer Nature for their excellent professional services, especially Mr. Srinivasan Boopathi, who exhibited maximum reliability and efficiency during the final production stages of this book. Thanks are due to Ms. Grace Jubert, teaching assistant in the Department of Communication at the University of Maryland, College Park, for her help in compiling the book's index. Last, but certainly not least, we are highly indebted to our families for all their unconditional love and support, and, most importantly, for believing in us and in our mission.

Sahar Khamis and Amel Mili, July 2017

Contents

1 Introductory Themes 1
Sahar Khamis and Amel Mili

Part 1 Unfinished Political Revolutions 25

2 Citizenship and Gender Equality in the Cradle of the Arab Spring 27
Amel Mili

3 Voices Shouting for Reform: The Remaining Battles for Bahraini Women 53
Nada Alwadi and Sahar Khamis

4 Lebanese Women's Rights Beyond the Cedar Revolution 73
Rita Stephan

5 Women's Space After the Arab Spring: Can We Generalize? 89
Deborah Harrold

Part 2 Unfinished Social Revolutions — 109

6 Religious Discourses and Gender Dynamics: Reflections on the Arab Spring — 111
Asma Nouira

7 "I Am Untouchable!" Egyptian Women's War Against Sexual Harassment — 131
Nahed Eltantawy

8 Stealth Revolution: Saudi Women's Ongoing Social Battles — 149
Namie Tsujigami

9 Social Media, Social Learning Systems, and the Women's Movement in Tunisia After the Jasmine Revolution — 167
Sana Jelassi

Part 3 Unfinished Legal Revolutions — 195

10 Gendering the Law in Egypt: A Tale of Two Constitutions — 197
Lubna Fröhlich (Azzam)

11 From Lalla Batoul to Oum Hamza: New Trends in Moroccan Women's Fight for Citizenship — 219
Brahim El Guabli

12 Concluding Remarks: What's Next? — 241
Sahar Khamis and Amel Mili

Index — 253

Notes on Contributors

Nada Alwadi is a journalist, writer, and researcher. She works as an Assignment Editor in the Digital Department at the Middle East Broadcasting Networks in Washington DC. In her current position, Alwadi is working on a project directed at countering terrorism through social and digital media. She is a Ph.D. candidate in public policy at Virginia Tech University. Alwadi has been working as a journalist, covering politics and human rights issues in her native country, Bahrain, and in the Middle East, since 2003. She worked with a number of reputable media organizations, including *USA Today* in Bahrain. Some of her writings appeared in *The New York Times* and *Open Democracy*. She holds a master's degree in Mass Communication with an emphasis on women's political empowerment in the media. She was a Humphrey/Fulbright Fellow at the Philip Merrill School of Journalism at the University of Maryland, College Park. She was one of the recipients of the first James Lawson Award for Nonviolent Achievement by the International Center on Nonviolent Conflict in 2011.

Brahim El Guabli is a Ph.D. candidate in the Department of Comparative Literature at Princeton University. El Guabli's dissertation titled "The Minor Re-writes the Nation: Memory of Loss, Archives, Historiography and State Cooptation in Morocco" investigates literature's engagement with the traumatic legacies of the "years of lead" in Morocco (1956–1999). Using a comparative approach, El Guabli places questions of loss, agency, citizenship, and history at the center of trauma narratives, as they pertain to the situation in Morocco, and the predominantly Arabic-speaking area.

El Guabli's work has appeared in *The Arab Studies Journal*, *The Journal of North African Studies*, *Francosphères*, and *Jadaliyya*. He is the co-editor of the forthcoming two-volume special issue of *The Journal of North African Studies* titled "Violence and the Politics of Aesthetics: A Postcolonial Maghreb Without Borders." El Guabli is the recipient of a 2017–2018 Laurance S. Rockefeller Graduate Prize Fellowship at the Princeton University Center for Human Values.

Nahed Eltantawy is Associate Professor of Journalism and Women & Gender Studies, and Chair of the Journalism and Sport Communication Department at High Point University's Nido R. Qubein School of Communication. Her research focuses on women and gender studies, media representation, social media activism, and critical and cultural studies. Her work has been published in various books and peer-reviewed journals, including *Feminist Media Studies*, *International Journal of Communication*, and *Communication and Critical/Cultural Studies*. Eltantawy presented her research at various national and international academic conferences and conventions. She has also been an invited conference speaker at various universities, including the Columbia Journalism School in New York, the University of Toronto, and the University of Southern California Annenberg School for Communication and Journalism.

Lubna Fröhlich (Azzam) is a political consultant currently residing in Berlin. She completed her college education with an undergraduate Master's/Diploma in Political Science at the Free University in Berlin. She worked overseas in many countries, including Senegal, Mali, Egypt, and several European countries. She was a research fellow at the German Institute for International and Security Affairs in Berlin (SWP). She was also a fellow at the Hanns-Seidel-Foundation between 2012 and 2016. Her primary research focus is women's legal rights and their codification.

Deborah Harrold is a senior lecturer in the Department of Political Science and the Liberal and Professional Studies program at the University of Pennsylvania. She is a political scientist specializing in the comparative politics of the Middle East and North Africa. Her research and teaching interests include economic policy and history, cultures of economics, comparative democratic processes and democratic thought, issues of gender and women's rights, and Islamic politics. Her research tackles the intersection of economics, culture, and politics, including publications on the informal economy, economic discourse, and business interest articulation in Algerian politics. She holds a Ph.D. in Political Science from the University of Chicago.

Sana Jelassi is the Head of the Gender Section in the Protection Division in UNRWA (United Nations Relief and Works Agency). She worked for 20 years in the area of gender equality and development management, especially in postconflict settings and protracted crises zones in the Middle East and North Africa (MENA) region. She holds a Medical Doctorate with a specialization in Psychiatry, a Master of Science in Development Management, as well as a master's degree in Systems Thinking.

Sahar Khamis is Associate Professor of Communication and Affiliate Professor of Women's Studies at the University of Maryland, College Park. She is an expert on Arab and Muslim media, and the former Head of the Mass Communication and Information Science Department at Qatar University. Khamis holds a Ph.D. in Mass Media and Cultural Studies from the University of Manchester, England. She is a former Mellon Islamic Studies Initiative Visiting Professor at the University of Chicago. She is the co-author of the books: *Islam Dot Com: Contemporary Islamic Discourses in Cyberspace* (Palgrave Macmillan, 2009) and *Egyptian Revolution 2.0: Political Blogging, Civic Engagement, and Citizen Journalism* (Palgrave Macmillan, 2013). She is the recipient of a number of prestigious academic and professional awards, and a member on the editorial board of many renowned academic journals. Khamis is a media commentator and analyst, a public speaker, a human rights commissioner, and a radio host.

Amel Mili served as the director of the Arabic Language and Culture Program at the Lauder Institute for International Studies, University of Pennsylvania, from January 2010 till May 2017. She is joining the Department of Global Studies and Modern Languages at Drexel University as a faculty member, starting in fall 2017. She holds a master's and a Ph.D. in Global Affairs/Political Science from Rutgers University, Newark. She also holds a JD in Private Law from the Law School of Tunis and a master's in Public Administration from the University of Tunis. Mili served as a Magistrate in the Administrative Tribunal of Tunisia, between 1991 and 2009. Her research interests include the intersection between religion and law; gender politics; constitutional transitions during the Arab Spring; and language education. Her professional and personal interests include advocating for gender equality, protecting minorities' rights, and promoting social justice.

Asma Nouira is an associate professor at the University of Law & Political Sciences of Tunis in Tunisia, since 2011. She is a member of the scientific council of the Center for Maghrib Studies in Tunis. She received her master's in Law from the Law School of Tunis in 2000 and her doctorate in Political Science in 2008. She was a visiting professor, teaching on the topic of Islam and human rights at the University of Bologna from 2009 till 2010. Nouira received numerous grants and fellowships, including a research grant from the Arab Research Support Program of the Arab Reform Initiative in 2014. Nouira's research focuses on state and religion, history of Islamic institutions, Islamic law, religious dialog, democratization, human rights, and secularization. She was a fellow at the Käte Hamburger Center for Advanced Study in the Humanities in 2014.

Rita Stephan is a research fellow at the Moise A. Khayrallah Center for Lebanese Diaspora Studies at North Carolina State University and the Director of the Middle East Partnership Initiative (MEPI) at the United States Department of State. She previously served as an analyst at the United States Census Bureau; a visiting researcher at the Center for Contemporary Arab Studies at Georgetown University; and a research associate at the Lebanese Emigration Research Center at University of Notre Dame in Lebanon. She received her Ph.D. in Sociology from the University of Texas at Austin with a Portfolio in Women's and Gender Studies. Her dissertation titled "The Family and the Making of Women's Rights Activism in Lebanon" earned her a P.E.O. Scholar Award and an American Association of University Women's Dissertation Fellowship. Her publications focus on the Lebanese women's movement, social movements, social networks, and Arab-Americans.

Namie Tsujigami is a project associate professor at the Centre for Middle Eastern Studies at the University of Tokyo (UTCMES) and a professor with the Sultan Qaboos Chair in Middle Eastern Studies. As a visiting researcher at the King Faisal Centre for Research and Islamic Studies since 2005, she conducted fieldwork research on women's movements, networks, agency, and transnational migration in Saudi Arabia. Among her publications is a book on Saudi Arabia titled *Gender and Power in Contemporary Saudi Arabia: A Discourse Analysis from the Perspective of Foucauldian Theory of Power* (2011, in Japanese). This book received a Grant-in-Aid for Scientific Research (KAKENHI), an award provided to creative and pioneering research. She also authored the book *Gender Order in the Muslim World: Women's Struggle after the "Arab Spring"* (2014, in Japanese).

ABOUT THE EDITORS

Sahar Khamis is an associate professor in the Department of Communication at the University of Maryland, USA. She is an expert on Arab and Muslim media, and the former head of the Mass Communication and Information Science Department at Qatar University. She is the co-author (with Mohammed el-Nawawy) of two books *Islam Dot Com: Contemporary Islamic Discourses in Cyberspace* (2009) and *Egyptian Revolution 2.0: Political Blogging, Civic Engagement and Citizen Journalism* (2013).

Amel Mili is the director of the Arabic Language and Culture Program at the Lauder Institute, University of Pennsylvania, USA. She holds a JD degree in private law and an MS degree in public administration from the University of Tunis, Tunisia, as well as a PhD degree in global affairs from Rutgers University in Newark, USA.

LIST OF FIGURES

Fig. 7.1	A screenshot of the map from HarassMap	136
Fig. 7.2	HarassMap shopping bags campaign	138
Fig. 7.3	"The Circle of Hell" graffiti	141
Fig. 7.4	"No to harassment" graffiti	142
Fig. 7.5	Queen Nefertiti graffiti	143
Fig. 8.1	Hacked website of http://www.oct26driving.com	156

LIST OF TABLES

Table 2.1	Female Participation in State Institutions, 2008	36
Table 2.2	Results of the Elections of the Constitutional Assembly, October 23, 2011	38
Table 2.3	Women Participation in Political and Economic Life, 2010	43
Table 2.4	Women Participation in Mass Media	44
Table 9.1	Community dimensions	179
Table 9.2	Boundary dimensions	180
Table 9.3	Identity dimensions	181

CHAPTER 1

Introductory Themes

Sahar Khamis and Amel Mili

1.1 The Parallel Political, Social, and Legal Struggles

When in December 2010 a street vendor from a small town in central Tunisia self-immolated in a desperate act of protest against both economic deprivation and the humiliation resulting from mistreatment by the police and local authorities, he unwittingly opened the floodgates of longstanding discontent and frustration at the regime of president Ben Ali, and inspired citizens across the region to stand up against their respective regimes, long perceived to be corrupt, incompetent, and illegitimate. The impact of the tweeted image of this young man setting himself on fire was so profound that it prompted some observers to claim that the flames metaphorically ignited a wildfire that engulfed the entire Arab region.

Following the example of Tunisians, citizens across the region conquered their fears, raised their voices, and felt empowered to stand up and challenge the authority of their tyrannical regimes, demanding political and social reforms. These sweeping regional uprisings came to be known as the "Arab Spring" or the "Arab Awakening." While different Arab

---

S. Khamis (✉)
University of Maryland, College Park, MD, USA

A. Mili
University of Pennsylvania, Philadelphia, PA, USA

© The Author(s) 2018
S. Khamis, A. Mili (eds.), *Arab Women's Activism and Socio-Political Transformation*, DOI 10.1007/978-3-319-60735-1_1

countries embarked on different journeys in their political transitions, all have experienced a level of public debate that was unprecedented, in both substance and boldness. In many of these countries, political parties and civil society organizations argued in favor of drafting and enacting new constitutions in an attempt to break away from the past, and to ensure that it never returns.

Very early on, gender issues took center stage in the sociopolitical transformations and debates that arose in the context of the Arab Spring uprisings. There are several reasons for the emergence of gender issues at the heart of these sociopolitical transitions and struggles in the Arab world.

One important reason for the prominence of gender issues is the fact that women played an important and prominent role in political transitions in the so-called Arab Spring countries. Women of all ages, socioeconomic backgrounds, religious orientations, and political ideologies emerged as prominent figures in the midst of these uprisings, carving new places for themselves, even in some of the most traditional, conservative communities, as heroines, public opinion leaders, and role models, for both men and women to look up to and emulate. Many of them took to the streets, side by side with men, facing the dangers of being killed, arrested, or harassed, with amazing bravery and unmatched courage. And many of them resorted to new media tools, such as social media applications, to advance their struggles and support their causes (Al-Malki et al. 2012; Heideman and Youssef 2012; Khamis 2011, 2013; Radsch 2011, 2012; Radsch and Khamis 2013).

Through engaging in these multiple forms of struggle, Arab women were, in fact, contesting and redefining new gendered spaces, politically, legally, and socially, which involved risk-taking and the exercise of agency, despite all forms of intimidation and in the face of many constraints. Images and records of the Arab Spring not only confirm the ubiquitous presence of women alongside men in virtually all stages of the uprisings but also attest to their visible and prominent leadership roles. Many women have been seen at the forefront of protests and marches, while others were caught on camera, defying army soldiers, and pushing through riot police and barricades.

These acts of heroism, on the one hand, confirm the historical continuity of Arab women's struggles, through both social and political movements, while, on the other hand, they signal important shifts in how Arab women articulate and perform their subjectivities as agents of change. This is especially true since, in engaging in these forms of struggle, Arab women were not just confining themselves to stereotypical gender roles, such as nurturing or supporting men in their struggle for freedom; rather, they assumed non-stereotypical gender roles by being in the front lines of resistance, risking their own lives, and exposing themselves to the dangers of arrest or assault. Therefore we can confidently say that the Arab Spring unveiled "numerous examples of courageous Arab women heroes risking not only their reputation but also their physical safety for the sake of reform" (Al-Malki et al. 2012, p. 81).

In doing so, they were determined to merge the struggle for equal citizenship and full participation in the political arena with that for greater gender equality in the social arena in their newly transforming societies and transitioning states. For this reason it has been said that while men were fighting one struggle in the midst of the Arab Spring movements—namely, the political struggle to end dictatorship and to pave the way for democracy—Arab women were fighting two parallel struggles: one to end political injustice and the other to end social injustice simultaneously (Al-Malki et al. 2012; Khamis 2013).

In other words, it could be said that another reason for the prominence of gender issues in the midst of the Arab Spring or Arab Awakening movements is the crossover from the political to the social realm, and vice versa, as illustrated by the myriad of overlapping issues and intersecting activities which Arab women took part in, and across these two domains simultaneously.

Nowhere is this more evident than in the case of Tunisia, where gender organizations were instrumental in steering the constitution towards higher gender standards, while mutually advocating for higher democratic standards. The stakes were particularly high for Tunisian women, who had secured significant gains from the legislation enacted in 1956, even before the Tunisian uprising, and who felt threatened by the regressive, or more restrictive, agenda of some religious parties, which started to emerge at the center of the political stage and to assume positions of leadership after the Arab Spring, especially when it came to gender issues and gender equity.

Another important reason why gender issues were so central in the midst of the Arab Spring movements was their relevance and connection to ongoing constitutional debates and legal reform efforts and initiatives. Drafting a new constitution is a social venture as much as it is a political venture. Indeed, the tone of a constitution is determined, to a very large extent, by the type of state that we want to build. Two state models were in competition in the countries that went through the constitution-building process—namely, a modern state modeled on Western-style liberal democracy, and a classical state inspired by Islamic constitutional traditions. While these two models may concur on general principles of political governance, they differ significantly in terms of social/societal features. At the center of the social debate is the role of women in the private and public spheres, an issue which has been very contentious and controversial, generating much debate and igniting much passion over time.

An important reason why gender issues played a key role in the constitutional debate is that whenever an Arab country had a fair and transparent election, religious parties seemed to win with a significant mandate. Whether that means that most Arab countries prefer to be ruled by religious groups remains to be seen. It is important to note in this context, however, that the most important element in winning an election is having better organization. And, interestingly enough, religious parties, such as the Muslim Brotherhood, in most Arab countries, despite decades of persecution and repression, seem to have better organization for three main reasons.

First, they have existed for much longer than any other party because they can survive long periods of political oppression by going underground, under the cover of religious activities. Second, they sustain an organizational infrastructure which can provide social welfare services and resources in their mostly economically challenged societies in the form of mosques, religious schools, hospitals, clinics, and subsidized food outlets across the region, which secure a popular base of support and popularity for them. Third, they appeal to the common voter through religious and cultural slogans that most Arab citizens are familiar with, can relate to and empathize with.

The emergence of religious parties on the political scene raises the stakes of constitution-building because they are mostly perceived as more prone to putting forward constitutional principles that are not favorable to women. However, it is important to avoid the danger of sweeping generalizations in making such a claim, taking into account the fact that there are many types of religious group, with varying degrees of conservatism or liberalism, when it comes to the issue of gender roles and women's place in the private and public spheres.

For all of the above reasons, the primary focus of this book is the gender struggles, which became particularly visible and salient in the context of the Arab Spring movements, but which had been going on for many years before the eruption of these uprisings, and which are still very much evident in many parts of the Arab region today, six years after the eruption of the Arab Spring movements of 2011.

In other words, although the connection to the Arab Spring is certainly clear for all the above reasons, the scope of this book is not just limited to these movements or restricted to this context, since there is ample evidence indicating the birth of gendered struggles in different parts of the Arab world before the eruption of the Arab Spring, as well as the continuation of these gendered struggles in many of the so-called "post-Arab Spring" countries.

In terms of the "pre-Arab Spring" context, we can give examples of how Arab women were actively involved in shaping the public sphere, through carving new places for themselves in the domain of political activism, even before the eruption of the Arab Spring. A good example is the uprising which took place in Redeyef, a mining area in the south of Tunisia, under the authoritarian regime of the ousted president Ben Ali in 2008. This was initiated by women, lasted a few months, during which citizens called for economic and social justice from the government, and was eventually crushed with the repressive machine of Ben Ali.

Likewise, Egyptian women played a crucial role in igniting and mobilizing grassroots activism in the context of previous uprisings, including the April 6 movement, which erupted in the industrial city of Al Mehala El Kobra, initially as an attempt to call for working-class rights, just like the case of Redeyef in Tunisia, which later snowballed to attract and mobilize more activists across the board. Egyptian women were also central in igniting and mobilizing activists within the ranks of the Kefaya movement (*Kefaya* is the Arabic word for "enough"). As the name implies, the movement was trying to send a clear message to ousted President Hosni Mubarak that the Egyptian people had had enough of his 30-year dictatorship, and that they could not tolerate any more corruption, autocracy, or repression.

All of these pre-Arab Spring movements are recognized today as important political developments that forged the space and paved the way for the sweeping uprisings in 2011. Women have been recognized as key actors, central players, and effective mobilizers during these uprisings.

In terms of the post-Arab Spring context, we can refer to some of the ongoing efforts to guard, and expand, women's rights and gender equity in the political, social, and legal spheres. For example, of the many Arab countries that experienced political upheavals in 2011, Tunisia and Egypt enacted new constitutions, and both were active in promoting civil rights and gender equality. Yet it would be naive to imagine that the constitution alone is sufficient to ensure the protection of women's rights in these countries. Much remains to be done within the legislative branch to ensure that future legislations consolidate the constitutional principles, and within the judicial branch to ensure the appropriate interpretation of the constitution and future legislation.

Also, gender equality is not merely a matter of law; rather, it is also a matter of social practice, cultural norms and traditions, and prevailing mindset. Here also, perhaps more than anywhere else, much remains to be done in terms of spreading much-needed awareness and proper education aimed at potential perpetrators and potential victims, in an effort to combat stagnant traditions and societal norms which hinder women's progress and limit their potential.

All of the above reasons explain why we extended the scope of this book to cover the periods before, during and after the Arab Spring uprisings; to tackle political, social, and legal issues; and to include both counties which witnessed the Arab Spring upheavals, such as Egypt, Tunisia, and Bahrain, as well as those that did not, such as Morocco, Lebanon, and Saudi Arabia. The main logic behind this inclusive approach is our belief that in many Arab countries, albeit with varying degrees and in different forms, of course, there is a need to tackle underlying structures of injustice and cultural practices of discrimination, which negatively impact Arab women and limit their potential for growth, development, and advancement, politically, socially, and legally.

1.2 Revisiting Intersectionality within an Arab Context

The conceptual notion of intersectionality was initially introduced by Western feminist scholars to resist "the assumption of a falsely universalizing unitary model of 'women'" (Carastathis 2008, p. 28). It was mainly an attempt to acknowledge the multilayered complexity and nuance of so-called gendered identity politics, which is created at the intersection between gender, race, and sometimes class, as in the case of black women, for example (Collins 1995, 1998, 2003; Crenshaw 1989). In other words, it could be said that "The intersectional model … consigns hyper-oppressed subjects to an intersection of axes of oppression" (Carastathis 2008, p. 28).

This book revisits the notion of intersectionality from a different angle. It explores how Arab women's complex forms of activism and resistance oscillate between binary opposites, such as the traditional vs. the modern, the online vs. the offline, the religious vs. the secular, the top-down vs. the bottom-up, the official vs. the popular, the formal vs. the informal, the private vs. the public, and the local vs. the global. It investigates how Arab women's multiple identities, struggles, and resistances are created and expressed at the intersecting crossroads, where all of these binary opposites overlap across legal, social, and political domains.

We argue that it is at the intersections between these binary opposites and overlapping categories that new gendered identities, new forms of activism, and new modes of resistance are continuously born and regularly manifested.

Our investigation of these intertwined, interrelated, overlapping and intersecting aspects adds new layers of analysis to the concept of intersectionality, as it moves beyond the overlapping categories of gender, race, and class to encompass competing subjectivities, clashing ideologies, varied modes of expression, and unique sites of struggle, in addition to national boundaries, historical contexts, and ongoing sociopolitical struggles and transformations.

The case studies which are presented here, stretching across various Arab counties, different historical phases, and multiple forms of gendered activisms, struggles and resistances, help to unpack the complexity of this revisited notion of intersectionality, with all its multiple dimensions, manifestations, implications, and effects.

We can argue that this intellectual effort attempts to take the concept of intersectionality to the next level on two fronts. First, it acknowledges "the discursive unrepresentability of hyper-oppressed subjects" (Carastathis 2008, p. 29) and the need to provide unrepresented, or underrepresented, groups (in this case Arab women), who are suffering from multiple layers of disadvantage and oppression, with platforms to make their voices heard, their views expressed, and their identities visible.

Second, it engages in "feminist politics of solidarity" which, according to Carastathis (2008), has three major functions: "performing a structural analysis of the ways in which systems of oppression 'interlock' and of the ways in which subjects are located in and reproduce these systems; involving an actional commitment to transforming the structural relations that subtend these systems; and distinguishing between being position*ed* or situat*ed* in relations of oppression and privilege ... and position*ing* or situat*ing* oneself in relations of solidarity" (p. 30) with "communities in struggle" (Mohanty 2003, p. 228).

Indeed, Arab women's multiple forms of activism, resistance, and struggle which are displayed throughout this volume could be said to meet the above criteria and to serve these three functions because these women have clearly engaged in multiple forms of action, both individually and collectively, to shake their autocratic regimes, fight the social systems of oppression, and defy the legal and cultural power structures by forming their own struggle movements and communities of action.

1.3 Three Stages of Arab Feminism(s)

The evolution of gender policies in the Arab region has been driven by the ebbing and flowing of four competing political forces: the international balance of power and how Arab regimes positioned themselves therein; the intolerance of Arab regimes towards any form of political activism, regardless of its agenda; the emergence of political Islam and its focus on gender matters as an integral part of its agenda; and the natural aspirations of Arab people for reform and their yearning for greater political freedoms (Mili 2015).

In the midst of these competing forces, and at their intersections, three distinct phases of Arab feminism(s) have evolved throughout their own unique historical contexts and distinct developmental stages, in response to myriad sets of political, social, and historical factors.

The first stage could be said to have been prompted by the tides of nationalism and fighting colonialism which swept the Arab region after World War II. In their quest to free their own societies from colonial forces, Arab citizens were, in fact, engaging in more than one struggle, on both the political and social domains simultaneously. All the discourses prevailing throughout the Arab region at that time agreed on the relationship between underdevelopment and colonialism and the necessity to end the latter. Yet they differed a great deal in the courses of action and the remedies societies should take to best build their future and to rid themselves of these unfortunate realities. The status of women and gender dynamics were central to these discourses. Competing forces, representing different ideologies and positions, adopted various discourses pertaining to women, which to a large extent set the stage for the frame through which Arab feminism(s) developed afterwards.

Broadly speaking, two competing visions of women's place and role in society were simultaneously evolving at that time, albeit in different directions: the "nationalist modernist discourse" and the "nationalist conservative discourse."

Proponents of the first position were mostly educated intellectuals and scholars who questioned the roots and causes of colonialism, and established a connection between underdevelopment, colonialism, and the "woman's question" or the "woman's situation," as it was refereed to. The nationalist modernists were mostly people from the upper classes of society who had usually been exposed in different ways to the West and considered it to be the model to follow, or at least to take as an example for inspiration in the building of a new developed society. These included educated Arab scholars and intellectuals who had spent significant periods of time in the West (mostly Europe), such as Qasim Amin, Rashid Rida, and Rifaat Al-Tahtawi in Egypt, and Tahar Haddad in Tunisia, who took the lead in raising this issue. Some nationalist women also took part in this newly emerging discourse, such as Bechira Ben M'rad in Tunisia, Huda Shaarawi in Egypt, and Nazirah Zein ed-din in Lebanon (Mili 2009).

These reformers called for a progressive change in women's status, presenting such a change as a precondition for a so-called Arab renaissance (*al-nahdah*). They vigorously denounced negative societal practices, which allowed the ill treatment of women on the basis of faulty interpretations of certain religious texts, and denounced the hypocrisy that reigned in society when it comes to dealing with women. They called for an end to the massive inequalities endemic in their contemporary societies, insisting on the need to address them for the sake of social and economic progress. At the heart of these calls for reform was asserting women's rights to visibly participate in public life, through seeking education, abolishing gender segregation, and ending all forms of discrimination against women (Mili 2009).

Proponents of the second position had a different outlook when it comes to women's role and place in society. The nationalist conservative narrative stems from a need to protect a "pure Islamic identity" as it arose during the acme of Islamic times. Thus the conservatives defended an absolute freeze on religious debate, and rejected any evolutionary interpretations based on new readings of classical Islamic texts, or revisiting them in light of contemporary conditions to best serve the public's interest. The struggle against colonialism centered on the preservation of Islam in its original form, as revealed many centuries ago. Maintaining women in a status of second-class citizenship was viewed as part of protecting the traditional way of life and preserving the authenticity of local culture, and was therefore viewed through the same lens as the struggle for liberation from alien colonial powers. One of these voices was that of Tal'at Harb, an Egyptian nationalist, who argued that women's liberation is another imperialist/colonial plot designed to undermine Egypt's social structure, religion, and morality (Mili 2009).

Unlike the modernists who called for the integration of women into the public sphere and their participation in political life, competing traditionalist, conservative movements have historically used a different meaning of gender to create an alternative legitimacy for a different audience. As progressive as it may seem, the "woman's question" has always been justified by them in reference to an Islamic framework, which puts public welfare and the good of society first, by glorifying and prioritizing a woman's role as a mother and a good wife. Never has it been framed as a question of autonomy, human rights, freedom, or liberty of choice for her as an autonomous individual.

Paradoxically and ironically, at the same time as these traditionalists and conservatives were restricting women's freedoms, they were also claiming, with some success and resonance among relatively wide segments of the public, that their efforts were intended to protect and honor women, by honoring and preserving their roles as devoted mothers and faithful spouses.

These push and pull mechanisms between these varying positions could be said to have been born out of an international nationalist discourse that arose in many occupied/colonized Arab countries, which placed women's rights and women's status at the center of their priorities, reflecting a tension between a need for "modernization" and the need to assert a "pure national identity." Interestingly enough, although the main aim of this nationalist discourse was eventually "liberation," mainly from the forces of colonialism and occupation in the political domain, the way in which the concept of "liberation" was understood and interpreted in the social domain varied widely.

On one hand, it was viewed by the modernists as liberation from stagnant social traditions and cultural practices which impeded social progress, as in the case of negative practices against women. On the other hand, however, it was viewed by the conservatives as liberation from the hegemony of the West, and from attempts to emulate the Western way of life, which was considered to be a threat to the pure values of society, as in the case of calling for women's liberation.

Simply put, from the conservative perspective, when colonial powers talked about liberating women, they were attempting to alter the purity of Islamic societies in order to weaken them and, therefore, better control them. And so the reformists and modernists who were echoing the same views were viewed with suspicion by the conservatives as advancing the very same colonialist agenda.

In a clever strategy, the traditionalists and the conservatives were able to portray the modernist view as adhering to the viewpoint of the colonial power, and to accuse advocates of the modernist view of being unpatriotic, and of betraying the national cause of liberation from colonialism. They argued that the modernist viewpoint is a colonial construction intended to affect the purity of Islamic society in order to weaken it.

Overall, the debate between modernists and traditionalists having gender at its core was at the center of the competition between groups interested in power at the time of access to independence. Therefore it could be said that the so-called "woman's question" in the Arab region has been central to this debate since the early nineteenth century and resurfaced with acuity during times of transition. While it is true that "The development of the feminist movement … is deeply rooted in the nationalist and reformist movement," (Charrad 1997) we argue that the nationalist movement was deeply shaped by the polarized debate revolving around the "woman's question." This relation made the "woman's question" and the "national question" intertwined in the nationalist debate, with the national question taking precedence (Charrad 1997).

When they emerged from their colonial past around the middle of the twentieth century, Arab countries had to take steps to build their respective nations (around newly defined identities) and their states (around newly defined constitutions and state institutions). We can argue that the political choices they made in terms of state model, at this stage, were intimately related to the social choices they made in terms of gender roles, so much so that their social choices, in terms of gender standards, were virtually an integral part of their political choices.

As they emerged from the yoke of colonialism and prepared to build their respective nation-states, many Arab countries had a unique opportunity to work from a blank slate. Different countries adopted different state models, from monarchies (e.g. Morocco and Jordan) and socialist models (e.g. Algeria, Egypt, Libya, and Yemen) to Western-style democracies (e.g. Lebanon and Tunisia) (Mili 2015).

These different state models yielded sharply varying gender policies, reflecting the interconnectedness between the political and social domains, and reminding us of the overlap between the structure of the nation-state and the nature of the gender dynamics which prevail within it. Whereas monarchies drew inspiration from religious sources, Western-style countries adopted policies that were based on secular principles of universal human rights, while socialist states took a middle ground, with a predominantly secular style of government which still pays respect to religion, at least nominally, even if it does not allow it to play a very significant role in the way the country is governed (Mili 2015).

In other words, at the time of their independence and the building of their post-colonial nation-states, the newly emerging Arab regimes made different decisions in the realm of gender policies according to the type of political and social project they wanted to build. Women, however, were, ironically and paradoxically, absent from the discussion that they were at the center of.

Therefore this post-colonial stage of nation-building witnessed the birth of a new type of Arab feminism, which could be best described as top-down state feminism. This second stage of Arab feminism, as the name implies, was characterized by the state's firm control over many aspects of political and social life, including drafting new laws regulating gender relations and family dynamics. Although this was sometimes executed in a fashion which seemed to best serve women's interests and to promote more gender rights, as in the case of Habib Bourguiba and his successor Ben Ali in Tunisia, or the three successive rulers in Egypt—Nasser, Sadat and Mubarak—the tradeoff was creating tame and domesticated feminist organizations, which simply echo the government's positions and operate within the confines of its policies.

In other words, although many of these rulers moved to create institutions that seemed to promote gender standards and to give a voice to gender concerns, as in the case of the National Council for Women, which was created by Mubarak's wife in Egypt and which could be considered an epitome of state feminism, the truth remains that these were all subservient to the state apparatus. Therefore they were not indicative or reflective of any truly autonomous or independent women's movements at the grassroots level.

Therefore it could be said that this second stage of state feminism was mostly characterized by a form of top-down, cosmetic, tokenistic feminism, which was mostly dictated and imposed by the regimes in power.

One of the most important functions which this type of state feminism serves is acting as a political prop, which is used to convey an image of a modern, secular, forward-looking country. This, in turn, is expected to increase the legitimacy of the regime internationally, especially in the eyes of Western governments and foreign allies. One of the most common techniques used in this regard could be referred to as "the first lady syndrome" (Khamis 2013)—in other words, the reliance on the image, fame, and credibility of the first lady to pass certain legislations or to take certain steps which are perceived to be favorable to women, usually with little trickledown effect to wider segments of the population at large. One good example is the establishment of the National Council for Women, the epitome of state feminism, by former Egyptian first lady Suzanne Mubarak.

This could be best understood in the context of international developments, since we cannot detach the local from the global in our attempt to better understand gender dynamics in the Arab region. In the late 1980s and early 1990s, the fall of the Berlin Wall, the breakup of the Soviet Union, and the democratic transitions in several Eastern European countries, put fresh pressure on Arab regimes to make political overtures and to move in the direction of political reform. This period coincided with a change of the guard in several Arab countries, such as Morocco, Jordan, and Syria, ushering in a new generation of young leaders, and further raising hopes for democratic reform. This necessitated and justified some of these cosmetic and tokenistic forms of state feminism to increase the new regimes' local popularity and international legitimacy.

Therefore it could be said that the 1990s in particular witnessed major international shifts with the fall of the Soviet Union and the rise of the liberal democratic system as the winner and the sole viable model in the world. This coincided in the Arab world with the regression of the ideologies of "secular" inspirations, which left a void that has been filled by a return to religion. This increased religiosity was sometimes equated with, or driven by, the rise of fundamentalism, which was financed by petro dollars. This was coupled at the same time with the birth of a new generation of young people in the Arab world who do not believe in the sole power of ideology, are increasingly disillusioned with their authoritarian regimes, and are yearning for more freedom.

The 9/11 attacks and the subsequent "War on Terror" created a new dynamic for many Arab regimes by giving them an opportunity to consolidate their power and legitimacy, both locally and internationally. Within their respective countries, Arab regimes were quick to highlight the dangers of religious parties and their agendas, and to present themselves as the modern, sensible alternative and as the forces safeguarding safety, stability and security inside their countries and in the Arab region as a whole. The events of September 11, 2001 gave these Arab regimes a new excuse to exercise unchecked persecution of opposition groups, especially religious opposition parties, under the cover of fighting terrorism. On the international stage, these regimes gained renewed legitimacy by offering to be partners in the so-called global War on Terror and presenting themselves as bulwarks against terrorist threats. Therefore Western countries that needed the cooperation of these Arab regimes in the so-called War on Terror were less prone to lecture them on their human rights record.

Part of the game of polishing their international image and reputation consists of presenting themselves as secular, modern state actors that are prepared to move against religious parties and to promote a modern state model along secular lines. Gender policies became an important (and risk-free) vehicle for these Arab regimes to burnish their credentials, promote their legitimacy, and consolidate their power, both domestically and internationally.

Therefore, in a bid to polish their credentials as modern secular regimes, many of these Arab governments took measures to promote gender-favorable policies and practices and signed up to gender-related international protocols. However, Arab gender organizations were suffering, as much as anyone else, from the restrictions imposed on grassroots sociopolitical activism, and the lack of a truly vibrant and dynamic civil society. It is not surprising, then, that when the political upheavals of the Arab Spring of 2011 started, Arab women were eager to play a leading role by merging their gender militancy with political activism as their first outlet of expressing true freedom for the very first time.

However, it is worth mentioning that the type of top-down "liberation by decree," or state feminism, which prevailed in many parts of the Arab world during this second stage of feminism, as in the case of the Tunisian experience under Bourguiba, for example, was not totally pointless, useless, or harmful. This was mainly because the formal codification of women's legal rights played a huge role in changing the social culture and prepared for a social change that helped women to access spaces and places that were totally out of bounds to them before. A good example would be drafting new laws and regulations which guaranteed women's rights to participate in the public sphere, through accessing the educational system and participating in the workforce, as well as laws protecting women against different forms of discrimination, domestic violence, and abuse (Mili 2009).

Although it is true that this type of state-imposed, top-down feminism was mostly tokenistic, elitist, and without a sufficient trickledown effect, owing to limited grassroots participation from women, we cannot deny that it did serve some useful purpose in terms of paving the way for Arab women to access new public spaces, and it was an important milestone in their journey towards gaining more rights. Therefore it is important, and fair, to acknowledge both the pros and cons, as well as the contributions and limitations, of this type of formal, state feminism.

At the heart of the debates and controversies which shaped and influenced women's position and status in these newly independent states was the centrality of religion and its role in determining the boundaries of women's legal, political, and social rights. Here again, there was no agreement across, or even within, different Arab countries, or between different women's groups, on how much, or how little, of a role religion should play in gender dynamics in these evolving societies.

Some women's groups attempted to strike a balance between Islamic teachings and women's rights, arguing that they do not have to be mutually exclusive, and that it is very possible to uphold women's rights within an Islamic framework, thus proposing the notion of "Islamic feminism" (Khamis 2010). Other women's groups, as in the case of some of the feminist organizations in Maghreb countries, for example, believed that upholding the notion of secularism is fundamentally important if the concepts of gender equality and women's liberation are to become reality. The advocates of this position were particularly threatened by the new dawn of political Islam because they believed that the rise of religious groups, which use religion as a tool to achieve political gains, constitutes a real threat to women's rights. For these women's groups, secularism is the solution, not new interpretations of religious texts, as advocated by other feminist groups (Mili 2009).

From the mid-1980s onwards, important international events, such as the end of the Cold War and the fall of the Soviet Union in 1989, which led to the rise of the USA as the sole superpower and the emergence of capitalism as the sole viable economic system, created a context in which religious and gender identities arose and developed in relation to one another. More recently, reactions to the Iraq War and to the War on Terror translated into a rise in religious sentiment, as evidenced in more Arab women wearing the Islamic veil (*hijab*), for example. This newly emerging generation of Islamic feminists is generally mindful of the burden of patriarchy. Most of them are affiliated with Islamic associations, Islamic political parties, or both, and do not represent themselves as antiliberal or anti-reform.

Rather, it could be said that they pretty much contextualize their activism within the framework of their own religiosity through claiming a new gendered identity, while respecting the dictates of Islamic teachings, and they focus on Islamic texts and quote them while expressing their demands. Vis-à-vis international feminism(s), they sought in Islam a characterizing identity and a strategy of liberation that standard Western explanatory frameworks, often based on egalitarian and individualistic assumptions, do not include (Mili 2009).

At the other end of the spectrum are the so-called "liberal feminists" who oppose this discourse because they choose to articulate their legal and emancipatory demands in terms of liberalizing society, without concentrating on religious texts per se. Faced with modernity issues, such as definitions of individual and collective identities in a fast-changing world where religion is assuming a bigger role, as well as a delineation of women's new roles in public space, liberal feminists sought to play down what they considered to be the narrow religious aspect of Islam (Al-Ali 2000; Mili 2009).

These liberal feminists are mindful of the use, or even exploitation, of Islam by the patriarchy. They challenge the patriarchal discourse by making an issue out of the separation of, and opposition between, the private and public spheres. This approach allows liberal feminists to politicize the private sphere and to attack the theological discourse that deliberately ignores women's real issues, including their political, economic, and social rights, by choosing to focus instead on narrow theological issues and debates (Al-Ali 2000; Mili 2009).

It could be said that the tension and battle between these two tendencies—namely, secularization and Islamization—was very much at the heart of defining the emerging nation-states' identity in the local, regional, and global arenas. A central and integral part of this identity formation, of course, was gender based, through determining the role and place of women in society.

Half a century after their independence, as many Arab countries prepared to transition from their postcolonial autocratic regimes to tentative democratic systems, the question of how they define their gender options, and how these affect their state models, came to the fore again. In this context, Arab women had two distinct incentives to participate in the democratic process: to ensure that their transition does lead to better democratic standards and a brighter future; and to ensure that women preserve and build on their gender gains. In other words, as previously mentioned, they had to fight their social, political, and legal battles simultaneously.

The golden moment for Arab women came with the eruption of the Arab Spring movements in 2011 as they started to assume unique positions of leadership and visibility for the first time, ushering in the third stage of Arab feminism. Here it is worth mentioning again how Arab women did not just enact their activism in the streets alongside men calling for the fall of autocratic rulers and toppling dictatorial regimes. Rather, they took their activism to the realm of seeking legal and social reform in an attempt to promote a gender-friendly agenda. In other words, feminist militants who were advocating for democracy and political rights used their fight to push for more rights for women, both socially and legally, since they felt that the best way to preserve democracy in the long run is to secure a greater political role for women, thereby sealing again the bond between gender militancy and political militancy.

The main distinguishing factor between this third phase of Arab feminism and the two previous ones was the visibility and centrality of women's leadership at the forefront of the new waves of activism and revolt. In the first stage of nationalism, it was mostly men, whether modernists or conservatives, who were key to charting the road ahead for social reform, including making decisions about women's position in society and their participation in it. Likewise, in the second stage of nation-building it was state leaders, again men, who took the lead by promoting a model of top-down, state feminism. In both cases, women's participation in the decision-making process was mostly limited, and their role was primarily restricted by and channeled behind male leadership.

The emergence of genuine women's voices, the building of authentic women's leadership, and the creation of many grassroots, gender-based organizations marks a shift in gender politics from a top-down approach, where progress is driven by state actors, to a bottom-up approach, where gender activists take matters into their own hands and drive the evolution of gender standards, according to their own needs, demands, interests, and agendas.

To fully understand the third stage of Arab feminism, it is important to bear in mind that the democratic movements that swept throughout the Arab region were about justice and dignity as much as they were about the spaces and sites within which justice and dignity were defined and redefined, claimed and fought, as well as contested and negotiated. Struggles over justice and dignity do not just take place in a vacuum, nor do the gender dimensions of these struggles. This is why feminist scholars of gender have been attentive to the meanings and implications of the spaces and sites of these struggles, which vary widely geographically, culturally, socially, and politically, as illustrated by the various contributions to this volume.

Struggles over gender justice and equity in the Arab world prior to, during, and after the Arab Spring reveal ways in which women (and men) have been engaged in processes of opening up, carving out, redefining, and reshaping different physical and metaphorical spaces. These processes take place in the real world (i.e. on the ground in various liberation squares in Arab capitals), as well as increasingly in virtual spaces (i.e. on social media, such as blogs, Facebook, YouTube, and Twitter). These processes are not always simple or unidimensional since they seek to transform gender relations in the public and private spheres simultaneously, and to redefine the meaning and practice of citizenship beyond gender hierarchies.

The idea of contesting and redefining spaces implies risk-taking and the exercise of agency, despite all forms of intimidation and constraints. The contributions to this volume illustrate how Arab women, and their groups and organizations, were able to reformulate their demands for gender rights within the context of activism for democracy, freedom, and sovereignty in the private and public sphere. In doing so, all of the chapters document the diversity of spaces and sites where Arab women struggled to secure democratic institutions and practices within their respective societies, and how, in doing so, they were, in fact, engendering both the political and social domains, as well as the private and public spheres, simultaneously.

Indeed, the focus on "cyberactivism" (Howard 2011), which has at its core blogs, social media, and multimedia performance, as part of this third phase of Arab feminism echoed the so-called "third wave of feminism" in its focus on practices of cultural production (Heywood 2006; Kearney 2006; Schilt and Zobl 2008; Bell 2002).

This could be said to be true since young Arab women created their own cyberactivist culture, linked by their participation and activism in social media networks. Like other networks of young women linked by their use and creation of content on particular platforms, such as the Riot Grrrl zine culture or Iranian feminist websites, the specific platform—in this case blogs and social media—"became a central element of the movement" (Bell 2002).

We can argue that the overlap between this third phase of Arab feminism and the so-called "third wave of feminism" stems from the fact they are both part of a universal, global movement to build on, and make maximum use of, digital technologies and new media tools to empower laypeople and members of marginalized groups, especially women, at the bottom-up, popular, grassroots level, and to enable them to make their voices heard and to have their stories told.

However, in drawing this comparison between this third stage of Arab feminism and the third wave of feminism in the Western context, we are aware of the fact that each of them is the byproduct of its own unique historical, political, and social contexts. Yet we believe that there is some value in highlighting the similarities and overlaps between them owing to their participatory tendencies and emancipatory potentials when it comes to promoting a bottom-up, grassroots model of feminism.

At the same time, it is equally important to highlight some of the discrepancies and differences between them. Most importantly, unlike critiques of Grrl Zines, or other manifestations of third-wave feminism, for focusing too much on a "narrowly construed type of individual expression without drawing out deeper political implication," (Bell 2002) cyberactivism via blogs and social media in the contemporary Arab world proved to be "both individual and political, which ultimately challenges the dichotomy between private and public spheres" (Radsch and Khamis 2013, p. 887).

In other words, the type of activism enacted by Arab feminists in the midst of these uprisings negates the narrow conceptualization of feminism as referring to the relationship between awareness and action, consciousness-raising, and the importance of autobiographies and the sharing of personal experience that take precedence over generic political and social discourse, including that about a "collective" voice (Armstrong 2004).

This is especially important to highlight since Arab women activists "adopted social media practices that enabled them to articulate their identities in the public sphere and to participate in the uprisings in multiple ways, resulting in a sense of personal empowerment and collective potentiality that was fundamentally linked to the communicative platform" (Radsch and Khamis 2013, p. 887).

Understanding how the different aspects of Arab women's activism in the political, social, and legal spheres have historically developed over these three stages, and how they are interrelated and interconnected to each other, on the one hand, as well as how they are connected to international dynamics and influences, such as the notion of third wave feminism, for example, on the other hand, is crucial to fully understanding the various case studies which are tackled in this book.

Overall, we can contend with confidence that there is a close connection between gender militancy and political militancy, and that women's liberation cannot happen without full political liberation, whether from external political forces, as in the case of colonialism and occupation, or from internal forces, as in the case of dictatorial and autocratic regimes. Under colonialism, feminism was seen as a tool for national liberation, social emancipation, and autonomy, especially by modern reformers. During the early time of independence and post-colonialism, feminism sought to provide the economic and social context and resources needed for state-building. With the rise of Islamism, feminism was used as a tool for the building of an Islamic state model by the advocates of political Islam.

In all of the above stages, however, we can argue that women's active participation was not as strong, active, or visible as it should have been because most of the decision-making in all of these stages was not made by women on issues which were central and essential to women and their wellbeing. It was not until the eruption of the Arab Awakening movements that we truly started to witness a strong, visible, and effective form of women's leadership at the grassroots level.

Therefore we can conclude that the creation of dynamic and evolving stages of Arab feminism(s) was continuously taking place at the crossroads between various push and pull mechanisms, and competing forces, including modernization vs. conservatism; localization vs. globalization; the public sphere vs. the private sphere; secularization vs. Islamization; and top-down state feminism vs. bottom-up grassroots activism.

To fully grasp this back-and-forth interplay between the concept of feminism and gender activism, on the one hand, and sociopolitical transformation and democratization, on the other hand, we should best perceive them as two sides of the same coin, which can only be perfectly understood and appreciated when historically contextualized and politically situated.

To better understand these historical, social, and political contexts, we have to be able to link the local, the regional, and the global, as well as the past, the present, and the future, all at once. As Marzouki (1993) reminds us, the debate about Arab women's autonomy, rights, and activism did not just take place at the national and regional levels. Rather, it involved concerns and narratives that crossed national borders, since the tangled web of women's destiny is also shaped by international events, and it links the history of the Arab region with its present and its future. Exploring this direct relationship between international political developments and the birth of feminist movements and organizations in the Arab world therefore is as important as understanding the historical development of these movements during several phases.

1.4 Seven Important Questions

This volume aims to engage in a theoretically informed and empirically supported constructive discussion to answer the following questions:

- How are Arab women's complex identities both shaped and reflected across different historical contexts, national boundaries, forms of activism, and sites of struggle?
- How are the different aspects of Arab women's activisms, struggles, and resistances in the political, social, and legal spheres interrelated and interconnected to each other, on the one hand, and to the wider political, social, and legal realities in their respective countries, on the other?
- How have these different aspects of Arab women's activisms, struggles, and resistances in the political, social, and legal arenas evolved historically, and how did they intersect and overlap, hence contributing to the birth of different forms, degrees, and phases of Arab feminism(s)?
- What role did Arab women's gender demands, struggles, and grievances play in triggering the Arab Spring protests, and how did they influence the course of these movements?
- How did the unresolved, ongoing gender demands, struggles, and tensions play out and manifest themselves before, during, and after the Arab spring uprisings?
- What were some of the most important sites and tools of struggle which Arab women deployed to enact their multiple forms of activisms and resistances, and how did they vary across different Arab countries, and during different phases?
- What new opportunities do the ongoing waves of political transition in the Arab region, with all their complexities, offer in terms of gender equality, and what challenges do they pose?

To answer all of the above questions, this book relies on both theoretical insights and empirical evidence. Indeed, the interaction between theory and empirical studies in this collection is reflective of the way in which the struggle for gender equality has been moving forward ... there is an alternating focus between the theoretical approach to the study of gender in Muslim-dominant societies and the need to pinpoint particular cases of women who have triggered widespread social movements, and been targets of state, gender-based violence. Theoretical considerations are dependent on the fleshing out of empirical changes and events. This volume reflects that dialectic. (Khalil 2014, p. 132)

Bibliography

Al-Ali, N.S. 2000. Secularism, Gender, and the State in the Middle East. In *The Egyptian Women's Movement*. Cambridge: Cambridge University Press.

Al-Malki, A., D. Kaufner, S. Ishizaki, and K. Dreher. 2012. *Arab Women in Arab News: Old Stereotypes and New Media*. Doha: Bloomsbury Qatar Foundation Publishing.

Armstrong, J. 2004. Web Grrls, Guerilla Tactics: Young Feminisms on the Web. In *Web Studies*, ed. D. Gauntlett and R. Horsely, 92–102. London/Oxford: Arnold/Oxford University Press.

Bell, B.L.A. Fall. 2002. Riding the Third Wave: Women-Produced Zines and Feminisms. *Resources for Feminist Research* 29 (3/4): 187–198.

Carastathis, A. 2008. The Invisibility of Privilege: A Critique of Intersectional Models of Identity. *A Multidisciplinary Journal on the Normative Challenges of Public Policies and Social Practices* 3 (2): 23–38.

Charrad, M. 1997. *Policy Shifts: State, Islam, and Gender in Tunisia, 1930s–1990s Social Politics*. London: Oxford University Press.

Collins, P.H. 1995. On West and Fernmaker's 'Doing Difference'. *Gender & Society* 9 (4): 491–494.

———. 1998. It's All in the Family: Intersections of Gender, Race and Nation. *Hypatia* 13 (3): 62–82.

———. 2003. Some Group Matters: Intersectionality, Situated Standpoints, and Black Feminist Thought. In *A Companion to African-American Philosophy*, ed. T.L. Lott and J.P. Pittman, 205–229. Oxford: Blackwell.

Crenshaw, K.W. 1989. Demarginalizing the Intersection of Race and Sex: A Black Feminist Critique of Antidiscrimination Doctrine, Feminist Theory and Antiracist Politics. *University of Chicago Legal Forum* 1989: 139–167.

Heideman, K., and M. Youssef. eds. 2012. Reflections on Women in the Arab Spring. Women's Voices from Around the World. Woodrow Wilson International Center for Scholars, Washington, DC.

Heywood, L. 2006. *The Women's Movement Today: An Encyclopedia of Third-Wave Feminism.* Westport: Greenwood Press.

Howard, P.N. 2011. *The Digital Origins of Dictatorship and Democracy: Information Technology and Political Islam.* New York: Oxford University Press.

Kearney, M.C. 2006. *Girls Make Media.* New York: Taylor & Francis.

Khalil, A. 2014. Gender Paradoxes of the Arab Spring. *The Journal of North African Studies* 19 (2): 131–136.

Khamis, S. 2010. Islamic Feminism in New Arab Media: Platforms for Self-Expression and Sites for Multiple Resistances. *Journal of Arab and Muslim Media Research* 3 (3): 237–255.

———. 2011. The Arab "Feminist" Spring? *Feminist Studies* 37 (3): 692–695.

———. 2013. Gendering the Arab Spring: Arab Women Journalists/Activists, 'Cyberfeminism,' and the Socio-Political Revolution. In *The Routledge Companion to Media and Gender*, ed. C. Carter, L. Steiner, and L. McLaughlin, 565–575. London: Routledge.

Marzouki, I. 1993. *Le mouvement des femmes en Tunisie au XXème siècle.* Paris: Maisonneuve et Larose.

Mili, A. 2009. Exploring the Relation Between Gender Politics and Representative Government in the Maghreb: Analytical and Empirical Observations. PhD dissertation, Rutgers University.

———. 2015. Political-Social Movements: Community Based: Tunisia In: *Encyclopedia of Women & Islamic Cultures*, General Editor S. Joseph. Consulted online on March 9th, 2017. doi:10.1163/1872-5309_ewic_COM_002018. First published online: 2015.

Mohanty, C.T. 2003. Under Western Eyes Revisited: Feminist Solidarity Through Anticapitalist Struggles. In *Feminism Without Borders: Decolonizing Theory, Practicing Solidarity*, 221–251. Durham/London: Duke University Press.

Radsch, C. 2011. Re-Imagining Cleopatra: Gendering Cyberactivism in Egypt. Paper Presented at the Middle East Studies Association (MESA) Annual Conference, Washington DC, December 1–4, 2011.

———. 2012. Unveiling the Revolutionaries: Cyberactivism and the Role of Women in the Arab Uprisings. James A. Baker III Institute for Public Policy of Rice University. http://bakerinstitute.org/publications/ITP-pub-CyberactivismAndWomen-051712.pdf

Radsch, C.C., and S. Khamis. 2013. In Their Own Voice: Technologically Mediated Empowerment and Transformation Among Young Arab Women. *Feminist Media Studies* 13 (5): 881–890.

Schilt, K., and E. Zobl. 2008. Connecting the Dots: Riot Grrrls, Ladyfests, and the International Grrrl Zine Network. In *Next Wave Cultures: Feminism, Subcultures, Activism*, ed. A. Harris, 171–192. New York: Taylor & Francis.

PART 1

Unfinished Political Revolutions

CHAPTER 2

Citizenship and Gender Equality in the Cradle of the Arab Spring

Amel Mili

2.1 Introduction: The Ongoing Struggle

The participation of women in protest movements is not a new phenomenon, even if this participation has often been overlooked and underreported. Hence, during the national struggle for independence from colonization, women have made significant contributions to the resistance movement, either by direct civil action or indirectly by supporting militants in their efforts. Yet, once independence was secured, women were for the most part excluded from the decision-making bodies that were to make fateful decisions about the direction the country would take as it charted its destiny and defined its identity; indeed, the early legislation pertaining to elections excluded women from membership of the National Constitutional Assembly and denied them the right to vote. Subsequently, under Bourguiba as well as under Ben Ali, women's messages in the political arena were a dissonant voice that was not in tune with the official discourse, as pointed out by Ahlem Belhaj in a 2013 interview. Their call for democratic reform was so genuine that it included support for their perennial nemesis, the religious parties. Furthermore, the protest movements that arose in the mining region of Tunisia in 2008, which set the stage

A. Mili (✉)
University of Pennsylvania, Philadelphia, PA, USA

for the revolution of December 2010/January 2011, were initiated by women who started the sit-in movement in protest against the Ben Ali regime. Nonetheless, women did not have a commensurate role in the first democratic structures that ruled the country after the Ben Ali regime fell in January 2011.

In previous research (Mili 2009), I collected empirical data on the evolution of gender standards and democratic standards in postcolonial Maghreb countries and found that, contrary to other countries worldwide, where these standards evolve hand in hand, in the Maghreb they are virtually unrelated. Upon analyzing the causes of this singularity, I concluded that it stems from a reversed Maslow hierarchy: the reason why gender standards and democratic standards are generally correlated in most countries around the world is that, according to Maslow's theory, people have a hierarchy of needs that they fulfill in increasing order of urgency and criticality; hence, after fulfilling their human development needs, they seek to fulfill their needs for human rights and political rights. In the Maghreb, that bargain was reversed in the sense that people conceded their political rights, viewing this concession as the price to pay to ensure the protection of their economic wellbeing and their human development. I have also found that human development (measured by the United Nations Development Programme's [UNDP] Human Development Index) and gender development (measured by its Gender Development Index [GDI]) are virtually indistinguishable, having a worldwide correlation of about 0.99, so my findings apply equally well to gender standards and human development standards.

In the euphoria that followed the 2011 protest movements in Tunisia, I felt compelled to revisit the paradox I had identified before (Mili 2009), and conclude with some relief that Tunisians have joined the worldwide community by rearranging their priorities in the right order (Mili 2013); hence they are now prepared to stand up for their political rights, after having secured their human development and gender development goals.

In the two years that followed the 2011 Jasmine revolution, Tunisians experienced their first exposure to democracy, with all the attendant chaos and uncertainty that characterize such political transitions. The euphoria of 2011 had given way to disillusionment with the democratic process, and Tunisians have come to realize that democracy is not a panacea but rather a long, tedious, painstaking process with a steep learning curve. The National Constitutional Assembly, which was formed in October 2011 for a one-year mission to write a new constitution and organize elections, had long since exceeded its term and exhausted its legitimacy, and was still struggling to come up with a viable constitution. In the meantime, the country's economy was stagnant at best, and the security situation was becoming precarious, raising concerns about the political stability of the country.

One of the most prominent points of discord holding up progress in drafting the constitution was the question of what kind of society we might wish to build in Tunisia: do we wish to build a secular society where religion is a private matter and all citizens are free to practice any religion they wish or no religion, or do we want to create a society where religion plays a central role in public life? It is a paradox of the Tunisian revolution that this question arises in twenty-first century Tunisia, let alone that it becomes the central question of the constitutional debate: indeed, Tunisia lived since the middle of the twentieth century under a fairly secular political climate, and Tunisians have long practiced a moderate, pragmatic form of Islam. Moreover, the revolution in Tunisia was fueled by decidedly secular principles and goals, and was driven by young people whose main aim is to live in a modern, free society. How, then, did the religious debate come to the fore? It did so because the religious party Ennahdha ("the Renaissance") won a majority of seats in the assembly. It is an axiom of electoral politics that to win elections one does not need better ideas nor better people, only better organization. Unlike all the other political parties that were competing in the 2011 elections, Ennahdha had been around for several decades, having survived in different degrees of hibernation under the previous two regimes. In the nine months between the collapse of the old regime (January 2011) and the election of the National Constitutional Assembly (October 2011), while other parties were being formed from scratch and were struggling to define themselves, attract activists, and gain some name recognition, Ennahdha merely picked up where it had left off and used the vast infrastructure that mosques afford it to mobilize its base and secure a comfortable victory in the polls.

The implications of the religious debate for gender policies are enormous: if Ennahdha were to succeed in using its numeric advantage in the assembly to impose its views, gender equality would be set back several decades. Recognizing this danger, progressive forces in Tunisia were trying to enshrine gender equality in the constitution. By doing so, they in fact raised the stakes of the debate, and made it more difficult to reach a consensus on the outlines of the constitution. Indeed, religious forces in Tunisia were insisting on enshrining in the constitution a competing principle to gender equality—namely, "gender complementarity". Needless to say, nobody has any illusion about the degree of inequality and unfairness that can be legitimized by the innocent-sounding concept of complementarity. Progressive forces realized that by agreeing to the wholesale revision of the constitution, they had jeopardized many gender gains that were enshrined in the original constitution of Tunisia, and must fight very hard to reclaim every inch.

On January 26, 2014, the National Constitutional Assembly finally concluded its deliberations with the approval of a new constitution, which was signed the next day by the president of the republic (Moncef Marzouki), the chairperson of the assembly (Mustapha Ben Jaafar) and the prime minister (Ali Larayedh). On January 29, 2014, a new government took office on a limited-term basis to organize elections according to the terms of the new constitution, and to manage day-to-day operations. Led by Prime Minister Mehdi Jomaa, the government was made up of technocrats who, pointedly, had no political affiliation and were not allowed to run in the upcoming elections.

In this chapter, I review the history of gender politics in Tunisia from the first state postcolonial building stage to the present, and discuss the constitutionalization of gender equality in the Tunisian constitution, along with the political and social prospects of the country at this stage of the Arab Spring. I show how, through the recent history of Tunisia, the political choices that are made in terms of nation-state building are intimately related to the social choices that are made in terms of the role of women in society. I then discuss in chronological order the political and social orientations that were at play in Tunisia from the postcolonial era to today, and assess the prospects of gender policies in Tunisia in light of this recent history, and of the political and social forces that it has spawned.

2.2 Postcolonial State-Building

Tunisia lived under a French protectorate from 1881 until its independence in 1956. The main actor in the struggle for Tunisia's independence and the main architect of the new state that emerged after independence was an attorney by the name of Habib Bourguiba. Having pursued his law education in France and married a Frenchwoman, he was in awe of the culture, glory, and history of France, and he admired the ideals of the French Revolution and the political regimes that it spawned in France, across Europe, and across the world. Hence, when the time came to build a young nation-state in Tunisia, he had a clear model to follow. However, he realized that what makes a nation-state is not only the political system in place but also the maturity and human development of the population. Looking at Tunisia in the first half of the twentieth century, Bourguiba saw a society that was very backward, uneducated, and in the grip of old regressive traditions, many stemming from poorly interpreted religious edicts. He was especially shocked by the biases that Tunisian society held against women, who were at a great disadvantage in terms of family law, civil law, and social status.

Bourguiba could ill afford to dismiss these longstanding traditions. Indeed, he was dealing with a population for whom religion played an important role in everyday life. Further, during his struggle to secure the independence of Tunisia, he often appealed to the religious and ethnic identity of his people, calling on them to resist occupation by an alien people practicing an alien religion. He could ill afford to then turn around and challenge this Tunisian identity, much less in favor of the alien identity he was railing against. To further complicate his position, Bourguiba was challenged for leadership by another attorney, Salah Ben Youssef, who was resolutely pro-Arab and pro-Muslim. Whereas Bourguiba was educated in France and influenced by European values and ideals, Ben Youssef was educated in the Middle East and appealed to the Arab/Islamic identity of Tunisians.

To resolve this dilemma, in a clever sleight of hand, Bourguiba cast his social reforms not as the radical revolution that they were but rather as a reinterpretation of Islamic law. While he was serving as prime minister, he promulgated a body of law whose focus was to achieve gender equality in Tunisia and free women from centuries-old traditions. Known as the Code of Personal Status (CPS), this was signed into law on August 13, 1956 and took effect on January 1, 1957. Among the main gains that the code achieved in terms of gender equality are the following:

- *Minimum age of marriage.* The CPS mandates a minimum age of 17 for girls and a minimum age of 18 for boys. This is a very important reform because it put an end to the practice of marrying girls around the age of puberty, before they had a chance to fully develop physically and mentally. It also made it more difficult for families to organize arranged marriages, since the girl was now grown up and would be more likely (than a child would) to want a say in her marriage.

- *Elimination of polygamy.* Strictly speaking, polygamy was permitted by the Qur'an under very onerous conditions, with the explicit qualification that if the husband was not sure about fulfilling the conditions, he was restricted to only one spouse. But the conditions are so onerous (that the husband be perfectly fair) that the clause can be interpreted as a prohibition. The practice was not widespread in Tunisia, and where it was practiced it was grossly abused. Soliciting the help of religious figures, Bourguiba was able to push this clause through tough measures, including heavy penalties for violators.
- *Abolition of repudiation.* Repudiation was a very unbalanced process for dissolving a marriage, whereby a man could divorce his wife through a mere verbal declaration, whereas a woman could not secure a divorce except under very exceptional conditions. Like polygamy, this practice was grossly abused by men, especially in a society where women had no economic independence. Under the new law, divorce could only be granted by the courts, and the two parties had equal rights and responsibilities towards the court and towards each other. Furthermore, the court carefully considered the grounds for divorce, and imposed penalties according to each party's responsibility in breaking up the marriage.
- *Family Law.* Breaking with tradition, the CPS gave women significant advantages in case of divorce (especially if the husband was found to be at fault), including child custody, child support, alimony, and the ability to keep the family home or an equivalent home.

On July 25, 1957, the monarchy was abolished, the Bey of Tunis deposed and the new Republic of Tunisia proclaimed, with Habib Bourguiba as its first president. Building on the social reforms he had enacted as prime minister, Bourguiba went on to draft a progressive constitution that consolidated the gender gains enshrined in the code of personal status. In addition to adopting a Western-inspired constitution that gives women equal rights and responsibilities, Bourguiba pursued an aggressive policy that supported gender equality, liberated women from centuries-old traditions, and limited the power of religious institutions, which were running a parallel state and were generally anathema to gender equality. Among the gender-relevant measures that he enacted are the following:

- *Elimination of religious courts.* There is no point in enacting new laws unless one also controls the application of these laws. To this effect, Bourguiba eliminated the Islamic and Jewish courts that were in operation at the time, and he unified the justice system across the country into a hierarchy of courts under the jurisdiction of the Ministry of Justice.

- *Elimination of the economic power of religious institutions.* The institution of *Waqf* allowed religious organizations to manage funds through the exploitation of agricultural properties for the purpose of charitable actions, or to fund the construction of mosques, religious schools, and so forth. Bourguiba put an end to this practice by placing all religious matters under the oversight of the state, through governmental institutions.
- *Elimination of gender-hostile inheritance regimes.* The regime of Habous, which was in effect under the monarchy, was an ownership regime whereby a family owns a property (usually real estate or agricultural) that it can use but cannot sell. Also, this property is inherited from one generation to the next following the male lineage of the family exclusively. Bourguiba eliminated this practice and reverted to inheritance rules dictated by unified civil law.
- *Amalgamating religious education into the unified educational system.* Bourguiba put an end to the educational mission of the Zitouna mosque and merged religious education into the state's education infrastructure, with general religious education in elementary schools and specialized religious education at the secondary and tertiary levels.
- *Legalizing abortion.* Legislation enacted in 1964 allowed women to carry out an abortion within the three first months of pregnancy. This right was granted to single women as well as married women, and in the latter case did not require the approval of the child's father. Combined with access to health care, this measure meant that very often women were able to have the operation done in hospitals, under adequate medical supervision, free of charge.

What is remarkable about this set of measures is that they enhanced the standing of Tunisia with respect to the GDI, several decades before it was even invented. Indeed, if one looks at how the GDI is defined and computed today by the UNDP, one finds that it measures minimum marriage age, fertility rate, level of education, and degree of economic autonomy, all of which were attended to by the CPS.

The position of Habib Bourguiba is that these reforms do not challenge Islam; rather, they adapt it to modern times. He advocates a sharp separation of religion from state, and views the state as an important construct in building a modern nation. Moreover, he judiciously nurtured in generations of Tunisians that were born in the following decades (1950s–1980s) a distinct Tunisian identity that is superimposed (and to some extent supersedes) Arab/Islamic identity. This identity was nurtured and developed around a set of symbols, such as a flag, a national anthem, a national creed, national institutions, passing references to the multicultural/ multiethnic background of Tunisia (a mixture of Berbers, Phoenicians, Carthaginians, Romans, Arabs, Turks, Europeans, etc.), and references to Tunisia's glorious pre-Arabic history (Carthage, Hannibal, Rome, etc.).

Bourguiba's gender-friendly social and political reforms, combined with policies that devote most of the country's (limited) resources to education and health care, have produced a modern society that is open to the outside world, and equipped to deal with the challenges of the contemporary global world. In keeping with its progressive gender policies, and with its desire to be an exemplary player on the international stage, Tunisia signed the UN's Convention on the Elimination of all forms of Discrimination Against Women (CEDAW) in 1985.

2.3 The Democratic Bargain

By the late 1980s, Bourguiba (born in 1903) was growing senile and was clearly unable to fulfill the functions of president, but he was nevertheless kept in power by his entourage, who were using him as a figurehead to perpetuate their hold on power, at the expense of his popularity and to the detriment of the country. A few years earlier, the national assembly had declared him president for life and had amended the constitution accordingly, thereby absolving him from the burden of campaigning. Using an article of the constitution that provides for the termination of the tenure of a president on medical grounds, Prime Minister Zinelabidine Bel Ali deposed Bourguiba and declared himself president on November 7, 1987. In his inaugural address, Ben Ali declared an end to presidency for life (a promise on which he would later renege), promised democratic reforms, and encouraged political participation. In a break from his predecessor, he made a number of concessions towards the Islamist opposition, freeing political prisoners, commuting the sentence of activists who were sentenced to death, and through a number of symbolic gestures, such as concluding his speeches with religious citations, letting religious holidays be determined by religious authorities (rather than civil authorities), and allowing the calls to prayer to be broadcast on national television.

Taking advantage of this (temporary) democratic opening, women activists formed a non-governmental organization (NGO) called the Tunisian Association of Democratic Women. The creation of this and similar organizations is important because it marked a shift in gender politics from a top-down approach, where progress was driven by state actors, to a bottom-up approach, where gender activists take matters into their own hands and drive the evolution of gender standards in Tunisia. Hence progress no longer depended on the goodwill of powerful state actors but rather on the dedication of the main stakeholders—that is, Tunisian women. The Tunisian Association of Democratic Women (TADW) established the first counseling center for victims of domestic violence in March 1993, and spoke out against all forms of violence perpetrated on women, including political violence directed at dissidents.

Under pressure from organizations such as TADW, and in an effort to show a façade of modernity, the Ben Ali regime preserved the gender gains achieved under President Bourguiba, and added some new privileges:

- In 1993, legislation was enacted to allow a Tunisian mother to give Tunisian citizenship to her children when the father is a foreigner, subject to approval by the father, prior to the child reaching the age of 19 years.
- This law was amended in 2002 to dispense with the approval of the father in case he was incapacitated.

In terms of economic measures to help women:

- A fund was created to provide child support to children of divorced parents, when the mother had custody and the father failed to pay child support.
- Legislation was passed that enabled the wife of a state pensioner to avail herself of the pension of her husband upon his death, for as long as she lived. If the couple had an unmarried daughter, she would inherit the pension when both her parents passed away, for as long as she lived or until she married.

In terms of political participation:

- In the legislative elections cycle of 2004, the political party of President Ben Ali adopted a voluntary quota of 25 % female representation in all of its candidate lists.
- In the 2009 elections cycle, this ratio was increased to 35 %.

A study conducted in 2008 showed the rate of female participation in the various sectors of public life (Table 2.1). These percentages are clearly low, especially in the most critical branches of the state (executive, legislative and judicial branches).

The presidency of Zinelabidine Ben Ali lasted from 1987 to 2011 and was characterized by political stability and economic development. Through a combination of oppression and appeasement, by showing enough resolve to silence some opposition and enough leniency to co-opt others' opposition, by jailing some hardcore opponents, forcing others into exile, and making cosmetic concessions to yet others, the regime was able to secure a long period of stability, which was favorable to foreign investment and economic prosperity. On the other hand, by providing economic prosperity, the regime gave Tunisians a stake in political stability and made political opposition sound like a futile intellectual exercise; in a way, political stability and economic prosperity nurtured each other and ensured the longevity of the regime. This, in essence, is the precarious bargain that Tunisians made with the political system—conceding civil rights and political freedoms in exchange for economic prosperity—but it is an unsustainable bargain.

Table 2.1 Female Participation in State Institutions, 2008

Institution	Percentage, female participation
City councils	27.4
Regional councils	32.0
Judicial council	13.3
Economic and social council	20.0
Constitutional council	25.2
Minister portfolios	12.0
Diplomatic personnel	24.0
Advisory council	15.2
National Constitutional Assembly	22.7

2.4 The Arab Spring

The bargain alluded to in the previous section came to a crashing end on December 17, 2010 as a result of a minor incident in a small town in central Tunisia. A policewoman named Fadia Hamdi harassed an unlicensed fruit vendor, Mohamed Bouazizi, confiscated his wares, and ordered him to close his stall. When he resisted, she slapped him in public. In the macho culture of small-town Tunisia, a public slap from a woman is a major affront to one's honor. When the local authorities refused to meet with him and hear his grievances, he set himself on fire. This triggered a wave of protests, which were fueled by pent-up discontent and resentment against the regime. These protests spread across the country, all the way to the capital, where they culminated on January 14, 2011 with the fall of the regime and the exile of President Ben Ali to Saudi Arabia. Fadia Hamdi was subsequently put on trial for her role in the December 17 incident but was acquitted. Mohamed Bouazizi was badly burned and he passed away on January 4 after two weeks of intensive care, without witnessing the momentous events of January 14, 2011 that he had helped to set in motion.

Following the flight of President Ben Ali, a succession of short-lived governments filled the power vacuum, characterized by decreasing participation of members of the Democratic Constitutional Rally, Ben Ali's party. By late March the consensus had settled on a provisional government presided over by a former minister from Bourguiba's regime, Beji Caid Essebsi. This government had a limited-term mandate to manage day-to-day operations while preparing for the election of the National Constitutional Assembly, whose mission was to draft a constitution and prepare elections for whatever legislative and executive structures the constitution called for.

A special commission was created to plan for the elections, draw up electoral maps, put forward rules for submitting candidacies, campaign, run voting stations, create maps of voting stations, and compile rules for counting the results and assigning seats accordingly. It also monitored the conduct of the elections, with the help of non-governmental organizations from abroad. Campaigning was allowed between October 1 and October 22, 2011, and voting was set for October 23. The spring and summer of 2011 were a period of great excitement and anticipation in Tunisia, as parties of all tendencies were emerging, scrambling to enroll members, and trying to gain some traction with the voting public.

Gender-related civil society organizations were very active during this period, having participated in many of the political actions that preceded and followed the fall of the Ben Ali's regime. In particular, they were instrumental in removing from power all the members of Ben Ali's party, which was subsequently dissolved. Furthermore, they were active in seeking to achieve gender parity in the assembly. In an effort to accommodate their wishes, the Electoral Commission agreed to mandate that all candidate lists alternate between men and women. However, as I discuss below, this did not produce the desired results.

The elections were held on Sunday October 23, 2011 under the auspices of the Tunisian Electoral Commission, and they were monitored by Tunisian and international bodies. They were universally hailed as a great success in terms of voter participation, poll organization, and transparency. According to the independent electoral council, the rate of participation among registered voters was 86.1 %, a very respectable figure by any standard, reflecting the faith that Tunisians had in the benefits of democracy. The results of the election, distributed by party and by gender (in terms of number of seats in the assembly) are shown in Table 2.2.

Table 2.2 Results of the Elections of the Constitutional Assembly, October 23, 2011

Rank	Party	Number of seats				
		Men	Women	Total	Percentage of vote	Percentage of women
1	**Ennahdha** (Islamist)	50	39	89	41.01	43.82
2	**CPR** (center left)	25	4	29	13.36	13.80
3	**Aridha** (petition, progressive)	22	4	26	11.98	15.38
4	**Takattol** (social democrat)	16	4	20	9.22	20.00
5	**PDP** (social democrat)	14	2	16	7.37	12.50
6	**PDM** (democracy, modernity)	3	2	5	2.30	40.00
7	**Moubadara** (The Initiative)	3	2	5	2.30	40.00
8	**Afek** (horizons, liberal)	2	2	4	1.84	50.00
9	**PCOT** (communist)	3	0	3	1.38	0.00
10	**MDS** (socialist)	2	0	2	0.92	0.00
11	**MP** (popular movement)	2	0	2	0.92	0.00
12	**Independents**	16	0	16	7.37	0.00
	Total	158	59	217	100.00	27.19

Notes: *CPR* Congress for the Republic, *PDP* Progressive Democratic Party, *PDM* Democratic Modernist Pole, *PCOT* Workers' Party, *MDS* Movement of Socialist Democrats, *MP* Popular Movement

The first observation we can make about the results is that, despite the efforts of gender-related NGOs and the goodwill shown by the Electoral Commission, the percentage of women in the assembly was far from parity, standing at 27.19 %. The second observation is that, paradoxically, the party with the largest female representation was the religious party, Ennahdha. These two facts stem from the way seats are assigned to parties, and from the level of organizational readiness of the various parties on the eve of the elections campaign.

- When it drew the electoral map, the Electoral Commission delineated electoral districts across the country and assigned a number of seats available for each district, on the basis of the latest population census. The list of candidates in a given electoral district must have the assigned number of candidates.
- The lists of candidates are ranked from 1 to N, where N is the number of seats in that district. When the votes in that district are tallied, each list is granted a number of seats proportional to the number of votes it has obtained; these seats are automatically assigned to the first candidates on the list.
- Very few lists had a woman at the top; most had a man at the top and then, say, women in positions 2, 4, 6, and so on.
- Most parties in the election were new and had no recognition beyond what they could build in the few months prior to the campaign, and then in the few weeks of the campaign itself. Of the 11 parties that fielded candidates in the election, only Ennahdha, the PDP, the POCT, and the MDS existed prior to the revolution. All of them had been ruthlessly silenced under the Ben Ali and Bourguiba regimes and were active only in the few periods of relative democratization in the past. Of these, the party that was most successful in surviving "under the radar," so to speak, was Ennahdha, the reason being that, as a religious party, it could hide its activity under the guise of religious activities. Given the importance of religion in Tunisian society, neither the Ben Ali regime nor the Bourguiba regime dared to interfere directly with religious activities. Furthermore, Ennahdha was successful in using the infrastructure of mosques across the country as an organizational tool to mobilize its base and remain active.
- When the electoral process was open and political activity was again legal, Ennahdha was quick on its feet, unlike other older parties that had been dormant for a long time. As the election results show, these

resuscitated parties did no better than brand new parties that had sprung up in the post-revolution period. Moreover, some of them, such as the POCT and the MDS, carried slogans that had meaning in the 1960s and 1970s but which had long since been discredited after the collapse of the Soviet Union.
- Because of the multitude of parties competing in the elections, most lists could only gather enough votes for one seat, sometimes two. The only party that often garnered enough votes to earn more than one seat in each electoral district was Ennahdha.
- Except for the few cases where a list was led by a woman, only lists that earned more than one seat had a woman in them.

These observations explain the following:

- Even though gender parity was scrupulously observed in the election process, it did not translate into gender parity in the composition of the assembly.
- Paradoxically, the party that represents the greatest threat to gender equality is also the party that has the greatest number, and greatest proportion, of women in its ranks. According to Lilia Labidi (2014), this statistic should push liberal women to revisit their position regarding the legalistic approach. It should also push Ennahdha women to reflect on the forces inside the assembly that defend women's rights, taking into account that it is more the fact of being a feminist rather than the fact of being a woman that is the best guarantee of political representation of women (indeed, some of the most conservative/reactionary positions in regards to gender issues were held by Ennahdha women, notably members of the Ennahdha caucus in the constitutional assembly).

In the morning after the elections, gender organizations were shocked by the results—so much so that they felt trapped by the decision to build a new constitution rather than amend the existing one, and they wished they had opposed it. Even though the elections were held with the greatest transparency, they did not appear to reflect the true political orientations of the majority of Tunisians. The decision to draft a new constitution was driven by a desire to break from the past more than the need to make profound changes to the current version. Yet by committing to draft a new one, and by electing an assembly where Ennahdha would hold the greatest number of seats, the country had exposed itself to the possibility of heading in a totally different direction from the trajectory it had followed for the previous six decades. For gender activists, this was a very serious situation. Not surprisingly, Ennahdha, emboldened by its success at the polls, and reading into it a bigger mandate than it was really given, did not hesitate to put everything on the table for reconsideration and revision: the gender gains achieved through the Code of Personal Status (CPS), the additional guarantees offered by the 1957 constitution, the secular/civil nature of the judicial system, the national identity, the role of women in society, gender equality in the workplace, principles of family law, and so on.

Gender equality advocacy organizations had grievances of their own: despite its revolutionary nature, especially in the context of 1956 Tunisia, the CPS had some gender-hostile language that ought to be fixed. It is conceivable that, in his efforts to get his gender legislation approved, Bourguiba had to make concessions to conservative forces in Tunisian society, but these are no longer needed in twenty-first century Tunisia. Some of the grievances of these organizations include:

- Article 23 of the code provides that a wife must obey her husband, and gives the husband the right to punish her in cases of disobedience.
- In its preamble, the code discusses the obligations of each party in a marriage, and makes explicit references to traditions and customs in Tunisia, opening the door to a wide interpretation that was used at the time to limit women's rights.
- The family home is decided exclusively by the husband, and the father maintains conservatorship of children regardless of custody decisions.
- When siblings inherit from their parents, a daughter gets half of what a son gets; this might have been a gain in the past, when women used to be excluded from inheritance altogether, but this law is considered to be a discriminatory measure by international standards. However, Ennahdha insists on its sacred character, taking its source from Sharia law to oppose its amendment.
- A Tunisian woman cannot marry a non-Muslim man, whereas a Tunisian man can marry a non-Muslim woman (*referred to as the Law of Houria*). It is very common to see foreign men convert to Islam before marrying a Tunisian woman.

In addition, gender equality advocates want to see Tunisia lift its reservations regarding the CEDAW and sign it as is.

When the National Constitutional Assembly convened for its first meeting on November 22, 2011 in the chambers of the assembly in Bardo, the battle lines were drawn, the stakes very high, and the possible outcomes were wide ranging. At stake for gender equality advocates was whether a modern society worthy of Bourguiba's vision and ready to meet the challenges of the twenty-first century would be built, or a society in the grip of millenary traditions where half of the country's human potential would be restrained and prevented from being deployed fully.

2.5 THE GENDER TRIBULATIONS OF THE ARAB REVOLUTION

When the National Constitutional Assembly convened, its first order of business was to elect its leadership and to form a provisional government that would run the day-to-day operations of the country until elections could be held according to the constitution that it was supposed to write. Pursuant to negotiations that started even before the first meeting, three of the top parties in the assembly agreed to a power-sharing arrangement, whereby

- Hamadi Jebali, from Ennahdha, was to serve as prime minister;
- Moncef Marzouki, from CPR, was to serve as president;
- Mustapha Ben Jaafar, from Takattol, was to serve as chairperson of the assembly.

Regarding other portions of the vote, the Aridha party was not a political party so much as a label on electoral lists. It was organized by an expatriate who lives in the UK and was not considered a viable political organization within the assembly. It was subsequently dissolved and most of its members joined other parties. The PDP, being the next biggest party in terms of the number of seats in the assembly, became the de facto voice of the opposition. Its spokesperson was Maya Jribi, a long-term pro-democracy activist. This party was expected to do well in the elections but, following its poor showing in the polls, it lost its appeal and morphed into a new party, the Republican Party (Al Jomhoury). Unlike its US namesake it is a left-leaning progressive party.

2.5.1 *Parity*

The first thing that gender-equality organizations aimed to address was the issue of gender parity in decision-making institutions within the state. The statistics in Table 2.3, collected in 2010 by the Center for Research,

Table 2.3 Women Participation in Political and Economic Life, 2010

Sector	Variable	Percentage
Economic activity	Women in the economically active population	27.9
	Rate of women's economic activity	24.8
	Women's share of the employed population	25.2
	Working women having a higher education	20.9
	Women's unemployment rate	18.8
	Unemployment rate among female university graduates	34.9
Legal professions	Women lawyers	42.5
	Women magistrates	28.9
	Women notaries public	31.0
	Women bailiffs	18.0
White-collar sector	Women pharmacists	72.0
	Women researchers	47.0
	Women journalists	44.6
	Women physicians	42.0
Public service sector	Women in administrative positions	25.5
	Women who are director general or secretary general of a company	13.4
	Women directors	22.0
	Women who are vice-directors/vice-chairs	23.6
	Women who are department heads	29.2
	Women who are supervisors of public health	28.5
	Women pedagogical guides	25.0
	Women who are directors of youth centers	18.1

Studies, Documentation, and Information on Women (http://www.credif.org.tn/), show that despite decades of progress, women still have some distance to go to achieve true gender equality in Tunisia.

Despite the debacle of the elections of the National Constitutional Assembly, gender equality activists continued to lobby in favor of gender parity in political institutions, soliciting support for their efforts from regional and international women's organizations. They were supported by an important organization in the Tunisian political landscape, namely the commission charged with protecting the objectives of the revolution, an NGO launched shortly after January 2011 to be the voice of the revolution, and to ensure that the gains of the revolutionary movement were not diverted by political forces. A quote from the coordinator of the commission, law professor Yadh Ben Achour, reflects a broadly held view of gender parity in political institutions: "This is an initiative brought forth by democratic political parties, civil society, and independent women and men, that has been approved democratically." Echoing his view, Rachida Bel Haj Zekri, president of the Association of Tunisian Women for Research and Development, declares:

> The principle of parity enshrined in the new electoral guidelines has a symbolic significance. It is a measure of positive discrimination that recognizes the right of women to gain access to political office and to the public space; this measure will certainly have a positive impact in the medium term on discriminatory practices within political parties. Its ultimate impact will be contingent upon the struggle that Tunisian women are pursuing at different levels within political parties to ensure that women be given prominent positions in electoral lists. The success of this measure is also contingent upon the dedication and political commitment of women in this critical phase, and of the effort of leaders of women's organizations to raise awareness of gender issues.

Given the importance of a free press in the democratic process, gender-equality organizations feel the need to ensure that parity extends to journalists and broadcasters so that women's voices are heard in the mass media. A study conducted by the TADW, seeking to assess the degree of participation of women in the mass media found very low female participation, revealing the statistics shown in Table 2.4, divided by sector.

The TADW formulated the following recommendations:

- Media organizations should learn to operate in a new, open environment, where they are free from political pressure, and have a responsibility to their viewership/readership more than anything.
- Media organizations should encourage participation of women and provide forums where women's issues are debated and shared with the public.

Table 2.4 Women Participation in Mass Media

Sector	Variable	Percentage
Mass media	Women in television	10.21
	Women in radio	10.40
	Women in the press	2.85

- Women's organizations should use mass media effectively to voice their concerns and promote their views.

The debate on gender parity in Tunisia is reminiscent of the debates about equal opportunities that take place in the USA: supporters argue that there is a need to redress longstanding injustices, and that the emphasis is temporary; while opponents argue that it is discriminatory, contrary to fairness, and encourages mediocrity. Like the debate on equal opportunities, the discussion about parity will most likely fade when the need for parity measures diminishes.

2.5.2 Constitutionalization of Gender Equality

When the National Constitutional Assembly opened the debate about the new constitution, many parties assumed that the starting point of the discussion was the 1959 constitution. Many were shocked when some parties in the assembly proceeded to open up fundamental questions that many Tunisians assumed were long since settled, such as national identity, the role of religion, the type of state, and the role of women. Some would talk about a deviation in the path of the revolution as the demands of the youth during the revolution had been freedom and dignity. Gender-equality organizations were very concerned about this situation and they decided to advocate in favor of strong language in the constitution that enshrined equality between men and women. Two competing views were under consideration:

- One is supported by many gender organizations, civil society, and many parties represented in the assembly, and it provides for a separation of state and religion, makes reference to the International Human Rights Framework, and emphasizes the separation between citizenship and religious affiliation. Gender organizations such as the Association of Democratic Women and the Association of Women for Research and Development demand the removal of all exceptions raised by the Tunisian state on the CEDAW.
- The other is supported by the most powerful party in the assembly, which favors the application of Sharia law, considers religious affiliation as part of citizenship, and argues in favor of a principle of complementarity between the genders rather than a principle of equality.

The threat that the assembly might adopt the second view has energized civil society in general and women's organizations in particular, and has mobilized a vast movement of protest that has remained active for the duration of the assembly proceedings (nearly two years). The reason why many feel the need to include this principle in the constitution now is that the 1959 constitution failed explicitly to do so, and this omission caused a great deal of subsequent ambiguity. Indeed, in Arabic and many other languages, the masculine plural is used to designate a plurality that might include masculine subjects and feminine subjects. In addition, Arabic gives a different form to nouns depending on whether they designate a male or a female subject. So when the 1959 constitution stipulates that all (male) citizens are equal before the law, it may have meant to designate male and female citizens, but it could also be (mis)interpreted as referring to males alone and so cannot be used to claim that male citizens and female citizens are equal before the law. Therefore when subsequent legislation provides that the testimony of a man before a court is worth the testimony of two women, one cannot strike down such a law on the grounds that it is unconstitutional. The same applies to civil laws that provide that a woman inherits half a share compared with her brother's share. Both laws are inspired by Sharia. Another questionable aspect of the 1959 constitution is that it provides for equality before the law but does not explicitly provide for equality of rights and duties. Thus it cannot be used to strike down articles of family law that provide different rights and duties to spouses.

The formula that women's organizations advocated then was (to reflect the Arabic) that the (male) citizens and the (female) citizens are considered equal before the law, and have the same rights and obligations. Such a formulation would capture the political dimension of equality (that all men are treated equally and all women are treated equally) but also the social dimension (that a man and a woman are treated equally).

August 13 is a national holiday in Tunisia, called Women's Holiday. It celebrates the enactment of the CPS in 1956. It is usually seen as an occasion for the nation to reflect on this legislation and on its role in the development and shaping of the nation. In 2012 the holiday coincided with the time when the assembly was opening the debate on very fundamental political and social orientations, and in the process putting some issues that most Tunisians consider off limits back on the table. Sensing a danger to women's rights, women's organizations used the holiday to launch a large-scale campaign intended to draw people's attention to the debate taking place in the assembly, and to the possibility that the nation stood to lose a great deal of the social advances it had achieved during the previous few decades. Tunisians were very receptive to this campaign because most recognize the role that these gains have played in making Tunisia what it is, and most would never want to let them slip away. Interestingly, Tunisians from all walks of life, including men and women, young and old, women dressed in Western style and those wearing Hijabs (usually part of Ennahdha's political base), walked side by side, calling on the assembly to maintain the gender progress enshrined in the CPS. Presumably the significance of such unanimity was not lost on the leadership of Ennahdha, who were watching the mood of the country in preparation for the next election cycle.

What started out as a one-day event turned into an ongoing nationwide debate that saturated the airwaves, the printed press, and public forums across the country for the duration of the assembly's deliberations The overwhelming majority of citizens, civil society organizations, labor organizations, and political figures spoke out in clear terms against any rollback of gender-equality gains. Furthermore, as the assembly and the provisional government stayed in place well beyond their original one-year term, more and more people started questioning their mandate and opposing their argument that they represented the will of the people.

Two events in 2013 further weakened the Ennahdha, and shredded much of its legitimacy and popularity, even within its core base: the assassination of Chokri Belaid on February 6 and of Mohamed Brahmi on July 25. Both were political figures from the left who had spoken out vigorously against Ennahdha. Much of the blame for their deaths was placed on the government—if not for carrying out the murders, at least for creating such a climate of insecurity as to make them possible, and for dragging its feet in investigating the crimes and bringing the perpetrators to justice. Everyone suspected that these murders were carried out by religious extremists, and by association they blamed religious parties for them. The assassinations caused a great deal of shock and outrage because Tunisia is not accustomed to political violence; they also produced calls for the sitting administration to be dissolved and replaced by a caretaker government of national unity. Popular pressure to dissolve the government remained strong through the remainder of the year, until a new constitution was approved in January 2014, and a new government was formed to organize the first full-term elections based on the political structures dictated by the new constitution. It is conceivable that during the last few months of the constitutional debate in the assembly the religious parties felt very weak and therefore did not have the clout to impose their views as much as they wished. It is also possible that they felt that muscling their way through the constitutional debate to impose their views against the will of the majority of Tunisians might cost them dearly in the upcoming elections. Whatever the reason, the constitution that was enacted on January 26, 2014 reflected many of the views held by women's organizations in Tunisia and elsewhere.

2.6 The Constitution of the Second Republic

The new constitution was approved by the National Constitutional Assembly late in the evening of January 26, 2014 by 200 votes in favor, 12 votes against, and 4 abstentions. It replaced the 1959 constitution, which had been suspended since March 2011. It is divided into ten chapters and 149 articles. If the constitution of 1959 formed the basis of the first republic of Tunisia, it is possible to consider the political regime outlined in the 2014 constitution as the second republic. Among its most interesting articles are the following:

- Articles 1 and 2 are declared immutable. Article 1 declares that Tunisia is a free, independent and sovereign state. Its religion is Islam, its official language is Arabic, and its political regime is a republic. Article 2 declares that Tunisia is a state that has a civil character, based on citizenship, the will of the people, and the primacy of the law. Many analysts feel that these two articles, both immutable, appear to contradict each other. Whether they do depends on whether one interprets them as descriptive or prescriptive; it is possible to view them as a clever compromise that enables all parties to recognize their views therein.
- Whereas Articles 1 and 2 appear to contradict each other, Article 6 contradicts itself. The first paragraph declares that the state is the guardian of religion, and that it guarantees freedom of worship and belief, and freedom of conscience. It also guarantees the neutrality of mosques, and opposes their use for partisan purposes. Yet the second paragraph declares that the state also commits to promote values of moderation and tolerance, and to protect sacred artifacts, and it prohibits accusations of apostasy. Many secular-minded subjects see massive contradictions between these distinct missions.
- Article 21 provides (with the qualification that Arabic conveys gender when referring to people) that (male) citizens and (female) citizens have the same rights and duties. They are equal before the law and are

free from any form of discrimination. The state guarantees its citizens freedoms, and individual and collective rights. It provides them conditions for a decent lifestyle. The following articles (22–24) build on this theme by declaring the sanctity of life and virtually excluding the death penalty, prohibiting torture, protecting the sanctity of the home and the confidentiality of communications. From the standpoint of gender equality, Article 21 is of the utmost importance because it provides gender equality in all its forms: equality before the law but also equality in terms of rights and duties. The article should put an end to such practices as assigning different weights to the testimony of men and women, awarding different shares of inheritance to men and women, and recording different information on identification papers (marital status is recorded on women's documents but not men's). Article 22, which cites the sanctity of life and the state's responsibility in protecting life, raises an issue for women's organizations, however, who fear that it may be used to interfere with a woman's abortion rights.

- Article 39 mandates free education until the age of 16, and declares that the state must guarantee the right to free public education at all levels (primary, secondary, tertiary). This is clearly a legacy of Bourguiba, who was a champion of free education as a key to human development. It provides an obligation for citizens to educate their children until age 16, and an obligation for the state to provide free education at all levels. The article goes on to mandate that the state nurture in children an Arab/Islamic identity, in addition to the national identity, and to encourage the use of Arabic at the same time as it supports an interest in foreign languages and civilizations.
- Article 42 protects access to culture, encourages cultural creativity at the same time as it supports the national culture in its authenticity and diversity, and encourages the overture to foreign cultures and the dialog of civilizations.
- Article 46 is even more explicit than Article 21 in its protection of women's rights. The state commits to protect the rights gained by women, to sustain them, and to improve them; it ensures equal opportunities between men and women in assuming different responsibilities in all domains; it seeks to achieve parity between men and women in all elected bodies; and it takes the necessary steps to eradicate violence against women. By acknowledging violence against women, taking up the issue as a matter of state and committing the state to the eradication of this scourge, the Tunisian constitution is clearly charting new territory.

While critics may highlight the seemingly contradictory nature of this constitution, it is possible to view it instead as an attempt to reconcile many worthy goals that it is attempting to achieve. If one excludes the possibility of hidden agendas, most Tunisians would gladly endorse the goals therein. Speaking of Article 42, Professor Yadh Ben Achour sums up the dilemma of the authors of the constitution in the following terms (translated into English):

> This magnificent article, open on the world, contradicts once more Article 39. It is a faithful reflection of our society, which is itself full of contradictions. What is important, in my opinion, is that these questions are finally debated. This was never done before in Tunisia, neither under Bourguiba nor under Ben Ali. Under Bourguiba, we were under a regime of modernity imposed by the shepherd, the leader. With Ben Ali, we were under absolute dictatorship. Today, these debates are taking place in the open for the first time, and are the subject of intense discussions in the assembly, in the printed press, and on television platforms. I believe this is the beginning of a genuine secularization of our society.

2.7 Concluding Remarks

In this chapter I have summarily reviewed the recent history of statebuilding in Tunisia, and shown how the decisions made and the options chosen are intimately related to those made with regard to gender equality and gender roles in society. I conclude with three observations:

- First, it is important to bear in mind that women have played a crucial role in the Tunisian revolution. While everyone likes to point out the Sidi Bouzid incident as the trigger of the revolution, I would suggest that it caused a spark, and the spark would have been fruitless if it were not for a climate of discontent that pervaded that area of the country, pursuant to a wide protest movement that was initiated in 2008/2009, in which women played a central role. Women and women's organizations continued to adopt key roles in all subsequent phases of the Tunisian revolution: participating in the sit-ins that resulted in the fall of successive governments formed in the spring of 2011 with members of Ben Ali's party; mobilizing progressive forces in the period leading up to the elections of October 2011; raising awareness about gender issues and civil rights on Women's Day in 2012 and 2013; and campaigning vigorously against two draft constitutions that were floated by Ennahdha prior to the final version.

- Second, it is important to remember that the participation of women in the Tunisian revolution has led to advances not only in gender standards but also in democratic standards. Indeed, women's organizations were instrumental in pushing a progressive constitutional agenda that stressed religious tolerance, openness to the outside world, and adherence to international standards in terms of human rights and freedoms.
- Third, it is essential to recognize that, as political transitions go, the Tunisian revolution has been exceptionally smooth and peaceful, and has led to a hopeful, positive outcome in the form of a revolutionary constitution and an orderly transfer of power. From the early days, international journalists referred to this transition as the "Jasmine Revolution" in the same way that the transition of power from Bourguiba to Ben Ali, which took place in compliance with the constitution, was referred to as the "Jasmine Coup d'État". In addition to being a regional leader in gender standards and in progressive constitutions, Tunisia can also pride itself on specializing in fragrant political transitions.

Acknowledgments I gratefully acknowledge the following political figures and scholars who graciously agreed to meet me and answer questions: Mr. Taieb Baccouche, PhD, scholar, university professor, political activist, and former minister of education in the first post-revolution government (interviewed in Tunis on July 17, 2013); Ms. Boshra Bel Haj Hmida, attorney, political activist, feminist, and former president of the NGO Tunisian Association of Democratic Women (interviewed by phone on January 15, 2014); Ahlem Belhaj, medical doctor and professor of medicine, director of a hospital ward for child psychology, and president of the NGO Tunisian Association of Democratic Women (interviewed in Tunis on August 22, 2013); Ms. Emna Jebloui, university professor at the University of Tunis, a consultant for the UNDP, director of the Tunisian Institute of Political Science, and an advisor to the president of the National Constitutional Assembly (interviewed in Tunis on August 18, 2013); and Mr. Neji Jelloul, university professor, political activist, and expert in Islamic studies (interviewed in Tunis on August 10, 2013).

Bibliography

Charrad, M.M. 2002. *Nation States, Kin-Based Formations, and Gender in the Maghrib*. Annual Meeting the Middle East Studies Association, November. Washington, DC.

Charrad, M.M., and A. Zarrugh. 2014. Equal or Complementary? Women in the New Tunisian Constitution After the Arab Spring. *The Journal of North African Studies* 19 (2): 230–243.

European Parliament. 2012. *Gender Equality Policies in Tunisia*. http://www.europarl.europa.eu/egData/etudes/note/join/2012/462502/IPOL-FEMM_NT(2012) 462502_EN.pdf

Fakir, F. 1997. Engendering Democracy and Islam in the Arab World. *Third World Quarterly* 18 (1): 165–174.

Fregosi, F. 2004. *La Regulation Institutionnelle de l'Islam en Tunisie: Entre audace moderniste et tutelle etatique*. CNRS, Universite Robert Schumann. Reference:Technical Report, http://www.ceri-science-po.org/. May 2004.

Haddad, T. 1977. *Imraatuna fi Chariaa wal Mujtamaa*. Tunis: M.T.E.

Inglehart, R., L. Harrison, and S. Huntington. 2000. *Culture Matters: How Human Values Shape Progress*. New York: Basic Books.

Inglehart, R., and P. Norris. 2003. *Rising Tide: Gender Equality and Cultural Change Around the World*. Cambridge, UK/New York: Cambridge University Press.

Khalaf, U.A.A. 2013. *Constitutions and Constitutional Amendments in the Arab World*. Technical report, University of Baghdad, Baghdad, Iraq, 2013.

Khalil, A. 2014. Tunisia'a Women: Partners in Revolution. *The Journal of North Africa Studies* 19 (2): 186–199.

Labidi, L. 2014. *Electoral Practice of Tunisian Women in the Context of a Democratic Transition*. Washington, DC: The Wilson Center.

Marshall, S.E. 1984a. Politics and Female Status in North Africa: A Reconsideration of Development Theory. *Economic Development and Cultural Change* 32 (3): 499–524.

———. 1984b. Paradoxes of Change: Culture Crisis, Islamic Revival, and the Reactivation of Patriarchy. *African and Asian Studies* 19 (1–2): 1–17.

Mili, A. 2009. Gender Standards vs Democratic Standards: Examples and Counter Examples. *International Journal of Women Studies* 11 (2): 100–120.

———. 2013. Gender Standards vs Democratic Standards: Revisiting the Paradox. *International Journal of Women Studies* 14 (2): 3–11.

Moghadam, V.M. 1994. *Modernizing Women: Gender and Social Change in the Middle East*. Cairo: American University in Cairo Press.

———. 2003. *Gender and Social Change in the Middle East*. Boulder: Lynne Rienner Publishers. isbn:1-58826-195-6 hc 1-58826-171-9 pb.

Nazir, S.C. 2005. *Women's Rights in the Middle East and North Africa*. New York: Freedom House.

UN Authors. 2009. *Les quotas de genre en politique en Algerie, au Maroc et en Tunisie*. Institut International de Recherche et de Formation des Nations Unies pour la Promotion de la Femme.

Welzel, R.I.C. 2005. *Modernization, Cultural Change, and Democracy: The Human Development Sequence*. New York: Cambridge University Press.

CHAPTER 3

Voices Shouting for Reform: The Remaining Battles for Bahraini Women

Nada Alwadi and Sahar Khamis

3.1 Introduction

There is no doubt that social media helped young women to play a central role in the uprising in Bahrain, similar to the rest of the so-called "Arab Spring" countries. Cyberactivism became one of the main catalysts to put many young Arab female activists on the map, providing them with respect from their own communities, lots of online followers, media exposure, and, in some cases, international fame.

According to Courtney C. Radsch and Sahar Khamis,[1] female cyberactivists are redefining the boundaries of private and public spheres, linking political and social domains, connecting national and international audiences, and performing mainstream and citizen journalism. This was the case in many Arab countries during the popular uprisings of 2011, and Bahrain was no exception.

Since 2011, the portrayal of women in Bahrain has shifted dramatically. Women are now being portrayed as proactive leaders, vocal, and brave, a

N. Alwadi (✉)
Virginia Tech University, Blacksburg, VA, USA

S. Khamis
University of Maryland, College Park, MD, USA

portrayal which is somehow new to the small island. When Jalila Alsalman, a Bahraini teacher and mother, was released after spending months in prison for her activism, people treated her like a hero. Thousands of Bahrainis gathered in front of the prison to receive and cheer her and her family. Huge banners showing her picture were hung on the houses of her conservative village for months to demonstrate the pride in her role in the prodemocracy movement. Many people in Bahraini villages who had previously been hesitant about voting for women in the election now treated one of their own as a hero and a leader.

This chapter explores the role of women in the ongoing popular uprising in Bahrain, and how social and online media facilitated the way in which women on the island are now seen as leaders in their community. It also examines whether gender demands were one of the triggers for this uprising in Bahrain and, if so, how?

We begin by giving an overview of the political struggle in Bahrain and the popular uprising of 2011. We argue that cyberactivism was one of the main factors that shaped the Arab movements, including that in Bahrain. We also claim that the social and online media were a golden opportunity for Bahraini women to be seen as leaders in their community. Several online female activists from Bahrain were interviewed for the purpose of this chapter. Stories of other female activists are highlighted as examples to support our arguments.

This chapter also sheds light on one of the most controversial gender issues in Bahrain—The family law—and explores how this was affected by the ongoing political struggle there.

3.2 Bahrain: The Popular Protest of 2011

Inspired by the so-called "Arab Spring," Bahrain witnessed major popular protests on February 14, 2011. Tens of thousands of Bahrainis, men and women, joined the protests in their capital, Manama, demanding political reforms and democratic transition. Social media was essential in organizing this movement and mobilizing people to join it. The discussion began on an online popular public forum called Bahrain Online, where the idea of organizing protests on February 14 was introduced. As political events escalated in Bahrain during February and March, social media, particularly Twitter and Facebook, became the main sources of information for those who wanted to follow the news.

Meanwhile, state-controlled media, including television and radio, were largely one-sided in their coverage, and most newspapers, except for *Alwasat*, also reflected the state's agenda by portraying the protesters as violent and sectarian.

The uprising was crushed a month later by the Bahraini authorities, and Emergency Law was declared in the country for three months. Major human rights violations were committed during this time, including imprisonment and torture, in some cases leading to death, and the dismissal of thousands of employees for participating in the protests. Doctors, journalists, college professors, and many others—men and women—were targeted, imprisoned, tortured, and dismissed.

After the worst of the violence in Bahrain, the government appointed an independent body to investigate the factors that led to the protests and ensuing chaos. The Bahrain Independent Commission of Inquiry (BICI), which included a reputable team of international human rights experts, released a 513-page report in November 2011 detailing the investigation. The report documented 46 deaths, 559 allegations of torture, and more than 4000 cases of employees being dismissed for participating in protests.

According to many international human rights organizations, at the time of writing, most of the BICI recommendations have not yet been implemented in Bahrain despite the fact that the government accepted the results of the report and pledged to implement its proposals. In fact, the latest moves in Bahrain appear to be towards more restrictions on freedom of speech rather than fewer.

3.3 How Did Cyberactivism Affect Popular Movements in the Arab World?

New media, especially social media, played a critical role in triggering the wave of revolt and upheaval which has been sweeping the Arab world since 2011. These new communication methods managed to put many Arab women in the spotlight. In their article "Cyberactivism in the Egyptian Revolution," Khamis and Vaughn[2] (2011) argue that the role of new media before, during, and after the Egyptian revolution was especially important in three intertwined ways: enabling cyberactivism, which was a major trigger for street activism; encouraging civic engagement, by aiding the mobilization and organization of protests and other forms of political expression; and promoting a new form of citizen journalism, which provides a platform for ordinary citizens to express themselves and document their own versions of reality.

This is true in many Arab countries, including Bahrain, a small country with a large internet population. Bahrain has witnessed a great surge in social media activism, which both inspired and paralleled political activism on the ground. However, it also witnessed governmental efforts to resist and halt this activism, both on the ground and online, which was evidenced in many cases of shutting down websites, blogs, and Twitter accounts, and arresting political opponents who were also social media activists. As a result, Bahrain was added to the "Reporters without Borders" list of "Enemies of the Internet in 2012"[3] after a number of journalists, bloggers and social media users were allegedly arrested and tortured by the authorities. According to this report, the online activists' community in Bahrain is very well organized but closely watched by the government. The report indicates that,

> Because of Internet filtering, a lot of online content is in theory inaccessible to the general public. The filtering obviously targets 'pornographic' content, but also, and above all, political and religious opinions that [are] at variance with the regime. Content about the ruling family, the government, and the opposition is strictly regulated, although there are ways to circumvent the filtering.

The effective role that new media played in the Egyptian and Tunisian revolutions has broad implications for repressive states in the Arab region and, indeed, throughout the world. Given the demographic, economic, and political conditions in the broader Middle East region, uprisings and political movements are likely to continue to foment. Howard[4] (2011, pp. 20–21), presciently, given the Egyptian example, noted that nations with significant Muslim populations show "modular political phenomena" (i.e. "political action based in significant part on the emulation of successful examples from others"), that "successful democratization strategies in particular countries are transported into the collective action strategies of movements in other countries," and that "democratization movements appear to be learning to use information technologies from each other, linking up to share experiences and transporting successful organizational strategies."

The true implications of the current wave of political upheaval in the Arab world, and the extent to which it will be influenced by social media, remain to be seen over the course of the coming years. As Jeffrey Ghannam[5] (2011) states in a report to the Center for International Media Assistance, "Social networking has changed expectations of freedom of expression and association to the degree that individual and collective capacities to communicate, mobilize, and gain technical knowledge are expected to lead to even greater voice, political influence, and participation over the next 10 to 20 years."

3.4　The Rise of "Cyberactivism" in Bahrain after 2011

It is evident that the Bahraini government adopted many methods to curb the press and force it to endorse the views of the regime. However, it was very difficult to contain the flow of information after the political crisis and the February 14 movement, since they took place in the digital age. The previous role of the press as a supporter of authority has weakened, and new dynamic and popular tools are available to individuals to use free of charge. New and digital media started to fill the information gap created by the biased traditional media in Bahrain. These new media channels were equipped with photos, videos, and documented recordings. This officially declared the era of "citizen journalism" in Bahrain.

Three years after the crackdown in 2011, the number of citizen journalists and photo journalists is on the rise in the country. There were many cases of imprisonment, torture, and targeting of these individuals, which sometimes led to death, such as citizen videographer Ahmad Ismael who died after being shot while he was filming a protest in 2012. However, the harsh treatment of citizen journalists doesn't seem to be effective in preventing others from spreading news, photos, and videos via social media, Twitter in particular.

The July 2012 Arab Social Media Survey,[6] prepared by researchers at the Dubai School of Government, found that #bahrain was the most-tweeted hashtag in the Arab world in February and March 2012, being mentioned 2.8 million times in English and 1.5 million times in Arabic. In fact the use of Twitter has been thriving in Bahrain after 2011 by both anti and pro-government individuals, not only among the youth but also among political leaders and public figures. This is also the case for the rest of the Gulf countries, which have relatively high income levels that allow the widespread use of smart phones.

According to the same report, the penetration of social media usage in Bahrain is among the highest in the Gulf area, with 25.93% of internet users in Bahrain being on Facebook, and 5.33% on Twitter. These percentages even exceed the penetration of social media usage in Saudi Arabia, a country which is well known for the widespread use of social media, with 19.18% of internet users being on Facebook and 2.89% on Twitter.

Jane Kinninmont[7](2013) argues that Twitter has played a major role in allowing like-minded people to network across national borders and may be contributing to the continued formation of a 'Khaleeji' (Gulf) identity. However, she also mentions the "darker side" of Twitter in the region, which is that it is now being used as a source of misinformation, propaganda, and hate speech. This has resulted in polarizing Bahrain society more than ever, as well as given space for sectarian language and the incitement of violence. Twitter has also become a new battleground for censorship owing to political and religious sensitivities. Censorship on Twitter and other social media in Bahrain increased to the maximum in recent years, and harsh punishments were imposed against those who are critical in social media. More than 38 Bahraini citizen journalists were arrested over the past three years for their activism on Twitter. Many of them have been convicted of "slandering the king" on Twitter and have received prison sentences ranging between one and seven years.

Therefore using social media for political activism in Bahrain is becoming harder and riskier than ever. But those who consider themselves online activists are still strong believers in the power and effectiveness of social media.

The issue of censorship of cyberactivists in Bahrain—whether they are journalists, bloggers or photographers—has become a pressing one addressed by many organizations focusing on human rights, and freedom of opinion and expression around the world. The many arrests of journalists, human rights activists, and politicians resulting from internet censorship have added to the urgency of the issue and created an unhealthy environment for political debate on social media in Bahrain.

The 2012 report of the press-freedom group Reporters without Borders classified Bahrain as one of the countries that are "enemies of the internet."[8] According to the organization's criteria, the listed countries impose restrictions on the internet, monitor the published contents, and imprison bloggers. Though the group considered 2011 to be "the most dangerous year" for internet users, Bahrain was chosen among the top five enemies of the internet in 2012. It added Bahrain to its list after the death of the Bahraini blogger Zakariya al-Ashiri while in government custody in 2011. It also suggested that the Bahraini authorities have arrested many internet users and launched a campaign to defame those who protest for freedom of expression and communications.

Bahrain Watch, a volunteer initiative led by a group of cyberactivists and specialists, is the first scheme to document the use of British spyware by the Bahraini government to spy on activists. It documented this in its report published in 2012.[9] According to this, several methods used by the Bahraini government to censor activists were documented. These include sending online messages containing spyware that automatically uploads to the recipient's device, and hacking Facebook and Twitter IP addresses to determine the identities of their users and arrest them. In addition, the government demanded the passwords to the online accounts of arrested cyberactivists to access their personal contacts and investigate their associates. The report documented the cases of five people who were arrested on the charge of insulting the king on Twitter. Some of them confirmed having been targeted and pursued through spy links. The report documented more than 120 pro- and anti-regime accounts that have been targeted in 2011 and 2012 with spy links using a public mention, such as a tweet that is visible to the public.

3.5 Bahraini Women Activists: Champions of the Cyber World

The wave of uprisings which swept the Arab world in 2011 did not just instigate a "political awakening" that has shaken the power structures in a number of Arab countries and resulted in dictators fleeing their countries, resigning from office, or facing brutal death. Rather, it also triggered a "social awakening" that has shaken Arab societies' commonly held assumptions about gender roles and women's ability to challenge them. This was evident in the many heroic examples and iconic images of Arab women's multiple activisms and resistances, in both the political and social spheres, which stunned the world and earned its respect and recognition, as evident in the selection of Tawakkul Karman, as the first Arab Nobel Prize winner ever, in what has been seen by many as a recognition to the "Arab Spring" movements, in general, and to Arab women's roles in them, in particular (Khamis 2011; Radsch and Khamis 2013).[10]

Since the uprising in February 2011, Bahraini women activists have emerged as new leaders in their society, thanks to the increasing role of social media and their effective utilization of this new media platform to spread their political opinions and exercise their social and political activism. Their ideas, voices, and activities have been receiving stronger support from within their—often conservative—communities. It is now more accepted by the public that democratic transition cannot be achieved without the participation of women. However, women's activism in Bahrain is not new. The women's movement in Bahrain dates back to the 1950s. Young, educated Bahraini women started their activism work back then. It not only revolved around empowering women in their society but also involved their engagement in its political struggle. New generations of women activists rose in Bahrain during the political unrest of the 1990s.[11] However, social media gave them a new opportunity to be presented as "leaders" in their own community after the political unrest began in 2011. Women activists were very active in social media as well as on the ground, and their role continues to be essential in the political struggle in Bahrain.[12] The participation of women in opposition and pro-government movements has been an important feature of the political struggle there. However, it marked a growing sectarian split in society. Female supporters of the government have gained a voice to express their concerns in the National Dialogue, which was a series of events organized by the government. It is just a matter of time before we can assess whether their voice will be heard and their recommendations implemented. Female opposition members are active in the ongoing protests and are concentrating on pushing for political reforms, while keeping gender-related demands absent from their agenda. All in all, despite improvements, Bahraini women still face challenges to female empowerment. So far it is clear that the way ahead lies in the hands of the Bahraini authorities, whose role in female empowerment is paramount. As a result, they are able to promote a pro-female image abroad, which sets them apart from the opposition, which can easily be accused of stalling female empowerment.

Women participated widely in the movement alongside men, and, as the crackdown on the uprising became a reality, they bore the consequences of their actions, just like their fellow male activists. Although the facts are disputed, the opposition claims that so far 14 female protesters have died, mostly from tear gas suffocation. Furthermore, women have been detained and incarcerated. Among the imprisoned female protesters, the case of Ayat al Qurmezi, the young female poet who dared to publicly read a poem which harshly criticized the ruling family in Bahrain, made headlines throughout the world. She was incarcerated and then released after a forced apology was aired on Bahraini television.

It is hard to mention Bahraini online female activists without mentioning Zainab Alkhawaja, or "Angry Arabiya," which is her profile name on Twitter. She is a young Bahraini activist who became widely known from early 2011 for her online activism. She has almost 48,000 followers on her Twitter account and she has been recognized as one of the most influential people in the Arab world online. Zainab and her sister Mariam, who is also another well-known activist, are the daughters of human rights activist and former president of Bahrain Center for Human Rights Abdulhadi Alkhawaja, who is now serving a life sentence in prison for his political activism. Zainab has been on hunger strike several times demanding her father's release. She also has been jailed several times. The world will never forget the moving photos[13] of her being dragged by a female police officer back in late 2011 during a sit in organized in Manama. On November 2011, a US journalist witnessed Alkhawaja standing her ground alone in front of oncoming riot police. He reported that tear gas shells were being fired just past her head. Because of her fame, officers were ordered not to remove her from the road and were finally forced to advance their vehicles by another route.

According to Magdalena Karolak (2012), women activists who supported the pro-government movement participated in numerous sit-ins and rallies as well as shows of loyalty organized throughout the country. They had no specific demands targeted at female empowerment behind their participation but strongly believed in an "Iran/Shi'a takeover" of Bahrain. The aims of the pro-government movement were centered on the preservation of the monarchy and the Sunni identity of the country.[14]

The impact of women's activism on supporting the uprising in Bahrain was very alarming to the Bahraini authorities, which is why they were punished just like their fellow male activists. Bahrain is still the only country in the Gulf region that has cases of jailing and torturing women for their political engagement, as well as several cases of women being killed by the police. The crackdown on women activists in the country created a lot of admiration for them from the general public. People in very conservative villages started chanting for those women, they began viewing them differently, following them on Twitter and listening to them speak in the media, or on the stage when they organized public protests. Suddenly the image of the Bahraini woman as a political leader became popular and acceptable, as Bahraini women became as active as their male counterparts, both online and on the ground.

Online activist Asma Darwish recalls her experience in 2011 as an example of how social media can glorify the role of women activists. She says:

> I still remember when I participated with [a] few other women in a strike campaign at the UN [United Nations] building in Bahrain during the status of Emergency law 2011, social media, Twitter in particular, picked up the story and in it went viral in [a] few hours. International media were calling us and reporting our story. I will never forget this moment as I felt the whole world was watching what those Bahraini women [were] doing, it was very empowering.

If there is something that the Arab Spring has achieved in Bahrain, it is giving women an outlet to prove themselves as real, and equal, political players for the general public to see. This was not previously available to ordinary women; only to those who were privileged by the state. However, the uprising witnessed the rise of regular Bahraini women who were given a golden opportunity for the first time to emerge into the public sphere as iconic role models and public opinion leaders, who have captured the public's attention and earned its admiration and respect. By doing this, they proved themselves to their own communities as political and social leaders, while, most importantly, proving that no political transition could be achieved without the full participation of women.

3.6 The Family Law in Bahrain: One of the Remaining Battles

According to Glosemeyer I. (1998),[15] Bahrain is for the most part a peaceful nation, but friction between the Sunni-led government and the largely Shiite opposition persists. Although they constitute the majority of the population, Shiites face discrimination in employment, government services, and education. While the ongoing ethnic and sectarian tensions are deeply troubling, they have acted as a catalyst for increased women's participation in political movements and demonstrations calling for social equality and the promotion of democratic rights.

Regardless of the increased role of women in different aspects of society in Bahrain, many women's issues promoted by women activists since the 1950s are yet to be a reality, with enacting a "family law" that protects women's rights in court being at the top of the list. With pressure and encouragement from local non-governmental organizations (NGOs), unions, and international bodies, the Bahraini government took steps towards improving the standing of women in Bahrain from 2002. The quasi-governmental Supreme Council for Women (SCW) which has played an important role in this process, and NGOs—including the Women's Union umbrella group—also promote women's rights. In particular, these entities have worked for the promulgation of a personal status code, in part to mitigate injustices in the arbitrary application of Sharia in family-related matters, as well as towards amending the nationality law, which still allows only men to pass citizenship to their children and their foreign-born spouse. Women have long been subjected to severe forms of discrimination in Sharia courts by judges who have issued rulings based on their personal interpretations of Islamic texts instead of codified law. The process has been so arbitrary that in some instances women's petitions were turned down even before the plaintiffs had an opportunity to present their case.

Bahrain is a signatory to the 1979 UN Convention on the Elimination of all forms of Discrimination Against Women (CEDAW). In 2002 it ratified the convention with "reservations." These mostly applied to the nationality clause, Article 9, which holds state signatories responsible for granting women equal rights with men to acquire, change, or retain their nationality as well as the right of women to pass their nationality on to their children and husbands. Bahrain had reservations on the following five provisions by the convention:

1. Article 2, paragraph two, states that a country should condemn all types of discrimination against women.
2. Article 9, paragraph two, states that women should enjoy the same rights as men in terms of giving citizenship to their children.
3. Article 15, paragraph four, states that women should be given the same rights as men in choosing their homes.

4. Article 16 states the need to provide equal marital rights for females and males, particularly in marriage contracts, raising children and custody.
5. Article 29, paragraph one, relates to disputes between two state parties.

Lifting these reservations could mean that Bahrain would finally introduce a family law, which would specify in writing how family issues such as divorce and child custody cases should be resolved.[16]

In May 2009, Bahrain approved a family law code for the first time (Law No. 19) which applies only to its Sunni citizens. In Bahraini Shiite sharia courts, personal status matters are still decided on a case-by-case basis by judges, who use their discretion to interpret the Islamic tradition, drawing on Islamic sources. It is evident that Sunnis and Shiites each have their own Sharia courts that deal with marital conflicts and other personal law issues in Bahrain. The approval of law No. 19 came after years of lobbying by civil society activists, as well as quasi-governmental organizations, like SCW. The original draft legislation was conceived to be applicable to both Sunnis and Shiites, and it contained separate chapters for the two sects. However, the Shiite portion was excluded from the draft after hardline Shiite scholars and legislators, who perceive the codification of a family law as the first step towards secularization, threatened to incite country-wide protests.

The new law, although encompassing many traditional Sharia provisions deemed unfair to women under international conventions, institutionalizes important protections, such as the woman's consent to marriage, her ability to include conditions in the marriage contract, and her right for separate residence if her husband takes another wife. Women's rights organizations nevertheless protested against the adoption of a divisive law that does not apply to more than half of the population, preferring instead to wait until the parliament passes a law applicable to both sects.[17]

Although it was centered on political demands, the 2011 uprising in Bahrain had a direct effect on the issue of adopting a family law in Bahrain, particularly that this issue has long been polarized and politicized. In 2005, the SCW led a public campaign to spread awareness about the importance of implementing a family law. It was motivated to promote such a law in order to add it to its achievements in front of the CEDAW committee at the UN. However, the substantial religious reservations forced the council to shut down its campaign and to refer it to women in civil society and women activists. The strongest reservations came from the Shiite religious community, which has long been known politically as the "opposition." Both the Alwefaq National Islamic party and its spiritual leader Sheikh Isa Ahmad Qasim were at the forefront of objecting against the law back then. A member of the Alwefaq party, Afaf Aljamri, explained this objection to one of us: "the party and the Shiite community saw this as a threat to its religious leadership, and in the long run a door which can open a state interference in the Shiite community's affairs". She explained the demands of this community: "The Shiite religious leadership didn't object to enforcing a family law in general, rather, they required legal guarantees that this law is not going to be changed by a secular force or body."[18] Those guarantees have been mentioned by the leadership of the Shiite opposition whenever asked about the issue of enforcing a Shiite family law: amending the constitution to include an article to protect the family law from any changes; and if this law needs to be amended at any time, this should be referred to the Shiite religious scholars in Najaf, Iraq.

There were several reservations regarding these demands which were refused by the Bahraini authorities. The government was not ready to amend the constitution for any reason, and it wouldn't allow any referral to an outside power regarding its own local law. The Shiite opposition knew these reservations very well and used the family law as a political card in order to try to open the door to amending the 2002 constitution, which has been a battle between the government and the opposition for years.

Therefore, the attempt to enforce a Shiite family law stopped in 2009, after the SCW worked with the Sunni religious leaders and enforced the first half of the law, which applies to the Sunni courts. This was mentioned as an "achievement" of the SCW in front of the CEDAW committee in 2010, but no one has taken the lead in fighting to enforce a Shiite family law since then.

After the 2011 political uprising in Bahrain, which was led by the Shiite opposition groups, there was a major turn of events. Some 18 out of 40 Shiite opposition members withdrew from the parliament as a protest against the crackdown on the protesters at Pearl Roundabout in 2011. As a result, there was a better opportunity for pro-government women—some of whom were Shiite themselves—to win in the re-elections and become members of parliament, especially given that the majority Shiite population boycotted the elections and were under attack by the government. A few of the new female members reintroduced[19] a Shiite family law in front of parliament in 2012 and tried to pass it as a law, seizing the opportunity that there were no Shiite members who would represent the opposition's mainstream objection to the law. The parliament kept delaying until the end of the term in 2014 owing to fears about the political implications of its enforcement under the tough political circumstances that the country has been enduring since 2011.

To this day, the road towards enforcing a family law to secure women's rights in front of the Shiite courts in Bahrain remains blocked. The family law dictates the marriage relationship and all matters arising in connection with marriage, such as engagement, dowry, maintenance, parentage, separation, and custody. The implementation of this law remains controversial because the family law has become a symbol of Islamic identity, and some Bahraini religious scholars view codification as a foreign imposition or a challenge to religious authority.

3.7 Concluding Remarks

The ongoing political resistance and civic engagement movements which have been sweeping the Arab world since 2011 and which came to be widely referred to as the "Arab Spring" or "Arab Awakening" have empowered large segments of the region's populations across different countries, especially in the Gulf region. In an article written by Jane Kinninmont,[20] a senior research fellow at Chatham House in 2013, titled "To What Extent Is Twitter Changing Gulf Societies?", she argues:

> The economic process of telecoms liberalization has facilitated a surge in social media technologies that are having a profound impact on the distribution of information and of power over communications, with a dramatic impact on political, religious and cultural debate. This is a prime example of the ways in which economic and demographic change can lead to social and political changes in the dynamic and rapidly evolving societies of the Gulf.

The most obvious example is Bahrain, a small Gulf island which has been witnessing a popular movement aiming for political and democratic transformation since February 2011. Taking into account the significant impact which the media, in general, and social media, in particular, has had in tilting the balance in favor of democratic transitions and popular revolt in the Arab region (Khamis and Vaughn 2011),[21] it becomes especially important to analyze the transformative media landscape in this country, with a special focus on the growing role of social media and its many implications on the equally transformative political landscape. Therefore, in a country like Bahrain, where political transformation is yet to be visible in the political arena but is prevalent in the content of many social media platforms, it becomes especially important to examine the role which social media may have played in paving the way for political transformation in the country, and whether it could be considered an instrument for inspiring change on the ground, or whether it simply reflects this change.

The rise in the use of social media in Bahrain was related to the popularity of these new technologies but was also largely triggered by the political crisis in the country and the lack of freedom of expression in the public sphere through traditional, state-controlled, mainstream media. Bahrainis used to deploy social media only to communicate socially and to network. However, social media is now used for much more. It offers an open space for Bahrainis, especially women, to express their oppositional views and alternative political opinions, and to share information and exchange knowledge related to the ongoing political struggle.

The use of social media in Bahrain has increased dramatically over the past few years, especially since 2011, due to the political situation. In fact, it is safe to say that social media has become one of the major sources of information for Bahrainis, to a level that competes with, if not exceeds, the reliance on traditional media, including television and newspapers. This observation highlights the major changes in the media landscape in this small Gulf island over a short period of time in favor of new media. This environment created a golden opportunity for female activists to shine as leaders and influentials in their own community, and has changed—perhaps forever—the way the community looks at women in the political activism sphere.

Although Bahraini women have fought alongside men to enforce democracy and bring about political change in their country, they also fought another battle to achieve real change in their societal status to become fully equal to their male counterparts." This is evident in the issue of a family law, which has been used as a political card in the battle between the government and the opposition in Bahrain. This law has not yet been enforced in the Shiite family court, and the road to achieving this remains blocked, especially while the political crisis is yet to be resolved.

Women activists in Bahrain have a hard battle ahead of them that goes beyond the political battle for democracy and justice, which they are waging alongside men everyday, both online and offline. Their fight includes securing a space for women to be empowered and included in decision-making positions, so that they can treat issues such as family law, criminalizing violence against women, nationality for the children of women who are married to non-Bahrainis, and many other women-related issues as a top priority in their daily battle for a democratic society. It is safe to conclude that Bahraini women have been raising their voices, both online and offline, and are still shouting for change in the two parallel, and equally challenging, remaining battles for political and social reform.

Notes

1. Radsch, C., and Khamis, S., "In Their Own Voice: Technologically Mediated Empowerment and Transformation among Young Arab Women", *Feminist Media Studies* 13(5):881–890, 2013.
2. Khamis, S., and Vaughn, K., "Cyberactivism in the Egyptian Revolution: How Civic Engagement and Citizen Journalism Tilted the Balance", Arab Media and Society, Issue 14, summer 2011. http://www.arabmediasociety.com/index.php?article=769&printarticle
3. Reporters without Borders, Enemies of the Internet 2012. http://surveillance.rsf.org/en/bahrain/
4. Howard, P.N. (2011). The Digital Origins of Dictatorship and Democracy: Information Technology and Political Islam. Oxford: Oxford University Press.
5. Ghannam, J. (2011). Social media in the Arab world: Leading up to the uprisings of 2011. A Report to the Center for International Media Assistance. Retrieved April 14, 2011, from: http://cima.ned.org/publications/social-media-arab-world-leading-uprisings-2011-0
6. Arab social media report, 2012. From: http://www.arabsocialmediareport.com/Twitter/LineChart.aspx?&PriMenuID=18&CatID=25&mnu=Cat
7. Kinninmont, J., "To What Extent Is Twitter Changing Gulf Societies?". Chatham house, February 2013. From: http://www.chathamhouse.org/publications/papers/view/189413
8. The enemies of the Internet, Reporters without borders report 2012. Available here: http://surveillance.rsf.org/en/bahrain/
9. The IP Spy Files: How Bahrain's Government Silences Anonymous Online Dissent, Bahrain watch, 2012 Available here: https://bahrainwatch.org/ipspy/viewreport.php
10. Radsch, C., and Khamis, S., "In their own voice: Technologically mediated empowerment and transformation among young Arab women", Feminist Media Studies 13(5):881–890, 2013.

11. Khalaf, A., "Double efforts to minimize women's movement in Bahrain", Alsaffir Alarabi, 2012. Available in English at: http://bahrainspring.com/index.php/bahrainspring-articles-2/item/143-double-efforts-to-minimize-woman-movement
12. Alwadi, N., "Social Media as an Opportunity to Bahraini Women", CyberOrient, Vol. 8, Iss. 1, 2014. Available here: http://www.cyberorient.net/article.do?articleId=8815
13. Washington Post, "Bahraini activist 'Angry Arabiya' arrested", 12/15/2011 http://www.washingtonpost.com/blogs/worldviews/post/bahraini-activist-angry-arabiya-arrested/2011/12/15/gIQA73gKwO_blog.html
14. Karolak, M., "Bahraini women in the 21st century: disputed legacy of the unfinished Revolution", Journal of International Women's Studies, 2012. From: http://vc.bridgew.edu/cgi/viewcontent.cgi?article=1002&context=jiws
15. Glosemeyer, I., "Political Parties and Participation: Arabian Peninsula," in Encyclopedia of Women and Islamic Cultures, 551–553; M. Seikaly, "Women and Religion in Bahrain: An Emerging Identity," in Y. Haddad and J. Esposito, eds., Islam, Gender, & Social Change (New York, Oxford: Oxford University Press, 1998), 169–189.
16. Bahrain Center for Human rights report, Feb10, 2014, "Family Law in Bahrain". http://www.bahrainrights.org/sites/default/files/BCHR%20Report%20on%20Family%20Law%20in%20Bahrain.pdf
17. Freedom House report, 2010 "WOMEN'S RIGHTS IN THE MIDDLE EAST AND NORTH AFRICA". https://freedomhouse.org/sites/default/files/inline_images/Bahrain.pdf. This report is a chapter in *Women's Rights in the Middle East and North Africa: Progress amid Resistance*, ed. Sanja Kelly and Julia Breslin (New York, NY: Freedom House; Lanham, MD: Rowman & Littlefield, 2010), available in paperback, as a CD-ROM, and online at http://www.freedomhouse.org
18. Skype Interview with Afaf Aljamri, member of the Alwefaq political party, May 1, 2015.
19. Alwasat newspaper, August 28, 2015 "Tqui: family law is a priority for our political block" http://www.alwasatnews.com/3643/news/read/697357/1.html
20. Kinninmont, J., "To What Extent Is Twitter Changing Gulf Societies?". Chatham house, February 2013. From: http://www.chathamhouse.org/publications/papers/view/189413
21. Khamis, S., and Vaughn, K., "Cyberactivism in the Egyptian revolution: How civic engagement and citizen journalism tilted the balance", *Arab Media & Society*, issue 13, summer 2011. From: http://www.arabmediasociety.com/?article=769

Bibliography

Alwadi, N. 2014. Social Media as an Opportunity to Bahraini Women, *CyberOrient* 8 (1). Available: http://www.cyberorient.net/article.do?articleId=8815

Alwasat Newspaper. 2015. Tqui: Family Law Is a Priority for Our Political Block. http://www.alwasatnews.com/3643/news/read/697357/1.html

Arab Social Media Report. 2012. From: http://www.arabsocialmediareport.com/Twitter/LineChart.aspx?&PriMenuID=18&CatID=25&mnu=Cat

Bahrain Center for Human Rights Report. 2014. Family Law in Bahrain. http://www.bahrainrights.org/sites/default/files/BCHR%20Report%20on%20Family%20Law%20in%20Bahrain.pdf

Freedom House Report. 2010. Women's Rights in the Middle East and North Africa. In *Women's Rights in the Middle East and North Africa: Progress amid Resistance*, ed. S. Kelly and J. Breslin. New York/Lanham: Freedom House/Rowma & Littlefield.

Ghannam, J. 2011. *Social Media in the Arab World: Leading Up to the Uprisings of 2011*. A Report to the Center for International Media Assistance. Retrieved April 14, 2011, from: http://cima.ned.org/publications/social-media-arab-world-leading-uprisings-2011-0

Glosemeyer, I. 1998. Political Parties and Participation: Arabian Peninsula. In *Encyclopedia of Women and Islamic Cultures*, 551–553.

Howard, P.N. 2011. *The Digital Origins of Dictatorship and Democracy: Information Technology and Political Islam*. Oxford: Oxford University Press.

Karolak, M. 2012. Bahraini Women in the 21st Century: Disputed Legacy of the Unfinished Revolution, *Journal of International Women's Studies*. From: http://vc.bridgew.edu/cgi/viewcontent.cgi?article=1002&context=jiws

Khalaf, A. 2012. Double Efforts to Minimize Women's Movement in Bahrain, *Alsaffir Alarabi*. Available in English at http://bahrainspring.com/index.php/bahrainspring-articles-2/item/143-double-efforts-to-minimize-woman-movement

Khamis, S. 2011. The Arab "Feminist" Spring? *Feminist Studies* 37 (3): 692–695.

Khamis, S., and Vaughn, K. 2011. Cyberactivism in the Egyptian Revolution: How Civic Engagement and Citizen Journalism Tilted the Balance. *Arab Media and Society* 14: 37. From: http://www.arabmediasociety.com/index.php?article=769&printarticle

Kinninmont, J. 2013. To What Extent Is Twitter Changing Gulf Societies? *Chatham House*, February 2013, from: http://www.chathamhouse.org/publications/papers/view/189413

Radsch, C., and Khamis, S. 2013. In Their Own Voice: Technologically Mediated Empowerment and Transformation among Young Arab Women. *Feminist Media Studies* 13 (5): 881–890.

Reporters Without Borders, Enemies of the Internet 2012. From : http://surveillance.rsf.org/en/bahrain/
Seikaly, M. 1998. Women and Religion in Bahrain: An Emerging Identity. In *Islam, Gender, & Social Change*, ed. Y. Haddad and J. Esposito, 169–189. New York/Oxford: Oxford University Press.
Skype Interview with Afaf Aljamri. *Member of Alwefaq Political Party in Bahrain.* May 1, 2015.
The Enemies of the Internet, Reporters Without Borders Report 2012. Available here. http://surveillance.rsf.org/en/bahrain/
The IP Spy Files: How Bahrain's Government Silences Anonymous Online Dissent. Bahrain Watch, 2012. Available here. https://bahrainwatch.org/ipspy/viewreport.php
Washington Post. 2011. Bahraini Activist 'Angry Arabiya' Arrested, 15 Dec 2011. http://www.washingtonpost.com/blogs/worldviews/post/bahraini-activist-angry-arabiya-arrested/2011/12/15/gIQA73gKwO_blog.html

CHAPTER 4

Lebanese Women's Rights Beyond the Cedar Revolution

Rita Stephan

Roula Yacoub was found dead at her home in north Lebanon on July 8, 2013. Her husband, Karam Bazzi, had beaten her to death. Over the following two weeks, activists staged several demonstrations to protest about Roula's brutal death and the Lebanese government's inability and unwillingness to protect women from domestic violence (Al-Akhbar 2013). In response to this national campaign, on July 22, the parliament approved a revised draft of the proposed law to protect women from domestic violence under the title "The law to protect women and members of the family from domestic violence" (Merhi 2013). Not without many flaws in its approved version, this law represents a victory for the campaign against domestic violence and recognition for women's rights activism. Lebanese women's rights organizations have been advocating against domestic violence for years, but only in the aftermath of the 2005 Cedar Revolution has the issue gained momentum, leading to several campaigns on a national scale.

In 2005 a million men and women became a liberation movement that fulfilled Lebanese dreams for independence and sovereignty in

R. Stephan (✉)
The Moise A. Khayrallah Center for Lebanese Diaspora Studies, North Carolina State University, Raleigh, NC, USA

© The Author(s) 2018
S. Khamis, A. Mili (eds.), *Arab Women's Activism and Socio-Political Transformation*, DOI 10.1007/978-3-319-60735-1_4

what became known as the Cedar Revolution or the Lebanon Spring Revolution. From a dozen individuals grew the revolution, the aim of which was to liberate Lebanon from 15 years of foreign influence (Stephan 2005). A series of protests and demonstrations ultimately led to significant political and social changes in the country. The revolution was the first in a series of national protests that stormed the Arab world and collectively became known as the Arab Spring. Some claim that the 2011 Arab Spring was inspired by the Cedar Revolution, whereas others say that the Arab Spring in fact started with the revolution. Some 11 years later, the Cedar Revolution is the only case in the context of the Arab Spring that provides some historical depth for analysis. It provides answers to an important question related to gender politics: Did the fight for national freedom produce a political environment committed to advancing women's rights in the Arab world?

Since 2005, women's rights activists have intensified their battle for women's rights by strengthening their lobbying and public campaigns. Yet despite an increase in their efforts, little legal success has been achieved and the struggle is ongoing. While the Cedar Revolution liberated Lebanon from its Syrian occupiers, women remained restrained by the confessional, social, and political frictions in the country. Those who fought alongside of men and filled the streets in demonstrations continue to demonstrate for the same rights they fought for before 2005.

This chapter examines three historical periods: women's fight for rights before the Cedar Revolution, women's role in the revolution, and their activism since the revolution. These permit us to conclude that although the legal achievements are minimal, the political opportunities that have become available to women's rights activists in Lebanon as a result of the revolution are significant. I argue that while activism for national causes did not have a manifest impact on women's rights, the latent effect has created openings in the public sphere, showcased emerging leaders, and rendered the patriarchal politicoreligious apparatus less legitimate. Contextualizing women's rights as basic human rights, this chapter reveals how women's rights organizations have been able to reformulate their demands for women's rights within the context of activism for democracy, liberty, and sovereignty in the private as well as the public sphere.

The chapter relies on in-depth interviews with women's rights organizations and Lebanese activists who participated in the 2005 protests. These interviews were conducted in 2006 and 2009 in Lebanon. Additionally, the content of newspaper and internet articles and photographs related to the 2005 demonstrations, as well as more recent events, are analyzed to vividly illustrate the connection between advocacy for national causes and women's rights. The significance of this chapter is to highlight how women's participation in collective political action reflects on their activism for equal citizenship rights.

4.1 The Road to Women's Rights

Early women advocates were influenced by a number of events: the emancipation of Turkish women by Mustafa Kemal Ataturk, which came before the French gave women the right to vote, and by the Egyptian Huda Shaarawi shedding her veil and leading a movement for women's rights in 1923 (which was, incidentally, the decade in which woman's suffrage made strides in the West) (al-Qaderri 2001). Lebanese women's activism has its roots in journalism, educational programs, and charity organizations (Stephan 2010a). A politically conscious advocacy for women's rights emerged in the Arab world during the decolonization and nationalism period of the early 1900s. The pioneers of the Lebanese women's movement considered women's integration into society through education and work as essential for their participation as equal citizens in building a strong nation-state. They were influenced by the message from and efforts of American and French missionaries to educate girls.

Charitable organizations, *al jameyat al khayrieh*, emerged in Lebanon in the late 1800s and have continued to sustain their presence and their historical leadership roles to date (Stephan 2011). Led mostly by elite women, these organizations concentrated on increasing women's participation in public life through education and vocational training (Hijab 1988: 144). By the early nineteenth century, elite women were extensively involved in charitable organizations, viewing them as opportunities to participate in the public sphere without violating social norms and expectations.

The shift to political activism accompanied the formation of the Lebanese Council of Women in 1952. The council, which remains today as the most representative umbrella group of women's organizations, holds consultative status in the Lebanese parliament. Political advocacy began with the council's fierce fight to obtain suffrage for women. It succeeded in gaining voting rights for all Lebanese women by a decree that was enacted on February 18, 1953. By the end of the twentieth century, women's advocacy organizations, *al jameyat al matlabiyeh*, had emerged throughout Lebanon and the Arab world (Stephan 2011).

In the early 1970s and prior to the Lebanese 15-year civil war, women's sections were created among several political parties to encompass highly political women. Feeling marginalized and compartmentalized within their political parties, these sections gradually separated from their party of birth and gained autonomy. National women's organizations that had emerged among leftist middle-class women before the war reinvented themselves after the war through projects targeting the economic development and education of Lebanese women.

Between 1975 and 1990, Lebanon witnessed a bloody civil war that divided the country into a Christian East and a Muslim West. The war destroyed Lebanon's social and economic structures and forced many of the country's most productive citizens to flee. Women's organizations channeled their efforts into humanitarian needs. They launched many projects that provided social welfare services, especially for women who were left behind by their male family members who had emigrated. The war only underlined the urgency of creating a national policy to integrate female citizens into public life.

Although the council became inactive during the civil war, Laure Moghaizel—lawyer and founding member of the Lebanese Council of Women, the Lebanese Human Rights Association, the Democratic Party, the non-violent movement, and the National Commission for Lebanese Women—in 1985 established with her husband Joseph (also a lawyer) the Lebanese Association for Human Rights (Stephan 2011, 2010b). Laure and Joseph Moghaizel became significant figures in the women's movement in Lebanon through their efforts to reform important but often overlooked laws that impacted women's lives.

Under the leadership of Laure Moghaizel, women's rights became a matter of equal and fair treatment for all citizens. Laure declared: "Nothing justifies subjugating women to legal discrimination. Nothing shall prevent or restrict women from their human rights which they ought to enjoy and practice fully" (Moghaizel 1985: 7). Women's rights organizations scored a number of achievements, which included succeeding in eliminating legal penalties for the use or sale of contraceptives, and successfully campaigning to change the retirement age to 64 for men and women (at the time, forced retirement came at 55 for women and 60 for men). They also successfully campaigned for women's rights to witness in real-estate contracts, to practice commerce without being obliged to obtain the consent of their husbands, and to obtain life insurance on their own. Finally, they achieved partial reforms in honor-crime laws: defendants deemed guilty of only some charges could now be sentenced with reduced penalties rather than be granted total acquittal (Stephan 2011, 2010b). These were all small reforms but they chipped away at the edifice of patriarchy and discrimination.

Many of the opportunities that opened up the space for women in the 1990s were the results of the Taef Peace Accord, the agreement that ended Lebanon's 15-year civil war and the 1995 Beijing Conference for Women. This United Nations (UN) Fourth World Conference on Women: Action for Equality, Development and Peace witnessed the representation of 189 governments and more than 5000 delegates from 2100 non-governmental organizations. It brought the Lebanese government into partnership with women's organizations to provide social welfare services and to design the future of gender relations in the country, specifically the adoption of the UN Convention on the Elimination of all Forms of Discrimination Against Women. Multiple advocacy groups emerged during and after the Beijing conference and became effective in reaching out to women and increasing their political awareness. For ten years after Beijing, women's organizations enacted strategies to advance women's rights that benefited from the shifting international trends for gender equality. They fought to eliminate discrimination against women in five areas of the law: political rights, legal competency, economic and social rights, punitive laws, and the Personal Status Law (Moghaizel 2000). Women's continuous campaigns that focused on raising public awareness of political and legal rights might have had an indirect impact on the empowerment that some women felt as they participated in the Cedar Revolution. However, while women's organizations participated fully in the 2005 protests, they did not take a leadership role in the revolution. That task was assumed by two women: Nora Jumblat, the Sunni Syrian wife of the prominent Druze leader Walid Jumblat, and Asma-Maria Andraos, who was featured in *Time* magazine as one of the 37 heroes of 2005 (Ghazal 2005a).

4.2 The Road to Freedom

On February 14, 2005 a massive car bomb exploded in Beirut, taking the life of former prime minister Rafiq Hariri and several other people. This tragedy left the entire country in shock, and in a general state of insecurity and political instability. Immediately, individuals gathered at the location of the assassination, which became known as "ground zero."

The day after Hariri's funeral, Nora Jumblat was recruited by the protesters at ground zero. For almost three months, she managed many of the protest's logistics and organized various aspects of the revolution (Jumblat 2006). She became the natural mediator between demonstrators in the street and members of the élite class. Likewise, Asma-Maria Andraos, a 34 year-old Christian woman, found herself in the role of organizer and activist overnight. As a public relations consultant and event planner, she had been working to promote Lebanese businesses. The day after Hariri's funeral, she and her friends began a sit-in at ground zero to express their anger. They drew up a petition calling upon the pro-Syrian Lebanese government to resign. Four days later, they had 400 meters of signatures and a movement to sustain. From a dozen individuals grew a series of protests and demonstrations, which ultimately led to significant political and social changes in Lebanon.

Thousands of people gathered every night and the government grew weary of them. On February 28, 2005 the minister of the interior claimed the demonstrations to be unlawful and a military judge imposed a ban on assembly (Sheea 2005). This declaration set the stage for the largest collective show of civil disobedience in Lebanese history, as thousands of people from all over the country crowded into the streets. That same day, as a result of popular pressure exerted by the crowd, the pro-Syrian prime minister resigned. Five days later, the Syrian president Bashar al-Assad announced plans to withdraw his forces from Lebanon (Ghazal 2005b).

The Syrian-backed government along with the Hezbollah[1] leadership organized a counter-demonstration of 800,000 protesters on March 8 at the Riyad al-Solh Square. The purpose of the counter-movement was to express their support for and loyalty to Syria, and to reject Western interests in the region. However, on March 14, 2005, 1.2 million Lebanese filled the streets of Beirut and its suburbs, setting a record for Lebanon's largest demonstration ever. Syrian troops left Lebanese soil on April 27, 2005 and, less than a month later, the anti-Syrian alliance led by Saad Hariri—the son of Rafiq Hariri—won control of the parliament (Stephan 2010a).

Observers note the much enlarged role played by Lebanese women in these events, which energized political activism among women where it had, perhaps, grown tired. The feminization factor was eloquently depicted in Anisa al-Amin Merei's description of the significant contributions women made to the revolution:

> They turned their country into a flag, an anthem, a candle and a flower.
> Does the country need more than love? This is an emerging language that the youth created and the women dedicated: mothers, friends, lovers and sisters. This language became a flag and a national anthem of a country that has been historically suppressed. They are guarding this nation for a beautiful tomorrow for their men by protecting them from war, submissiveness and helplessness. (Merei 2005)

By openly protesting in the streets and non-violently resisting the Syrian occupation, these women in essence added a feminist dimension to the liberation of Lebanon. Because the trajectory of the Lebanese Cedar Revolution has come into focus through the lens of recent events in the Arab world, particularly the Arab Spring, it is important to emphasize this point.

When the events of the Arab Spring were reported in the Western world, some commenters wondered how women appeared out of nowhere, not only to participate in non-violent revolutions for freedom but also to lead them and, in the case of Yemeni Tawakkul Karman, become a Nobel peace laureate. Robin Morgan reports in *Ms.* magazine that although women leaders of the Arab Spring surprised the world, their participation "doesn't surprise those familiar with Arab feminism, since women have been the most consistent advocates of civil society across the region" (2011). Women, who were often considered indifferent to political processes and outcomes, became liberators and resistors in Lebanon's Cedar Revolution as well as in the Arab Spring.

Imbued with the spirit of democracy, Lebanese activist Mona Modad asked after the revolution: "Will this wonderful phenomenon finally prove that Lebanon is ready to embrace democracy and accept women as equal citizens?" (Modad 2005). Although women participated in the revolution to achieve freedom and independence, their quest for equality and rights was not achieved. But for them, having taken a remarkable step towards democracy, going back to restrictive gender relations was not an option.

4.3 Women's Rights after the Cedar Revolution

New organizations emerged around the Cedar Revolution to lead campaigns to raise awareness of domestic violence and protest about the vulnerability of its victims in the legal system. They partnered up with activists struggling for the legal protection of constituents who were not previously represented, such as migrant workers and sexual minorities. Some feminists ventured to find their own voice in the Lebanese struggle for women's rights and gender equality. Their position between East and West also exposed them to the rhetoric of global and multicultural feminisms. This rhetoric in particular appealed to them as they centered their demands on restructuring social and cultural norms and redefining legal rights and political participation in Lebanon. Like radical feminists of the West, these activists adopted a progressive feminist discourse instead of the typical feminine indirect rhetoric that had been used by Lebanese women's rights activists for years. Nonetheless, these Lebanese feminists insisted, like their previous comrades, neither to assume an inferior position vis-à-vis Western feminists nor to embrace Western politics that target the Arab World and Islam.

Taking on issues such as domestic violence and the abuse of female domestic workers, as well as issues such as the environment, women's art, male-centered knowledge, and sexual diversity, organizations such as Nasawiya and KAFA emerged in the post-2005 era and relied on traditional and social media outlets to disseminate information, recruit supporters, and raise awareness (Stephan 2013). According to its website, Nasawiya is a group of young feminists working to eliminate sexism, classism, heterosexism, racism, and capitalism. Members feel that these problems jointly silence women and other minorities, as their website states:

> We see all these problems as interrelated and equally oppressive, yet we insist on addressing them from a progressive grassroots feminist perspective … We believe … it is time we embraced the people that have long been silenced, by our society and then by many of the human rights groups in it.

Claiming their voice as the subalterns in the Lebanese society and the Lebanese women's rights movement, they claim to represent the voiceless in Lebanese society:

> We strive to not only be a movement of educated and privileged women, but a movement by and for the single mothers, the refugees, the disabled, the sex workers, the migrant workers, the people of non-conforming gender identities and non-conforming sexualities, etc … Having been united in marginalization, we can make an effort to unite in seeking a change in ourselves and in our society.

They relate sexism to the feudal/patriarchal Lebanese culture and demand non-judgmental sexual health services and sexual education. They also want to eliminate all forms of harassment and gender-based violence. Considering equal rights of employment, and equal treatment and pay in the workplace, as a fundamental right, they demand that it be extended to domestic migrant workers who currently hold minimum rights in Lebanon and the Arab world.

Nasawiya partners with organizations such as KAFA (Arabic for Enough) and Beit el-Hanane (Home of Tenderness) on the issue of domestic violence. The aim of KAFA is to achieve a democratic and just society that is free from violence and exploitation, whereas Beit el-Hanane was established in 2008 to support women victims of abuse. In addition to promoting community awareness and education, Beit el-Hanane supports gender-based violence survivors emotionally, psychologically, and physically through its counseling centers.

These organizations have come together to organize campaigns and protests to raise awareness of these unpopular causes. On January 14, 2012, for instance, more than a thousand men and women marched in the morning rain to demand the deletion of Article 522 from the Lebanese Penal Code. According to the Delete-522 Campaign website (http://www.delete522.com/about-campaign-522-rape-lebanon/), the article exonerates a man who commits a rape crime if he marries his victim. Included in the category of victims are minors, persons with a mental or physical disability, children he molests or sexually harasses, a person in a weak position he exploits or forces into sexual acts, or women or girls he kidnaps (with or without the intention of marriage). In addition to the march, the organization's websites have succeeded in collecting more than 1500 signatures in support.

In similar efforts to extend legal protection to victims of domestic violence, on March 12, 2012, men and women dressed in black marched silently through the streets of Beirut demanding the immediate mandate for the legal protection of female victims of family violence. They carried banners stating that "one woman dies in Lebanon each month as a result of domestic violence" and "Roula died but her voice did not" as well as "my silence killed me, scream for me."

After the death of Roula Yacoub, KAFA proposed a law to protect women against domestic violence. According to Roula Awda, a lawyer working with KAFA, the proposed law would enable law-enforcement officers to enforce the removal of a husband from his family home, in the case that his presence threatened the livelihood and well-being of his wife and children. It had also called upon the state to take up the responsibility of housing and caring for women of domestic violence—in the case that they are forced to leave their homes or resort to fleeing. (BBC 2013)

On July 4, 2013, KAFA invited two Lebanese women who had fled their abusive husbands to speak at a press conference. The two victims, Rim Zakaria and Zainab Awada, speaking boldly, encouraged other women to speak up and report their abusers. Two days later, the speaker for the Lebanese parliament, Nabih Berri, listed the proposed draft law for the protection of women from domestic violence as the first item on the agenda of the joint parliamentary committees. The law was approved on July 22 (Merhi 2013). Although KAFA and the National Coalition for Legislating the Protection of Women from Family Violence welcomed this step, they were concerned about the amendments made to the law. The approved version separates the powers of religious and criminal courts but it fails to explicitly criminalize marital rape; the harm that accompanies marital rape is instead penalized under the law. Moreover, minors do not profit from the protection order unless they are still under the age of custody, as set differently by the different religious laws. Hence the current status of this law, according to the coalition, discourages women from reporting abuse as a result of fear of their inability to protect their children owing to custody restrictions. The coalition continues its efforts to achieve revisions to the law and to protect it from being overturned (KAFA 2013).

Women's rights organizations in Lebanon are skeptical about lawmakers' commitment to advancing women's rights. Although the parliament passed their proposed law, it changed much of its original wording. Activists viewed the adoption of their proposed law and the renewed discussion about domestic violence as crucial, but they also know that real social and legal changes remain distance goals.

KAFA's campaign to combat domestic violence in Lebanon has focused on raising awareness through protests, collaborations with other organizations, and convening conferences. However, no legal advances have been made until recently 2013 (stated above July 22). Since 2010, KAFA has worked on four major campaigns: advancing the rights of domestic immigrant workers; organizing a campaign against the sexual harassment of women; raising awareness of and combating child molestation and child sexual abuse; and protecting women against domestic violence (KAFA 2013).

According to its Facebook page, Nasawiya is campaigning to further the protection of domestic workers' rights; defending the rights and fate of the missing (those who have disappeared or were kidnapped—women and children—during the Lebanese civil war); supporting women in trade unions; guaranteeing safe access to abortion; expressing solidarity with Egyptian women in their fight against sexual harassment; staging the Uprising of Women in the Arab World Facebook campaign; and voicing the grievances of Sudanese refugees (Nasawiyah 2013).

The Collective for Research & Training on Development Action (CRTD.A) has produced reports, hosted conferences and conducted various workshops and campaigns that focus on five projects: Active Citizenship and Gendered Social Entitlements, which encourages civic engagement in the social, political, and economic components of society; Arab women's right to nationality campaign, which advocates Arab women's right to pass on their citizenship to their children; women's economic empowerment, which calls for sustainable economic opportunities for women; women's leadership and democratic participation project; and a personal status laws and cross-confessional marriages advocacy project (CRTD.A 2013).

These are all efforts to chip away at the edifice of patriarchy and discrimination. However, given the premise that the Lebanese woman's rights movement continues to function within the parameters of Lebanon's political, religious, and social structures, feminists have had to espouse strategies that overcome local political cleavages, accommodate foreign interests, and take advantage of political opportunities that create openings to advance women's rights.

Today, women continue their struggle to achieve the aforementioned goals. They battle in the area of political rights to gain the ability for women to grant citizenship to their families, to guarantee a quota for women representatives in parliament, and to encourage a more vigorous role for women in all political parties in Lebanon. In regard to economic rights, they fight for the right to maternity leave, and for equality in pay, social security, and retirement plans. They also advocate for the removal of certain punitive laws against women (prohibiting adultery and abortion), and the normalization of laws to punish honor crimes, calling for them to be treated like any other violent crime. Also, personal status law must still be changed across the denominations to abolish the limits on women's rights in marriage, divorce, filiations, adoption, and guardianship. Women in both the Christian and Muslim personal status codes cannot initiate divorce and have no guardianship rights over their children.

4.4 Lessons for the Arab Spring

In the beginning of this piece I posed the question: Did the plight for national freedom produce a political environment that led to advancing women's rights? As this condensed historical overview of the women's movement in Lebanon shows, the answer is both yes and no. Although Lebanese women's rights activism was embedded in the struggle for an independent Lebanon and continues to be an essential element of social movement efforts for a democratic and equal Lebanon, women's rights activism in the country continues to face significant resistance.

In Lebanon's Cedar Revolution, women demonstrated, protested, expressed their opinions, and demanded the right to decide their destinies. In 2005, this was an entirely unique phenomenon in the Arab world, which has been notoriously unreceptive to both democratization and women's political participation. In the past, women's participation was mostly "individualistic, timid, uninformed, complicated with social restrictions, and alienated from contemporary politics" (Al-Turk 2005). However, women joined the ranks of leaders in Lebanon's struggle for independence, thereby giving the revolution a feminine face.

Women, often considered indifferent to political processes and outcomes, became liberators and resistors in March 2005. In order to frame the participation of women in this revolution, I have constructed the sociopolitical context in which the protests occurred. I have also demonstrated the diverse backgrounds of those women engaging in the movement and have discussed their reasons and motivations for doing so. As women assumed leadership roles in the Lebanese freedom movement, they created a more tolerant, less violent, and more feminized style of protest. The Cedar Revolution left an indelible image of women as active and equal citizens in their society. Their spontaneous, dynamic activism reveals an unmistakable sense of ownership. When the need presented itself, Lebanese women demonstrated an unprecedented political maturity, bringing new meaning to the word "patriotic."

Women in the Arab world unknowingly followed the footsteps of their Lebanese sisters, assuming key roles in the Egyptian, Tunisian, and Yemeni freedom movements and achieving similar results.

In the Cedar Revolution, women participated without being manipulated by political parties or restricted by their gender roles. Even though no manifest benefits were intentionally sought, the outflow of women leading and joining the protests resulted in the normalization of women's involvement in the political sphere. Women stormed the streets advocating their country's independence and pursuing their rights as equal citizens.

The revolution was nonetheless embedded in the Lebanese gender relations as well as cultural mores and symbols. Although women participated as equal citizens, their quest for equality and rights was not changed as a result of the revolution. In fact, the manner in which they participated has recreated gender relations that are significant to Lebanese culture. Gender roles were reinforced, the family's central role in politics was emphasized, and since the revolution politics has been conducted as usual.

As this overview shows, the struggle for an independent Lebanon which maintains basic human rights across the confessions is intertwined with the development of Lebanese women's rights activism, which coordinates with other social movements to pressure for democracy and equality.

While Lebanon is a unique case of semidemocratic culture, its broad ethnosectarian composition, and its postcolonial history, its confessional family law system and the tribal criminal code make it similar to other Arab countries (Stephan 2011). It is within the latter jurisdiction that women's rights lie unaffected by any political change on the national level.

Lebanon has been characterized as the "only Arab country to sustain a form of democracy, albeit of the consociational variety, for a significant period of time…" (Huntington 1991: 308). Unlike other countries that experienced the Arab Spring phenomenon, Lebanon's multisectarianism is mostly responsible for its semidemocratic governing system. Democracy, according to Salem (1993), emerged as "an unintended outcome of the social and confessional diversity in Lebanon." No other Arab state enjoys this form of multiculturalism and power-sharing.

Lebanese exceptionalism, which was the result of the forceful combination of heterogeneous and opposing social and political elements, continues to accommodate the confessional family law system and the tribal criminal code, according to Hamadah (2000: 15). In these two areas, Lebanon is sometimes worse than some other Arab countries. Egypt, for instance, has granted women the right to pass on their citizenship to their children, while Lebanon is still debating women's full citizenship. This contradiction promotes democracy on the "outside" and perpetuates inequality and patronage on the "inside." Staying true to democratic principles, activists point out that democracy really begins at home, in the private sphere, where women's rights also lie. However, discrepancies exist between democracy and equality in the public sphere and women's rights in the private sphere.

Democracy has not entered Lebanese or Arab homes. Women who participated in liberating the public sphere were unable to bring this liberation to their homes. Fahmieh Charafeddine claims that "Achieving equality between the sexes is a true thermometer of the presence of equality in a society and of the wide public participation, and both constitute the actual foundation of democratic processes" (2004: 397). Another Cedar Revolution is needed at home.

Some 11 years after the liberation of Lebanon from Syrian occupation, the country is still not ready to embrace full democratic processes or accept women as equal citizens. In this chapter, I have attempted to illustrate how the Lebanese resistance movement gained new meaning when Lebanese women demonstrated alongside men in 2005. The demonstration crystallized into a liberation movement that succeeded in peacefully expelling the Syrian army but did very little to liberate women from inequality and discrimination imposed on them by their own society. Still, this chapter has shown that while activism for national causes did not produce a direct impact on enhancing women's rights, women's penetration of the public political sphere has weakened the armored separation of the home and rendered the patriarchal politicoreligious apparatus less legitimate. In that sense, women's participation in the Cedar Revolution produced a political environment that is more amenable to advancing women's rights.

Acknowledgments I wish to thank Mounira Charrad and Jana Suleiman for their comments and suggestions; and Guita Hourani, Rudy Sassine, and Elie El-Mir from the Lebanese Emigration Research Center at Notre Dame University in Lebanon for their assistance in obtaining the data. This research was supported by the American Association of University Women and PEO International. All translations are mine, except where a translated document is cited.

Disclaimer The views expressed in this chapter are those of the author and do not represent the views of, and should not be attributed to, the U.S. Department of State.

Notes

1. *Hezbollah* literally means "the party of God." Founded during the 15-year Lebanese Civil War (lasting from 1975 to 1990), it continues to be known for armed resistance to Israel.

Bibliography

Al-Akhbar, E. 2013. Lebanese Man Accused of Killing Wife to Remain in Prison. http://english.al-akhbar.com/content/lebanese-man-accused-killing-wife-remain-prison. Accessed 26 July 2013.
Al-Qaderri, N. 2001. Lebanese Women's Journalism and Organizations in the Twenties, Two Faces-One Coin. In *al-Nisa' al-'Arabiyat fi al-ishrinat: huduran wa-huwiyah*, ed. J.S. Makdisi, N.S. Yarid, and T. al-B al-Lubnaniyat, 71–98. Beirut: Tajammu' al-Bahithat al-Lubnaniyat.
Al-Turk, J. 2005. Women in the Martyrs Square: Their Strategic Participation by Shaking of Political Inhibitions in Order to Resurrect Lebanon. *Al-Mustaqbal*, March 10, 2005.
BBC Beirut, in Al-Hoor Electronic Newspaper. 2013, July 17. Legal Dissatisfaction Following the Death of a Lebanese Woman at the Hands of Her Husband. http://hooor.org/news14079.html. Accessed 25 July 2013.
Charafeddine, F. 2004. Musharakat al-maraa al Lubnania fi al hayat al siyasiya: al waqe' wa al afaq. In *al-Musharaka al-Siyasiya lil maraa al-arabiya*, ed. A.-t. al- Bakoush. Tunis: The Arab Center for Human Rights.
CRTD.A. 2013. Reports Page. http://crtda.org.lb/reports. Accessed August 2, 2013.
Ghazal, R. 2005a. Asma Andraos Honored as 'Hero of Change'. *Daily Star*, October 14, 2005.
———. 2005b. Anti-Syrian Protests Continue Despite Announced Redeployment: Campers Determined to Stay Until the Complete Withdrawal of Troops. *Daily Star*, March 8, 2005.
Hamadah, N. 2000. al-Muwatiniyah: Tafkikuha wa iadat siyaghataha min manthour genousi. In *al-Muwatiniyah fi Lubnan bayna al-rajul wa-al-marah: min waqai Mu'tamar al-Muwatiniyah fi Lubnan*, ed. N. Hamadah, J.S. Makdisi, and S. Joseph, 13–24. Beirut: Dar al-Jadid.
Hijab, N. 1988. *Womanpower: The Arab Debate on Women at Work*. Cambridge/Cambridgeshire/New York: Cambridge University Press.
Huntington, S.P. 1991. *The Third Wave: Democratization in the Late Twentieth Century*. Norman: University of Oklahoma Press.
Jumblat, N. 2006. Personal Interview. Beirut, Lebanon.
———. 2005. KAFA "News and Campaigns". http://www.kafa.org.lb/kafa-news
KAFA. 2013. Enough Violence and Exploitation, Joint Committees Approve the Law to Protect Women. http://www.kafa.org.lb/kafa-news/65/joint-committees-approve-the-law-to-protect-women. Accessed 25 July 2013.
Merei, A.A. 2005. A Shiite Progressive Woman. *Annahar*, March 30, 2005.

Merhi, Z. 2013, July 24. Lebanon Domestic Violence Law: A "Cosmetic" Gain for Women? Al-Akhbar English. http://english.al-akhbar.com/content/lebanon-domestic-violence-law-%E2%80%9Ccosmetic%E2%80%9D-gain-women. Accessed 25 July 2013.

Modad, M. 2005. Is it Time for Women's Participation in Social and National Politics? *Annahar*, March 13, 2005.

Moghaizel, L. 1985. *al Mar'a fi al tashree' al Lubnani fi daw' al itifaqiyat al duwaliya ma'a muqarana bil tashri'at al 'Arabia*. Beirut: Institute for Women's Studies in the Arab World, Lebanese American University.

———. 2000. *Huquq al mar'a al insan fi lubnan: fi daw' itifaqiyet al qada' ala jamyi' ashkal al tamyeez did al mar'a*. Beirut: The National Commission for Lebanese Women and Joseph and Lore Mogheizel Foundation.

Morgan, R. 2011. "Women of the Arab Spring" in MS. *Magazine*, Spring. http://www.msmagazine.com/spring2011/womenofthearabspring.asp

Nasawiya. 2013. http://www.nasawiya.org/web/. Accessed 31 July 2013.

Salem, P. 1993. al-dimukratia al-alamia wa al-arabia wa al-hala al-Lubnania (Global and Arab Democracy and the Lebanese Case). In *al-intikhabat al-ula fi Lubnan baad al-Harb*, ed. P. Salem and F. Khazen. Beirut: Lebanese Center for Politicy Studies.

Sheea, M. 2005. The Sky Is Their Cover and the Flag Is Their Weapon, Along with the White Flowers Which They Offered to the Soldiers, Demonstrators in the Freedom Square Awaited a New Dawn: We Will Not Leave Unless the Syrians Apologize and the State Shows Remorse for their Crime. *Annahar*, March 1, 2005.

Stephan, R. 2005. Qira'a fi Asbab Intifada al-Haqiqa wa Mustaqbalaha. *Al-Mustaqbal Newspaper*, March 28, 2005, p. 4.

———. 2010a. Leadership of Lebanese Women in the Cedar Revolution. In *Muslim Women in War and Crisis: Presentation and Representation*, ed. F. Shirazi. Austin: University of Texas Press.

———. 2010b. Couples' Activism for Women's Rights in Lebanon: The Legacy of Laure Moghaizel. *Women Studies International Forum* 33: 533–541.

———. 2011. Women's Rights Movement in Lebanon. In *Mapping Arab Women Movements: A Century of Transformation from Within*, ed. N.A.H. Golley and P. Arenfeldt. Cairo/New York: American University of Cairo Press.

———. 2013. Political Implications of Cyberfeminism for Women in the Arab World. *e-International Relations*. http://www.e-ir.info/

CHAPTER 5

Women's Space After the Arab Spring: Can We Generalize?

Deborah Harrold

Women participated vigorously in the events of the Arab uprisings of 2011, present in the street, on social media, and in planning sessions. Their participation put them at risk from security forces as well as regime supporters. Some were beaten, sexually assaulted, shot, and, in Egypt, subjected to invasive and punitive "virginity tests" by military authorities. Despite brave participation and broad public acceptance of women's public roles, subsequent events indicate a straitened situation for women. Greater sexual harassment and violence in public spaces, including the public space of the university, has become marked in Egypt and Tunisia. While the police and security forces, and hostile Islamists, have been implicated, the attackers have also included men who are not in these categories. New political arrangements everywhere obliged all parties and groups to struggle over a broad set of issues in transitional committees and councils; women were minor participants, largely excluded. New constitutions are equivocal, the result of struggles and compromises. Where state control is weak (as in Libya), as well as where state control is firmer (as in Egypt), women suffer from increased insecurity. Do these outcomes challenge the vast scholarship and knowledge on women's issues in the region?

D. Harrold (✉)
University of Pennsylvania, Department of Political Science, and Liberal and Professional Studies, Philadelphia, Pennsylvania, USA

Does the expansion of women's rights in the West offer generalizable insights into women's struggles in the Middle East and North Africa, or are these histories and the theories derived from them too specific? Can we theorize from the wealth of information we have, narratives and events, or is the future contingent, the outcome of unfinished struggles? While strong modernizing states in the region have been the historical guarantors of women's rights, and the state's strength relative to civil society has been a long-term indicator of women's rights, other forces are shaping these outcomes beyond the strong state/weak state categories.

This chapter argues that two underexamined issues continue to shape outcomes for women following the events of 2011: first, the expansion of public space as a chaotic and dangerous space; and, second, the role of modernization discourse as a tactic. The other contribution of this chapter is to rehistoricize a larger trajectory of women's rights. While discourses on women's rights as part of universalist rights have played an important role in focusing and directing activism on behalf of women, the historical development of women's rights in the West problematizes an emancipatory trajectory and the value of public space for women's rights.[1] The experiences of women across North Africa and the Middle East today, and the historical development of women's rights in the West, suggest the limits of revolutionary participation and the value of public space in advancing universalist human rights discourses. After a short discussion of outcomes for women after the Arab Spring, this chapter moves to a more theoretical and historical discussion of public space and modernization as emancipatory sites and strategies, and then examines how the situation of women following the Arab Spring leads us to a more critical evaluation of these possibilities.

A note on women and gender. This chapter focuses on women and their rights, understood both in legal terms and in the realm of practices and assumptions. While gender has become a dominant frame for much scholarly work, encouraging an analysis of the construction of identities and categories of difference, larger power hierarchies, symbolic registers, and encouraging inclusion and analysis of masculinity and non-heteronormative identities, women are the focus of this analysis.

Women's rights after the Arab Spring do not appear to have advanced, but this is in the context of expanding war in Libya, Syria, and Yemen, the restoration of military rule in Egypt, and the consolidation of the monarchy in Morocco and Bahrain. Only in Tunisia have new institutions sustained elections at several levels: constitutional, national, and local.

Tunisians voted parties in and out, formed new governments, and maintained security against intermittent challenges in the form of attacks from Islamists outside the larger consensus. The Tunisian military has remained out of politics and, by its withdrawal, obliged opposing parties to negotiate. Women are not satisfied with continued sexual harassment on the streets, nor the involvement of the police in a well-publicized rape case in 2012, nor the lack of women high on party lists in 2014. Yet the main Tunisian political parties have worked to meet the requirement that women constitute half of party lists. By contrast, major French parties have paid millions of euros in fines for not meeting the quota, and less than 20 % of the United States Congress are women. In broader contexts, then, Tunisia's accomplishments are significant. Its constitution guarantees women's rights, seeks parity in all electoral institutions, and commits to women's rights as equality in all areas. While making this a reality will be a challenge for decades, the constitutional commitment cannot be underestimated. Perhaps more importantly, the participation in politics, in parliament, of women of different political parties, is bringing women into the continuous practice of politics. They exercise responsibility, men are increasingly habituated to working with women, and women are public and visible political figures. This is real progress, tempered by the struggles of constant negotiation among parties with major disagreements.

Outside of the real progress in Tunisia, new authoritarianism and war have made life more dangerous for women. In Egypt, the death of Shaimaa Al-Sabbagh, a 31-year-old poet, mother, and activist, embodied Egypt's recommitment to authoritarianism and astonishing explanations for violence. She died because she was "too thin," according to Egypt's head medical examiner, as headlined by the *New York Times* on March 22, 2015. Like many Egyptian activists, Al-Sabbagh had become committed to demonstrating until the regime fell, a utopian tactic. Unhinged from a politics of means and ends, participation in protests became important for idealistic Egyptians unable to accept the closing of political space marked by the Al-Sissi regime.[2] Several witnesses of the shooting came forward to give evidence against the security forces, including Azza Soliman, a lawyer and founder of the Center for Egyptian Women's Legal Assistance. They were charged by the state with "protesting without authorization and disturbing public order" as part of a larger effort of intimidation (Amnesty International 2015). On April 8, 2015, an Egyptian military court sentenced five supporters of deposed Egyptian president Muhammad Morsi to fines and two to three-year prison sentences, including Hagar Tobagi

(Muslim Brotherhood 2015). This reminds us that regimes may subject women to a benign sexism: their prison sentences seldom reach those handed down to men and they are less likely to be executed or shot. The consolidation of the military regime in Egypt has included mass death sentences for Muslim Brotherhood members and a massacre in a mosque of perhaps a thousand men. In Egypt, then, a consolidating authoritarian regime offers political women the benefit of comparatively benign sexism when it comes to political rights in public space, but that public space has practically vanished. Women's constitutional rights remain in place, and women's rights to education and work appear little harmed. The regime's lack of toleration for political dissent may come down harder on men but it affects women as well, sometimes to the point of death.

In Libya the lack of a strong state and the freedom of action afforded to militias produced a very different death: attorney and activist Salwa Bughaigis was shot and stabbed to death by several masked and uniformed men on June, 25, 2014. Her husband was abducted and is still missing. Salwa Bughaigis began her involvement in the important events in Libya by participating in demonstrations in Benghazi with other lawyers early in 2011. She went on to become a member of Libya's Transitional Council, resigning later to protest against the absence of women in the government. On the day she was shot, she had voted in the national elections and posted images of herself voting on her Facebook page, as reported by Agence France Press in Benghazi on June 25, 2014. These deaths may appear extreme—most women in Egypt and Libya are, after all, not shot in demonstrations or assassinated—but they suggest that expanded rights for women cannot be established or developed, and cannot be enjoyed, when militias, the state, or opponents attack women with deadly force for the crime of being a public and political person.

5.1 Public Space, an Essential Political Space

Public space as an essential site for the negotiation and expression of the political, and as an essential site for the expression of personhood, has a long history in and out of the region. Large street demonstrations or confrontations with colonial authorities in public space characterized nationalist movements in the region. Colonial authorities marked public space with statues, parks, avenues, and sometimes public executions and unveiling. Nationalist movements filled that space with speeches, conventions, marches, and sometimes uprisings. In public space, individuals presented themselves in cohorts or groups: labor movements, communists, religious scholars, students, and women. Yet in public space, together, they saw themselves not only as representing the nation but also as embodying it, being a true part of it. Not only were colonial authorities presented with a spectacle of the nation, but demonstrators saw each other in that space. For modern nationalism, then, the public space of the streets is a major site where the nation can be seen and can see itself.

Outside the frame of colonial and national, public space is also constituted in community or regional activities where women's participation is also marked: *mawlids* and religious processions, seasonal celebrations such as *sham al-naseem* in Egypt, the daily activities of market, mosque or church. And almost part of daily activities are political moments, when mosques are the site of critical sermons and markets the site of unrest over prices. While urban squares and streets are used for these events, villages offer smaller public spaces. Ceremonies and celebrations around life events also offer public-private spaces for women's participation. The creation of publics in space extends beyond nationalism in time, and those publics (both before and after the nationalist moment) have included women.

The role of public space as a marker of the political participation associated with modernity has a well-defined role in modern political theory. Jürgen Habermas is the canonical figure here with his conception of the "public sphere" and his associated account of the expansion of modern rights in early modern Europe. He begins with the prince's deference to merchants, as the merchants were allowed to direct their economic activities and manage their markets in relative freedom because of their value to the prince. The structure of rights became reified in law and eventually was extended to all. Not surprisingly, in this formulation, workers and peasants were the last to gain their rights (Habermas 1989). And, we could add, women. Yet the "space" of Habermas's public sphere is less the space of streets and squares than the *private* public spaces of markets and counting houses.

Only the outside, in streets and squares, could hold the greater publics that assembled in politics from the late eighteenth century onwards. The French Revolution brought a nation into a *parlement* and a mass movement moved inside and outside. Historical struggles over rights in the nineteenth century moved from interiors to streets: the mass meetings of the Chartist movement, the revolutions of 1848. Trade union movements and the left generally sought to assemble and show the power of the many in squares and streets, as well as in factories. As nationalism developed in the colonial North Africa and the Middle East, labor and left associations, with their commitment to mass presentation and participation, marked the many emerging movements and shaped their choice of tactics. The Étoile Nord-Africaine, founded by Messali Hadj, is a good example of this, with its extended association with communist and leftist groups; the Communist Party of Iraq, also founded in the 1920s, grew out of study meetings in a mosque, committed to equal rights for women, and it combined its communism with an immediate nationalist commitment (Batatu 1978). Iraqi nationalist struggles were marked by large demonstrations and marches. Egypt's nationalist movement, and Tunisia's nationalist movement, also featured large demonstrations, drawing in labor organizations for strategies and organizational capacity. Yet the demonstration and the march encourage the portrayal of the nation in groups, in segments, as components of the march as standing for the nation. The Western liberal narrative of individual rights appears to undervalue the contribution of the mass movements and mass participations of the left, as a liberal order dominated in the USA and the UK, and left theory has seen liberal democracy as the creation of elites (Collier 1999).

The democratization movements of Southern Europe in the mid-1970s that initiated a third wave of democratization, expanding to Latin America and Asia, and the color revolutions after the fall of the Soviet Union—to which we might add the 2009 Green Revolution in Iran— privileged the site of the streets and squares, with large demonstrations as the premier evidence and tactic of legitimate popular change. Their successes did, inevitably, depend on restraint from the top: that obscure combination of state coercive agency and institutional self-preservation from state elites, which would determine if the movement would proceed or be destroyed. In the cases where politics proceeded from demonstrations to change, security forces stood down, or were stood down, refused to be used, or prevented others from being used, as power-holders, and decided not to fire on crowds and begin negotiations. The dominant academic narrative has emphasized the crucial decision of the state not to use violence as the principle decision that makes revolution possible (Skocpol 1979; O'Donnell and Schmitter 1986).

Activists and popular media, though, have continued to situate the legitimacy of popular struggle in the street and the square. The magnitude of the assembled crowd, their fortitude in the face of security forces, the diversity of the crowd, or the domination of the crowd by middle and professional classes not associated with civic unruliness, or the youthfulness of the crowd, have all been advanced as evidence of the legitimacy of the demands. The expanding crowd, growing in number and diversity, is a sign of that expanding space of democratic possibility. The analytic narrative of democratization notes the increasing diversity of different and competing groups that fill public space when a democratic moment is permitted. Trade unionists, students, or anti-regime activists may start the demonstration. As it expands it takes in feminist groups, human rights activists, indigenous peoples' groups, professional groups, business groups, housewives, high-school students: an ever-widening presentation of the nation.

The emergence of lawyers on the street in Pakistan with the Lawyers Movement in 2007–2009 was remarkable and spoke directly to the legitimacy of the judicial system and its relationship to the executive. The demonstrations in Iran in 2009 included non-elite youth, whose arrival by motor scooter was noted with satisfaction by the young secular activist of the upper middle class (Moqadam 2010). So powerful is the legitimacy afforded to the large, collective, anti-regime demonstration that massive demonstrations against democratically elected regimes gain credibility: in Thailand in 2014, when the presence of youth and middle classes sustained a coup on behalf of the monarchy and elites; in the Ukraine in 2015, when a pro-Russian president was deposed, potential cabinet members presented to the crowd for approval by acclamation, and Russia took advantage of political collapse to seize territory; in Egypt, when idealistic pro-democracy demonstrators opposed the democratically elected Islamist government, accusing it of "stealing" the revolution, and ushered in a return to military authoritarianism; in Venezuela in 2002, when a range of anti-Chavez supporters sought US support for their cause but the Bush administration issued a statement in support of democratically elected regimes; in 2004 in Haiti, when elites with access to the latest US weapons organized demonstrations against a democratically elected president to prepare the way for a coup. Some massive demonstrations are part of political efforts to reorient the state. Others, such as the Occupy Wall Street project, see themselves as exemplary rather than part of a meanstoan end calculation of politics. They seek to connect to the power of political mobilization but for a more diffuse transformative project. While most marches and demonstrations have a concrete political goal—the downfall of the regime, establishment of political rights, attention to labor grievances, demands for rights—so powerful is the commitment and optimism generated by this form of mass mobilization that it appeals to diffuse and expansive proposals of community where no first step is apparent but where the goals seem now to be within grasp—a "moment of madness" (Zolberg 1972).

The demonstrations and marches of the Arab Spring drew on all these aspects of mass mobilization in space. People created tents to occupy parks and streets (Pearl Roundabout in Bahrain, Tahrir Square in Egypt, and in Tunisia and Yemen), and they sustained the idea of a new order, already born. People lived and demonstrated together, shared food, talked about politics, and saw a national unity in their own commitment to each other and in their diversity. This was particularly striking in Egypt, where the relatively *longue durée* of Tahrir Square brought together people from different walks of life, university students and manual laborers, Islamists and secularists, professors and housewives with young children. Young filmmakers filmed street theatre and then gave up their cynical distance to join what was already calling itself a revolution. Journalists came as interviewers and left traumatized and radicalized as they, too, were subject to the violence of security forces or regime thugs. The parks and squares of tents were structured to provide respite from the rigors of demonstrations where literal demonstrations of commitment were met with efforts to control, intimidate, and harm, isolating individuals or groups through targeted violence. Members of the Muslim Brotherhood were accustomed to protracted demonstrations, under pressure from the security forces, that appeared more like battles, and they remained organized and active, as noted by David Kirkpatrick's reporting for the *New York Times* on February 9, 2011. While banned from formal politics, the Muslim Brotherhood were a wide-ranging presence in professional unions, public charities, labor unions, and public space generally. They had also developed a tactical women's group. In contesting Egyptian elections over the past decade, the organization had mobilized women in part to visibly feminize its presence in the face of Egyptian security forces' control of polling places. Egypt's labor unions arrived in a march, en masse, when the Tahrir Square occupation was perhaps a month old and escalating, bringing an enormous group of employees, including women, into the public space. Intense strike activity in the few years before the 2011 events had developed and trained labor leadership at many levels. Women were a significant presence here (Beinin 2012). Women were integrally part of the crowds that constituted themselves as "the people" through the constitutive speech act of naming and speaking in that name (Kraidy 2016: 7). Women were present throughout the Egyptian protests, diverse in class identity, larger group commitments, and personal presentation. If an educated elite was more conspicuous in interviews with Western journalists, the constant stream of images showed a wider nation and broader inclusion. While Cairo was the center of the revolution from a media point of view, and perhaps from the regime's perspective, as Cairo is the capital of Egypt, occupied parks and massive demonstrations dominated space in regional centers such as Zagazig. Whatever the apparent losses in street safety or the ramping up of state repression, the visible presence of so many Egyptian women, in all sizes, shapes, styles, and dress, all struggling for change in Egypt, was overwhelming.

The Tunisian revolution may have had a more narrow planning base than the Egyptian revolution, but it started early and went more quickly. In the absence of a protracted occupation of space, massive demonstrations and the presence of the large public sector unions dominated in city centers. But smaller centers were the sites of intense demonstrations and protests, too. Tunisia's Islamist Ennahda party was more firmly underground, and it is not clear what it contributed to the rapid development of demonstrations. If Islamist organizations were less visible, Tunisia's major feminist party, Les Femmes Démocratiques, seemed to remove itself from the process of transformation when the head of the organization asked for support for the dictator, Ben Ali, on national television shortly before the deluge. This was a strategic commitment, not a tactical one; women's rights in Tunisia, as in Turkey, Iraq, and Iran, were understood as state feminism, and loyalty to the state that had guaranteed women's rights was a strategy that worked for most of the twentieth century. (Discussed in section 5.3 and 5.4 below.) Between the relative absence of a visible Islamist organization with women members, and absent feminists, Tunisia's public space and demonstrations did not promise the politics of public space to women. In addition, many of Tunisia's demonstrations took place as skirmishes between police and young men from the lower classes, unemployed and largely excluded from politics. While their cell phone images were picked up by Al-Jazeera, Tunisian women, especially those from the middle classes, and young university women, were not conspicuous in these early demonstrations, which were more tussles with security forces than demonstrations. Several things changed this: the Tunisian army quickly addressed the problem of units loyal to Ben Ali terrorizing neighborhoods and shut down regime violence. Tunisia's well-developed legal associations, such as the Tunisian association of constitutional lawyers, expanded into potential public space as if they had been working there for years. They had, albeit under an uneven dictatorship, but now they set to work constructing new constitutional possibilities for politics. The involvement of Tunisia's labor unions also helped reframe the demonstrations. These factors contributed to the quick expansion of demonstrations in Tunisia to include women, again, rapidly, from all walks of life, from different social classes, elite and poor, secular and Islamic.

5.2 Public Space, a Chaotic and Dangerous Space, Problematic Space

The public space of parks, squares, and streets that is so central to these events, and the exercise of a kind of public self, expands not as an extension of civil society but as a contested no-man's land of chaos and risk. Public space may become the space of insurrection, not demonstration, whether it is activists or regime actors who seek to escalate the level of violence. We see a variety of speech and actions that threaten women, individually and as a category. During and after the transformation in Egypt, women objected strongly to their treatment in the public space of street and square. Women reported an increase in verbal abuse and threats. Other public spaces were also threatened: university space became an area of harassment and groping, where individual men and groups threatened women students. This was partly due to state weakness, including the role of the security forces as they failed to police, were unable to police, or enacted revenge. It was also partly due to the expansion of civil society into this space, in which any man or group of men can express anger at women's presence. As the new state seeks a popular base, it has authorized expression from its supporters as well as raised expectations about expression from its opponents. Security forces, former security forces, Islamists, Muslim Brothers, Salafists, social conservatives, supporters of the former regime, and angry men all jostle in the public space of streets and city centers and in public forums of self-expression. The goals of the Arab Spring that included greater freedom for self-expression animated an array of speech acts in addition to the celebrated demonstration. We saw poetry performed publicly, social network posting, graffiti and art production, and protest art posted to global internet audiences. We saw street-cleaning as a political act. We may also have to confront the fact that sexual harassment, abuse, and rape are public and political speech acts and violent performances. This recognition disrupts the Western notion of a valorized public space but may be a more effective analysis of struggles there. And it disrupts the prevailing understanding of rape as violence, narrowly. Given a particular context, rape is violence about power not only over a woman, but over women generally; punishment of a woman, or of women generally, or of a kind of woman, be she deemed of little value, poor, and of no value, or of no morals, or of the wrong morals, wrong class, wrong culture.

Public spaces of streets and squares, workplace, and university have long been considered part of the stakes of women's expanded rights as well as one of the markers that differentiate the West from the Islamic world and connect to the vast discourse of place and propriety around women's dress, covered or uncovered. For Western spaces, places as diverse as the dissection hall in medical school and the golf course have been contested as women's different rights expanded. Women's access to diverse public spaces in the Arab world has been shaped by urban/rural and class divisions; poor women and rural women worked where they could or where they needed to; elite women were held to more exacting standards. Cairo as a site of long and settled modern habitation saw more women on the streets than in Algiers; a Tunisian seaside restaurant with outside tables will have many women; a Tunisian outside café will have only women tourists. Some urban streets may be used exclusively by men, others will be more heavily frequented by women. Access and comfort for women change according to the time of day: what is appropriate in the morning may become dangerous at dusk. What is reasonable with a male escort may be difficult or unthinkable without. A private car gives elite women new worlds of access that others attain with more difficulty on public transportation.

The informal policing of public space by men who pressure women in different ways, from the lighthearted sighs at the sight of a pretty woman to verbal harassment, groping, and sexual assault, is seldom noticed or appreciated by men. The presence of police may deter the more grave kinds of threats, but the aftermath of political transformation is a time of chaos, of new rules that look like no rules, when police are absent or resentful, and those men who feared police scrutiny might enjoy new impunity. It may also be a period, after the apparent equality of the people in the street together, when class divisions become meaningful again and old resentments enjoy new license.

5.3 Do Women's Rights Need a Strong State for Access to Rights and Public Space?

The importance of a strong state for the establishment and expansion of women's rights in the region has been well argued. Mounira Charrad (2001) argued that women's rights across North Africa directly reflected the relationship of state power to local clan and family authority. Where the state was strongest, in Tunisia, is where women's rights were established most firmly, maintained, and expanded. Morocco, where the state was weaker in the face of traditional social formations, had the weakest women's rights regimes. And Algeria, which she argued was in the middle regarding state strength, had a mixed set of laws and practices. It is not absolute state strength, she argued, that is important but state strength relative to traditional clan and family authority.

Two additional aspects are important here. First, war changes everything. Women may take on new roles that men are unable to accomplish and are additionally at risk. In Algeria, women have been targeted for being without headscarves, or for having headscarves. During the Algerian civil war (1991–1999), whole villages were killed and young women were abducted and raped. Journalists, police, teachers—men and women—were killed. Most of those killed by security forces and others, and most of those who disappeared, were men. Yet once the war had wound down rather than ended, with an incomplete national reconciliation and moderate Islamists in government (a Muslim Brotherhood party), women were more evident on public streets, headscarved or not; working in little restaurants, generally headscarved, or directing bus traffic at a major bus station, in modern young Islamic dress with leggings under a black cotton knit dress, all black and all fitted, bossing bus drivers in aviator sunglasses and leather jackets; or working in a small internet café in conservative Islamic dress. At the other end of the prestige scale, there were more women than ever in public sector management and in the justice department. These positions did not pay as well as jobs in the private sector but they represented the steady output of women graduates from university, despite the terrible years of civil conflict. Strong state, weak state—is this enough to explain an expanding norm in which women's access to education and work, need to work and right to work, have been increasingly taken for granted? Conservative families have educated girls, then we see young women seeking employment, then unmarried daughters want to go to France for more training, with parents torn between pride and concern.

Women choose to live alone not only for independence but also to avoid burdening family members and young families with children, and limited space. A world of work and possibility is expanding faster than imagined, sometimes as emancipation and sometimes experienced as hardship.

5.4 Modernizing State, Modernizing Society?

The modernizing states of the Middle East and North Africa committed to some vision of modern women as part of their larger commitment to modernity and rejection of tradition as part of backwardness. This is well known to scholars of nationalism in the postcolonial world generally. This commitment produced voting rights, expanded educational access, and access to jobs in the public sector for women. Critics of what has been called "state feminism" have argued that this historical development of rights for women precluded the development of a robust independent women's rights movement. In addition, a focus on the modernist sectors of education, higher education, and employment outside the home left poor and rural women largely untouched by the process (White 2003). Finally, the neoliberal state of the early 1990s turned away from these commitments and abandoned women's rights, as the private sector, including the family, and non-governmental organizations (NGOs) became more important for social strategies with the enormous cutbacks in state spending (Hatem 2005).

Yet several decades of state feminism, even lukewarm state feminism with equivocal commitments to women's employment, contributed to a changed social world in which women's access to education has become desirable for a wider range of social classes and groups. And this changed social norm regarding education affects a growing commitment to work outside the home. While elite women may seek a position in an NGO or foreign firm, middle-class and lower middle-class women seek an income to contribute to their family before they are married and to sustain their own children and family later. With advanced degrees and professional qualifications, women have gained access to prestigious positions although the salaries are often low. Although most media coverage of women's head covering emphasizes what we see on the street, and what is permitted or required by law in different Islamic countries, much of the development of women's modern Islamic dress is driven by women's desire to construct a modest and respectable public persona, for the workplace and for husbands, that also permits self-expression and a connection to fashion.

5.5 STATE FEMINISM, FAMILIES, AND INDIVIDUAL RIGHTS

While rights are generally attached to individuals, women live their lives largely in a family context. Women with professional careers, and those who publish, present as individuals, yet their cultural capital, education and professional trajectories may owe much to fathers and families. Marriages tend to be organized through family negotiations; educational and work strategies are again negotiated collectively. This means that commitments to women's education and women's work, support for women in public space, and the respect afforded women in public spaces, are not only the concern of individual women but of families, writ large. We see this in the massive demonstration in Cairo, organized by women, against the security service's mistreatment of women. The demonstration included women of different ages and social class, veiled, covered, and not. We also see support for women in the signs and support afforded by men. The dragging, by security services in Egypt, in the course of repressing demonstrators, of the young "woman in the blue bra", whose black overdress was pulled over her head, incensed a wide spectrum of the Egyptian population. Less obvious but no less important is this normalization of public support for women's public presence.

5.6 WHERE IS ISLAM IN ALL THIS?

Islamic commitments and Islamic organizations have largely supported women's access to education and employment. In their concerns about modesty and dress, they may have a sharper recognition of the insults women receive in public space, albeit a different solution than what secularists would like. The Muslim Brotherhood is a largely middle-class movement, in which women pursue educational goals and employment, within a larger assumption that marriage will be their primary occupation. In this they share the larger commitments of the country. Ennahda in Tunis was able to offer women places on its ballots; again this is a largely middle-class movement.

While much of recent concern about Islamic violence focuses on the Salafi movements, in North Africa and Egypt these are largely associated with the lower middle class and unemployed. Their economic grievances find expression in a discourse of Islamic justice. It is not surprising that the delightful cafés of coastal Tunis and film festivals have been the targets of attacks. The April 2015 attack on the Bardo Museum in Tunis, with its large collection of Roman mosaics, was an attack on tourism, privilege, and cultural capital. The Tunisian left understands itself as secular; it is largely urban and sees itself in a tradition of modernization. As the Tunisian state withdraws from rural Tunisia, spending less on education and social services, Islamic movements compete to be modern but also to recuperate an underclass.

5.7 Modernity as Strategy, Identity, and Policy

Today, modernization is a commitment and a strategy for feminists and liberals in the region, as well as important parts of the Islamic movement. "Modern" as an identity and a label in politics, though, risks assigning the opposition to a wholly negative category that must be overcome, or that will inevitably be overcome by history. When Tunisians speak of political affiliations as "modern" or "Islamist," they are adopting a Western history that created the frames of colonialism and exclusion. That this binary is redeployed in contemporary democratic politics seems a tragedy, but the power of the discourse with roots in Marx and French liberalism is undeniable (Marx 2005; Tocqueville 2001). Marxists in Afghanistan were deeply committed to undoing traditionalism with women's rights as modernity, and were less successful in advancing women's rights than they were in binding women's rights to the idea of secularism, against religion (Nawid 2007).

While Marx saw traditional life to be inevitably destroyed by capitalism and colonialism, French liberalism and universalism, so important for the construction of modernity in North Africa, saw Islam as primitive and superstitious, as well as an imported, alien creed. Although the nationalist movements in North Africa reaffirmed Islam as the moral basis of society, the idea of the universal understood as Western gained increasing salience with the importance of French in professional education and the greater deterioration of Islamic education. Modern states privileged Western education, expanding the gap between Islamic education and modern commitments. This gap is not so great in Egypt, where Arabic was maintained in the colonial period as the language of higher education and professional education, and the Islamic university of Al-Azhar was directed by a great Islamic reformer. The Azhar has had programs for women since the 1960s, and the modern Islamic movement of the 1980s included greater mosque attendance for women. The Islamic movement in Tunisia has been more repressed, making its incorporation into civil society more challenging and its alliances across the political and intellectual fields more difficult. In short, the greater political repression in Tunisia denied political actors the practice of negotiating different positions. Thus the commitment to the inclusion of women in Tunisia, in the parliament, across secular and Islamist parties, is more remarkable. The largely peaceful competition between parties, and alternation of power, is an unexpected and valuable political outcome. But the future expansion of women's rights in Tunisia and other countries of the Arab uprisings may be best sustained, in law and in practices and processes of daily life, if it can be bound and enhanced in broad religious or customary life and family life, and not be presented as belonging exclusively to a universalist discourse or secular vision (see Singerman 2004; Salima 2011). Open political processes bring conflicting views into politics, and the problematic state feminism of authoritarian states will no longer deliver women's rights against more traditional forces. Advances in women's rights will demand negotiation, compromise, and hybridity that will not satisfy purists.

The opening up of public space and the chaotic public space of insurrection thus threaten to become sites of conflict between democratic participation and modernization. Women's rights, advanced by patriarchal modernizing states, are confronted now by fractured patriarchal societies, yet societies in which women's access to education, employment, and a right to be present in political space has been increasingly taken for granted.

This chapter, then, has sought to recontextualize the understanding of women's rights post-Arab Spring, where the state's endorsement of women's rights was increasingly understood as inadequate or in bad faith, and where demands for greater participation appear to recast women's rights against political expressions of different social worlds. The demonstrations and uprisings of the Arab Spring were directed against authoritarianism generally, against inadequate governments that could not deliver basic services or disaster relief, governments whose economic policies did not benefit most people, and governments with particularly corrupt rulers. Women's rights were subsumed and included; women protested with men, assuming their right to protest and to work beside men for a better political and economic order. When the streets and public spaces became a place of insurrection and politics, regimes struck back violently, humiliating women and beating or killing people indiscriminately. Regime supporters, security forces, and other men also sought to humiliate, degrade, and assault women in public spaces. These efforts were refused by the protesters themselves, men and women, by large organized protests from women, and by networks of family and supporters. While police forces have been damaged, they will not be able to contribute to a public order of respect until they have been rehabilitated and reformed. Yet the larger effect of the Arab Spring events of 2011 will further consolidate women's rights in the region, both in terms of legal rights and in terms of practices and assumptions. So much of Western feminism is tied to individualism and to viewing women as a category separate from men. That understanding is altered by the nature of women's participation in the Arab Spring. Women made history with men; they worked beside them to create a new political order; they suffered and had losses, deaths, and humiliations; they have to live with unsuccessful negotiations and partial victories that sometimes feel like losses. That, however, is the nature of politics.

Notes

1. Despite vigorous participation in many aspects of the French Revolution, women's organizations were banned and no legislative measures to grant women greater rights were debated. Women's rights in the UK lagged behind the expansion of suffrage in the nineteenth century and the women's suffrage movement in real repression in the twentieth century. Women in Southern Europe also did not gain the vote and more equal rights until the second half of the twentieth century. Carole Pateman (1988), philosopher and scholar of democratic theory, has theorized that the construction of the Western liberal order created a public space where women's sexuality was exposed and rendered their civic aspect vulnerable.
2. Against this view is the evidence of an internal split in the ruling group over the repression of demonstrators, seen in the harsh criticism of the shooting from Al-Ahram considered to be a state media outlet, and in the announcement from the state prosecutor that the death would be investigated (Kirkpatrick 2015). The split within a regime, between *blandos* and *duros*, or soft-liners and hard-liners, is of enormous importance for the fate of a democratic movement (O'Donnell and Schmitter 1986: 15–16).

Bibliography

Amnesty International. 2015. Egypt: Human Rights Activist Among 17 Facing Spurious Charges in Security Forces' 'Cover Up.' April 2, 2015. https://www.amnesty.org/en/articles/news/2015/04/egypt-womens-rights-activist-among-17-facing-spurious-charges/

Batatu, H. 1978. *The Old Social Classes and the Revolutionary Movements of Iraq: A Study of Iraq's Old Landed and Commercial Classes and of Its Communists, Ba'thists, and Free Officers*. Princeton: Princeton University Press.

Beinin, J. 2012. Egyptian Workers and January 25th: A Social Movement in Historical Context. *Social Research* 79 (2): 323–348.

Charrad, M. 2001. *States and Women's Rights: The Making of Postcolonial Tunisia, Algeria and Morocco*. Berkeley: University of California Press.

Collier, R.B. 1999. *Paths Toward Democracy: Working Class and Elites in Western Europe*. Cambridge, UK: Cambridge University Press.

de Tocqueville, A. 2001. Essay on Algeria—1841. In *Writing on Empire and Slavery*, ed. and trans. J. Pitts. Baltimore: The Johns Hopkins University Press.

Habermas, J. 1989. *The Structural Transformation of the Public Sphere: An Inquiry into a Category of Bourgeois Society*. Trans. T. Burger and F. Lawrence. [1962 in German] Cambridge, MA: The MIT Press.

Hatem, M.F. 2005. In the Shadow of the State: Changing Definitions of Arab Women's "Developmental" Citizenship Rights. *Journal of Middle East Womens Studies*. 1 (3): 20–45.

Kirkpatrick, D.D. 2015. Coming to Mourn Tahrir Square's Dead, and Joining Them Instead. Killing of Shaimaa el-Sabbagh in Cairo Angers Egyptians. *The New York Times*, February 3.

Kraidy, M.M. 2016. *The Naked Blogger of Cairo: Creative Insurgency in the Arab World*. Cambridge, MA: Harvard University Press.

Marx, K. 2005. The Future Results of British Rule in India, [1852–1853]. In *Karl Marx Selected Writings*, ed. D. McLellan. New York: Oxford University Press.

Moqadam, A. 2010. *Death to the Dictator! A Young Man Casts a Vote in Iran's 2009 Election and Pays a Devastating Price*. New York: Farrar, Straus and Giroux. 2011.

Muslim Brotherhood. 2015. More Coup Opponents Court Martialed, Imprisoned—Including Woman. Ikhwan Web – The Muslim Brotherhood's Official English website, April 8, 2015. http://www.ikhwanweb.com/article.php?id=32085&ref=search.php

Nawid, S. 2007. Afghan Women Under Marxism. In *From Patriarchy to Empowerment: Women's Participation, Movements, and Rights in the Middle East, North Africa, and South Asia*, ed. V.M. Moghadam, 58–72. Syracuse: Syracuse University.

O'Donnell, G., and P. Schmitter. 1986. *Transition from Authoritarian Rule: Tentative Conclusions About Uncertain Democracies*. Baltimore: The Johns Hopkins University Press.

Pateman, C. 1988. *The Sexual Contract*. Stanford: Stanford University Press.

Salima, Z. 2011. *Between Feminism and Islam: Human Rights and Sharia Rights in Morocco*. Minneapolis: University of Minnesota Press.

Singerman, D. 2004. Rewriting Divorce in Egypt: Reclaiming Islam, Legal Activism, and Coalition Politics. In *Remaking Muslim Politics: Pluralism, Contestation, Democratization*, ed. R.W. Hefner, 161–188. Princeton: Princeton University Press.

Skocpol, T. 1979. *States and Revolutions*. Cambridge: Cambridge University Press.

White, J. 2003. State Feminism and the Turkish Republican Woman. *National Women's Studies Association Journal* 15 (3): 145–159.

Zolberg, A.R. 1972. Moments of Madness. *Politics & Society* 2 (2): 183–207.

PART 2

Unfinished Social Revolutions

CHAPTER 6

Religious Discourses and Gender Dynamics: Reflections on the Arab Spring

Asma Nouira

6.1 Introduction

Arab women have played an active role in the political movements that constitute the Arab Spring, as agents of political and social change, and as full-fledged citizens, equal to their male counterparts. The question of gender discrimination never came up in the early stages of the protest movements because the focus of all the efforts was on the overthrow of the regimes. So Arab women participated in all forms of resistance against repressive regimes, including protest marches, civil unrest, and online mobilization efforts, demanding freedom, dignity, equality, and democracy. Indeed, one of the main demands of the Arab Spring movements was for dignity, social equality, and economic opportunity.

Yet the issues of gender equality and women's role in society came to the fore very early in the political transitions of the Arab Spring, as a result of the emergence of religious parties to fill the power vacuum created by the downfall of the old regimes. In Tunisia as well as in Egypt, the religious

A. Nouira (✉)
University of Tunis El Manar, Tunis, Tunisia

© The Author(s) 2018
S. Khamis, A. Mili (eds.), *Arab Women's Activism and Socio-Political Transformation*, DOI 10.1007/978-3-319-60735-1_6

parties that rose to power proceeded to open up broad debates on alternative social models, based on traditional social and religious norms. Not surprisingly, gender issues were at the center of these debates, for any social model can be characterized to a great extent by the role that it assigns to women. The debates quickly mobilized the political forces of the country, opposing religious parties against secular parties. In Tunisia, which was the pioneer of both revolutionary gender standards and revolutionary political transitions, the debate on gender was framed by religious parties as one about the Islamic identity of the country, and as the alternative Islamic societal project.

During the transition period (January 14, 2011–October 23, 2011), the religious parties of Tunisia were advocating a moderate form of social evolution, through a return to traditional/authentic norms and standards that are part of Tunisia's sociocultural heritage. They broached the subject of gender standards indirectly through the more general subject of an Islamic societal model. The religious parties of Tunisia called for revisiting the secular modernist tradition of Tunisia embodied in the postcolonial state infrastructure, including in particular the Code of Personal Status (CPS), which represents the most important legal gains for Tunisian women. This is a fairly appealing agenda for a large segment of the society, as many Tunisians are eager to reconcile their traditional Arab/Islamic identity with the social and moral norms of the modern globalized world.

The elections of the National Constitutional Assembly of Tunisia on October 23, 2011 gave the religious party Ennahdha (the renaissance) a comfortable majority and emboldened it to be more assertive in its plan; the election results could legitimately be interpreted as a mandate for Ennahdha to implement its vision. In the wake of its electoral success, the party started intimating that it intended to implement Sharia law in Tunisia, in particular in what pertains to women's rights. In doing so, it feigned to consider that Sharia law is an integral part of its agenda of Islamic identity, and conveniently ignored that while most Tunisians have no problem embracing their Islamic identity, they are fiercely opposed to the application of Sharia law. Also, Tunisians are very attached to their specific multidimensional identity, which includes not only the Arab/Islamic component but also others, such as Phoenician, Carthaginian, Roman, Berber, Andalusian, and European. Finally, Tunisians are very proud of their role as trendsetters in gender standards, and they view the 1956 legislation that enshrines these standards as an important achievement to their credit, which they are reluctant to renounce.

By contrast with Tunisian women, Egyptian women did not have a body of progressive legislation that they could use as baseline in their demands for gender equality. With the exception of some minor amendments to the law of personal status, it is not possible to point to clear gains for Egyptian women prior to the revolution, so the struggle that they had to wage starting in the revolution of 2011 was focused primarily on acquiring new rights and privileges. The outcome of this struggle was to a large extent dependent on the outcome of many fateful elections that the country went through after the fall of the Mubarak regime, and on the attendant constitutional debates that these elections engendered.

The situation in Yemen was even worse for the cause of gender equality, as militants for women's causes were exposed to much denigration, slander, and accusation of misconduct from religious parties for the mere fact that they were protesting in the streets alongside men. A religious party, the Islah (reform) party, did support the participation of women in the proceedings of the revolution, but only within the bounds of religious parameters. Still, women were not intimidated, and they pressed on with their demand for political reform, and with the constitutionalization of their legitimate rights. In particular, they played a crucial role in the framework of the national debate, which lasted for six months starting in March 2013, and aimed to draft a new constitution and resolve the issue of power-sharing that arose in the wake of the downfall of the Ali Abdullah Saleh regime.

As for the situation for women in Libya, it is not very different from other countries of the Arab Spring, in that Libyan women first fought for political rights alongside men, only to find religious forces filling the vacuum created by the downfall of the Qadafi regime, and to find themselves compelled to continue their fight against the new power, but for higher stakes: political rights (democracy) and social rights (gender equality).

Despite some differences in the democratic transitions, the countries of the Arab Spring have witnessed similar circumstances where women find themselves compelled to fight against religion-inspired conservative forces, for the sake of preserving and consolidating their gains. Before we discuss the repercussions of the rise of religious parties in the countries of the Arab Spring, it might be useful to explore in some detail the raw agenda of these parties with regard to women's rights.

6.2　The Islamists' Gender Agenda

The political agendas of Islamist parties with regard to women's rights vary by country and by party, since they depend not exclusively on religious dictates but also on local customs and traditions. Yet they all have in common a patriarchal misogynistic streak that is compatible with the culture of most Arab countries. Also, they share a common rationale, which consists of the following elements:

- an emphasis on the premise that Islam brought great improvements to the situation of women in the Arabian peninsula by comparison with the period that preceded it;
- an emphasis on the poor condition of women in Western countries in the past, from the middle ages up to their recent history;
- an emphasis on the moral decadence of modern Western societies, in reference to sexual freedoms, lax moral standards, the demise of traditional family structures and values, the acceptance/normalization of alternative lifestyles and so on.

Hence these agendas discourage women from adopting modern Western-like lifestyles in favor of an original lifestyle that is inspired by Islamic guidelines and traditions, and adheres to the *natural* role of a woman in the family and in society.

The Islamist discourse in terms of gender roles revolves around the idea that men are superior to women in their physical, intellectual, and emotional attributes. The Qur'an makes repeated references to this effect, it provides that a woman inherits half the share of her brother in a family, and that the testimony of a man is worth the testimony of two women (which readily settles cases of "He said, she said"). Also, Islamists cite a quote from the Prophet to the effect that women lack wisdom and faith.

Consequently, the Islamist discourse does not adhere to the principle of gender equality and argues instead for the obscure principle of complementarity. This principle provides that men and women are different, and that they must play different and complementary roles within the family and within society. Within the family, the role of the woman is to bear and raise children while the role of the man is to provide for the family. This naturally determines their respective roles and spaces in society: the man occupies the public space while the woman occupies the private space of the home. This enables Islamists to blame women for the social ills of modern Arab societies on the grounds that these are caused by the failure of women to take up the function that is naturally theirs. Islamists argue that by being present in the public sphere, women create temptations in the eyes of men, which can lead to all sorts of social problems. Islamists argue that by focusing on her role as a housekeeper, the woman plays an important role by raising children in faith and supporting the family, and thereby contributing to the welfare and success of the nation.

6.3 Threats to Recent Gender Gains in Tunisia

Political Islam is broadly critical of modern social norms and presents alternative models under the heading "Islam is the Answer." In an attempt to denigrate modern social norms, Islamist activists point to the degradation of moral standards in society and place all the blame for this on women, and on women's liberation. As a result, they advocate the wholesale rejection of all the gender gains achieved by women, reserving their sharpest rebuke for the legislation of personal status enacted by Tunisia in 1956. However, rejecting this legislation puts them at odds with most Tunisians, who view it as an integral part of their identity and as an important component of the postcolonial modern state with which they identify.

The religious party Ennahdha has overplayed its hand by attempting to denigrate the modern state structures that the first president of Tunisia, a sworn enemy, had put in place from the mid-1950s; indeed, they have underestimated the extent to which president Bourguiba has nurtured in Tunisians a sense of pride in their state, and a strong loyalty to the Tunisian identity. This meant that when they attempted to play the Islamic identity against the Tunisian identity, not only did they fail but they lost the trust of the people in the process, which may have caused them to lose the elections of 2014.

In fact Bourguiba had co-opted the religious institutions of Tunisia in 1956 by involving them in his constitutional plan, and by casting his state-building initiative as interpreting religious guidelines rather than opposing them. But the reality is that many of the clauses of the CPS (1956) and the constitution (1959) contradict the letter of Islamic law. In particular, as far as gender issues are concerned, the Tunisian legislation differs from Sharia law in that it prohibits and criminalizes polygamy (Article 18), it forbids repudiation in favor of divorces that are declared by a judge (Article 30), and it does not prohibit a Muslim woman from marrying a non-Muslim, nor does it prohibit a non-Muslim from inheriting from a Muslim (Article 88). Through a combination of clout, diplomacy, and political dexterity, Bourguiba was able to push through his modernist state project in a society (Tunisia in the middle of the twentieth century) that was profoundly attached to centuries-old social and religious traditions, and despite the reluctance of powerful and entrenched religious organizations. But he did not silence the opposition to his project, nor did he put an end to the debate.

Despite the ruthless repression they were subjected to under the regimes of Bourguiba and Ben Ali, the Islamist forces of the country remained active, albeit in a state of relative hibernation, because unlike all the other forms of political opposition, they had a safe space to conduct their activity: the mosques. Thus when the democratic process opened up following the 2011 uprising, the religious parties sprung into action, picking up where they had left off, and reopening the debate about matters of national identity, gender roles, social norms, sources of legislation and so on. Against this background, gender organizations in Tunisia mobilized their energies to fight against the introduction of Sharia law, and in favor of the separation of religion and state. A large segment of Tunisian society, most notably the educated, liberated, modernized middle class, were very fearful that the emergence of religious parties would put the country at risk of losing all the advances that were achieved in terms of gender standards since independence. Gender organizations mobilized around two broad themes: no regression in gender standards and no revision of the CPS.

Most of the religious organizations in the country called for this revision, with the intent of making the CPS comply with the prescriptions of Sharia law. Religious organizations that are devoted to women were more ambiguous in the sense that they pledge their support for Sharia law at the same time as they acknowledge the importance of the CPS in shaping the social fabric of the country, and express their appreciation for its benefits to women. As for the religion-inspired political parties that emerged after 2011, only three of them (out of 20) declared their support for the CPS and expressed their commitment to protecting the gains of women:

- the party of justice and development, which defends women's rights and supports the participation of women in the political and economic life of the country;
- the party of dignity and development, which acknowledges Bourguiba's efforts to make the CPS compatible with Islamic teachings, and emphasizes the need to reconcile Islam with modernity;
- the party of reform and development, which includes the liberation of women as part of its social agenda.

All the while, other Islamist parties call for a literal application of Sharia law as it pertains to women, including polygamy, customary marriage, the mandatory hijab and so forth. Among these parties we cite the party of liberation (Tahrir), the party of mercy (Rahma), and the Zeitouna party. Many other Islamist parties remain ambiguous as far as women's rights. These range from those that adopt modern ideals in their philosophical platforms (e.g. the party of democratic reform) to those that adopt Islamic law as their source without declaring explicitly what their position is with regard to women's rights (e.g. the party of dignity and equality).

As for Ennahdha, the main religious party, which was the main party in the National Constitutional Assembly, it has managed to maintain its ambiguity with regard to preserving women's rights despite making repeated declarations to the effect that it does not intend to revise the CPS in case it gains power after the elections. As is typical in such cases, these declarations do not satisfy anybody: their political allies (including the Salafists and other religious parties) find that these declarations do not match their agendas, and that they are incompatible with a party that has long fought to establish an Islamic state. On the other hand, their political opponents accuse them of double-speak and suspect that they do not mean what they say. Observers believe that this ambiguity is part of the electoral strategy of Ennahdha, as it evolves from a stealth politicoreligious underground organization to a public political party poised to gain access to power, and as it tries to appease its extremist wing while reassuring its moderate base.

Part of the ambiguity is also a result of a lack of coordination within the Ennahdha party and between its leaders and spokespersons. Hence while leaders who have intuition for politics and political strategy (e.g. Rached Ghannouchi, the party leader) make reassuring pronouncements directed at the broad electorate at large, to the effect that the party intends to preserve gender standards enacted in the 1956 code, more dogmatic spokespersons (e.g. Habib Ellouze or Sadok Chourou) try to appease the extreme wing of the party by declaring that the constitutional debate will encompass fundamental choices about the societal model, state identity, sources of law and so on. Ennahdha perfected the skill of double-speak, saying different things to different audiences, and saying different things within the country and abroad.

At the same time as it was raging in civil society and political circles, the debate about national constitutional choices was taking place in the assembly, which had the mission of drafting a new constitution to replace the 1959 version. Even though the application of Sharia law was never mentioned in the political and electoral platform of the Ennahdha party prior to the elections of October 2011, many Ennahdha members of the assembly started talking about including an article in the constitution that explicitly provides that Sharia is the source of Tunisian law. According to Sadok Chourou, a prominent Ennahdha member of the assembly, the legislative body must draft the constitution on the basis of three sources—the Qur'an, the Sunna (the prophet's conduct and pronouncements), and a council of religious scholars—with the understanding that the role of the latter is to rule on matters where the Qur'an and Sunna are ambiguous or silent. Chourou considers that it is the duty of the assembly to use Islamic sources in its constitutional work, given that the population is majority Muslim and that Islam is the official religion of the country. Also, Ennahdha member Sahby Ateeg, the chairman of the Ennahdha caucus, considers that the constitution must be based on Islamic principles, on the grounds that Islam is an integral part of the Tunisian identity.

Yet Rached Ghannouchi, the spiritual leader of Ennahdha, insists in his declarations in Tunisia and abroad that his party does not intend to integrate Sharia law into the constitution. At the same time, he declared in a meeting with the extremist wing of his party that Sharia law can be applied by reinterpreting Article 1 of the constitution, which provides that Islam is the official religion of the state. This article has been approved by the vast majority of the assembly membership, mostly because it lends itself to a range of distinct interpretations. Several less prominent parties supported Ennahdha's position in the constitutional assembly, including:

- the Coalition of Freedom and Dignity, an independent Islamist party;
- the Popular Petition, a coalition of religious-leaning blocks that morphed into a party, led by an exiled former member of Ennahdha, who owns a television station in London, UK.

While this tug-of-war was ongoing within the assembly, pressure was building outside as well in favor of integrating religious principles and guidelines into the constitution. Several civil society organizations and political parties were organizing public events in front of the assembly's building demanding a constitution based on religion. In this context, the Tunisian front of Islamic associations organized a massive public demonstration in March 2012 after Friday prayer, called the Friday March of Sharia Supporters. This attracted thousands of participants affiliated with various movements, associations, and parties, including Ennahdha, the Liberation Party, and Salafist organizations.

Despite their best efforts, the religious organizations were not successful in integrating Sharia into the Tunisian constitution owing to pressure within the assembly from opposition parties, and as a result of the activism of secular civil society. A coalition of civil society organizations, women's organizations, and citizenship organizations remained vigilant throughout the constitutional process in 2012 and 2013, organizing counter-protests to express their support for separating constitution-building from religious interference, and to preserve the gains achieved by women though the 1956 legislation and the 1959 constitution.

Several factors contributed to the success of progressive parties in the constitutional debate that was taking place within the assembly and more broadly within the country. First, while the religious party Ennahdha was the largest party in the assembly, it did not have an absolute majority so could not impose its will arbitrarily. Second, virtually all the non-religious parties of the assembly were in favor of writing a constitution based on a modern state model rather than on religious-based constructs. Third, after two years of mismanagement, Ennahdha was fast losing support in the general population so may have felt that it had less of a mandate than from the election results of 2011, especially since the one-year mandate that those elections afforded was long over. Finally, as much as they wanted to integrate Sharia law, Ennahdha members of the assembly were also mindful of their popularity in the upcoming elections, which would follow the constitutional process, and they must have reckoned that if they overplayed their hand in the constitutional process, they might lose the elections.

As a result, the Tunisian constitution of 2014, which was enacted on January 27, 2014, reflected the will of the majority of the Tunisian electorate, which is profoundly attached to the state model that was inherent in the 1959 constitution, and to the gender standards of the 1956 CPS. In particular,

- Article 46 provides that the state commits to protect the rights of women, and to consolidate them and evolve them. When it talks about the rights of women, the article refers clearly to the CPS. It sparked much debate in the assembly and in particular in the committee on individual rights and freedoms, but it was finally approved

by a vote of 127 vs. 43 against. Half of those who voted against were members of Ennahdha.
- Article 49 provides that no constitutional amendment may alter the human rights and freedoms granted by the constitution. It places the gender gains of Tunisian women beyond the reach of any future constitutional amendments. The article is compared to Article 8 of the 1959 constitution, which precludes any violation of "the principle of popular sovereignty, republican values, human rights, and privileges granted by the code of personal status."

6.4 The Struggle for Equal Rights

By advocating for a brand-new constitution rather than a mere amendment to the 1959 version, Tunisian civil society in general, and women's organizations in particular, played a gamble of high risk/high rewards, and won. Women's organizations in other Arab Spring countries had a much more difficult struggle with far more mixed results. Yet the terms of the struggle were by and large the same: a debate about state models that quickly devolves into a debate about gender relations and the role of women in society, superimposed on a debate about the role of religion in public life.

In Egypt, gender activists had to fight against religion-inspired parties and organizations, such as the Salafists and the Muslim Brotherhood, who are vehemently opposed to women's rights and gender equality. In Yemen, women's organizations militated successfully in favor of laws that criminalize domestic violence against women, and laws that raise the age of marriage for young women, despite violent opposition from religion-inspired parties and advocacy organizations which claim that these laws are incompatible with Islam.

In Libya, religious parties and organizations kicked into action very soon after the fall of the Qadafi regime, seeking to enact laws that allow polygamy, forbid women from traveling without an approved male companion, and forbid mixing genders in public spaces. So much so that in one of his first official declarations as president of the National Transitional Council, Mustapha Abdeljalil announced that he would lift the legal constraints that were imposed by the Qadafi regime on polygamy on the grounds that they were in contradiction with Islamic law. This was followed by a religious edict that the religious authorities of Libya issued in April 2013 prohibiting women from traveling without an approved male companion. The climate of chaos and uncertainty that prevails in Libya, as well as the increasing political clout of religious factions, makes the struggle for women's rights even more difficult, and the prospects of positive outcomes for women even more remote.

Hence the pretext of applying Sharia law remains the weapon of choice of the opponents of women's rights. Interestingly, even though Sharia law deals with a broad range of legal issues, such as criminal law, civil law, constitutional law, and business law, the opponents of women's rights reduce it to the few articles that deal with women. Also, through the ages, Sharia law has merged with patriarchal social traditions that are alien to it, and it is being used as a convenient vehicle to enforce these archaic gender-hostile traditions under the cover of adhering to divine commandments.

6.5 Gender Discrimination

The constitutional debate that arose in the Tunisian constitutional assembly opposed two principles pertaining to gender relations: the principle of equality (advocated by secular parties) and the principle of complementarity (advocated by religious parties). The 2014 constitution of Tunisia reiterated the principle of equality, which was included in the 1959 constitution, and provides for equality before the law and equality in terms of rights and duties. However, the 2014 constitution goes one step further by referring to women by their Arabic gender, and by insisting on non-discrimination. Hence Article 21 of the 2014 constitution provides that "male citizens and female citizens are equal in terms of rights and duties, and are treated the same by the law, without any discrimination." It has emerged as a result of heated debate within the assembly and outside, as Islamists opposed the principle of gender equality and wanted to replace it with one of complementarity.

In July 2012 the Constitutional Commission on Rights and Freedoms, a committee of the National Constitutional Assembly, decided to approve an article submitted by members of the Ennahdha party, in which "The state guarantees the protection of women's rights and their gains on the basis of the principle of complementarity with women within the family, in their quality as partners of men in the development of the homeland." The debate that took place around this article reflects the extreme polarization in the assembly between religious parties and secular progressive parties. This polarization is also reflected in the principles that were adopted by the commission, which were, in order of priority, Islamic values, revolutionary imperatives, and universal human rights. To this hierarchy the commission added the cultural specificity of the Tunisian people, which generally refers to Islamic traditions and values.

These resolutions triggered much debate and elicited much protest from secular parties and civil society, who view with great suspicion the characterization of women as complements to men within the family; nobody is duped by the extent of inequality that can pass under the guise of complementarity. Many progressive parties and organizations viewed this development as an egregious regression of women's rights, and a serious strike against the social project that Bourguiba had built since the middle of the twentieth century on foundations of modernity and progress.

The principle of complementarity has raised sharp suspicion from gender organizations, civil society, and large segments of Tunisian society. Most viewed this concept as a thinly veiled attempt to return to an archaic division of gender roles whereby men work in the public sphere while women are confined to the home and the private space. Many stakeholders saw in this principle a prelude to giving priority to men in matters of hiring, and/or to forbidding women from working outside the home. The Tunisian Association of Democratic Women spoke out against this project and demanded the removal of the article for fear that it would legitimize gender discrimination on constitutional grounds. Taking advantage of the Women's Holiday (August 13 is a national holiday in Tunisia, celebrating the enactment of the CPS on August 13, 1956), women's organizations coordinated to organize a massive protest in front of the building of the assembly. Under the combined pressure of the street protests and the political opposition within the assembly, the leadership of Ennahdha blinked and withdrew its plan to include the principle of complementarity in the constitution. Also, to save face, the Ennahdha leadership downplayed the party's about-face and dismissed the opposition to their project as mere political escalation. Also, the Ennahdha member who presides over the Commission on Rights and Freedoms (Farida Labidi) accused the opponents of Article 28 of misinterpreting the article, of denigrating the commission and her party, and of misleading the public at large.

The episode of Article 28 gave the progressive forces of the country even more resolve to insist on equality, and to leave no possible room for misinterpretation, which can be used to chip away at gender gains. As an interesting side show, several women's organizations convened a fictitious constitutional assembly and drafted an egalitarian gender-centered constitution that emphasized non-discrimination and citizenship. The organizations included the Tunisian Association of Democratic Women; the Association of Tunisian Women for Research and Development; the Gender Committee of the General Labor Union of Tunisia; and the Gender Committee of Amnesty International. Back in the assembly, Article 28 of the August 2012 draft of the constitution was removed and replaced by Article 5 of the December 2012 draft, which provides for equality between male and female citizens without discrimination. This was in turn replaced by Article 11 of the April 2013 draft, which refers to men and women as associates in building society and the nation. This was followed by the June 2013 draft, which talks about equality between genders without discrimination. Finally this was replaced by Article 21 of the January 2014 constitution, which is very explicit in its adherence to equality. This article was approved by a majority of 159 votes with 7 against and an abstention.

In spite of this positive evolution, Article 21 of the 2014 constitution is not without flaws. First, it talks about equality between male citizens and female citizens rather than about men and women. Second, the article provides for equality of male and female citizens before the law, rather than in law. Third, while Article 21 excludes discrimination, it does not define discrimination in its legal meaning. All these ambiguities may reflect the very detailed bargaining that progressive forces and religious forces engaged in as they were drafting the constitution.

In addition to including the principle of equality, the 2014 constitution provides that women have a right to work equal to that of men. Article 40 provides that

> work is a guaranteed right for every male citizen and every female citizen and the state must make every effort to guarantee this right fairly, and based on competence. The state also provides to each male citizen and female citizen the opportunity to work in adequate conditions at a fair wage.

The article goes on to explicitly guarantee equal opportunity employment: "The state guarantees equal opportunity between men and women in assuming responsibilities at all levels and in all domains."

Observers believe that one of the main motivations for religious parties to avoid the equality principle is their desire to maintain inequality in the division of inheritance. Indeed, Islamic civil law provides that a brother inherits twice as much as a sister. This motivation appeared among the arguments that were put forth by religious parties when they recommended that the Tunisian government should declare its reservations with regard to the Convention on the Elimination of All Forms of Discrimination Against Women (CEDAW) on the grounds that what it calls for (the elimination of all forms of discrimination against women) is incompatible with the religion-inspired law of inheritance. Even though Tunisia signed this international convention in July 1985, it reserved the right not to apply any clause that was incompatible with its constitution. Tunisia has also formulated reservations regarding the CEDAW with regard to the second clause of Article 9, since Tunisian law treats men and women differently in terms of how Tunisian citizenship is given to children. Finally, Tunisian law differs from CEDAW recommendations in the way in which it handles the rights and duties of the two parties in a marriage.

The interim government that was in place right before the election of the assembly proceeded to subscribe to the CEDAW recommendations without any reservation, and lifted the reservations that had previously been formulated. However, on the election of the assembly, the religious parties started a vigorous campaign against the adoption of the CEDAW by Tunisia, arguing that it represents a wholesale challenge to the Islamic identity of Tunisia. This campaign was all the more effective because it was waged in large part by governmental agencies and ministries that were under the control of Ennahdha. This issue became a point of contention between the religious parties in power at the time and the secular opposition. Religious parties were portraying the CEDAW as a Western construct that encourages loose moral standards, and that is incompatible with traditional Islamic values. Secular progressive parties were praising the high-minded, universal principles that underlie this convention and were accusing the opposition of misinterpreting the convention to mislead the public about its contents. Despite repeated efforts by Ennahdha, the assembly, which acted as the transitional legislative body of the country at the same time as it was the Natipnal Constitutional Assembly, approved the lifting of the reservations that Tunisia had previously expressed, and approved the CEDAW convention in all its details.

In Egypt the 2014 constitution afforded women's organizations an opportunity to impose a constitutional/legislative framework that ensures the commitment of the state to its obligations towards the CEDAW convention, which Egypt had approved in 1981. All the parties in the constitutional debate had a stake in enacting a constitution that consecrates the civil nature of the state, and gives the constitution a modern look.

As far as other Arab states are concerned, they have generally adhered to the CEDAW convention but with some reservations on the grounds that some of its clauses are incompatible with their specific cultural/religious backgrounds.

6.6 WOMEN'S FREEDOM BETWEEN MODERN VALUES AND RELIGIOUS VALUES

The terms of the debate between religious parties and secular/modernist parties can be summarized as follows:

- Religious parties view many aspects of women's liberation as incompatible with the Islamic identity and traditions of Tunisia, and they implicitly blame women and women's liberation for the deterioration of moral standards. Also, they consider that women's access to the job market is enabled at the expense of men, and they advocate a societal model where women occupy the private space whereas men occupy the public space. Consequently, they feel that women ought to be confined to the home and, whenever they are in public, they ought to wear the *hijab* or *niqab*.
- Secular parties and civil society organizations view religious parties as being responsible for imposing their religious beliefs on others, and blame them for holding back the country and interfering with its progress and its development. Also, they view the Tunisian identity as a multidimensional attribute that includes dimensions other than the Arab/Islamic component.

Tunisians were generally shocked by the appearance of *niqabs* in their midst, a phenomenon which has never been part of the Tunisian tradition and a development they generally perceive to be negative. *Niqabs* started appearing around the time of the election campaign of 2011, and the trend continued after the elections, when Ennahdha was in power. Interestingly, in the debate around wearing the *niqab*, both parties refer to individual liberties. Those who support wearing the *niqab* argue that it is part of the individual liberty of the woman to wear it if she wishes to. Those who oppose wearing the *niqab* argue that most women wear it not of their free will but rather under pressure from their male minder or from social/religious pressures, and that individual freedom dictates that women free themselves from the obligation of wearing it. Also, opponents argue that the practice is based on the idea that women need to be excluded from the public forum, which is a first step towards confining women to the home. Be that as it may, wearing the *niqab* in public violates the basic rule of social interactions, which is that people identify each other when they share a public space. It also raises security issues since we now have individuals walking in our midst who can't be identified, and we don't know what gender they are or what they are carrying under their integral cover. This matter came to a head on the campus of the faculty of literature at the University of Tunis, Manouba campus, when two students wanted to take an exam in their *niqabs* but were forbidden from doing so unless they showed their faces for identification. It degenerated into student strikes and led to court proceedings against the university, alleging discrimination.

The same debate arose in Egypt after the overthrow of the Islamist party from power in the summer of 2013 between the religious parties on the one hand and the secular parties on the other. The Egyptian journalist Sharif Choubani started a vigorous debate about the matter when he called for a million-person demonstration in Tahrir Square in April 2015 to support removing the *hijab* and the *niqab*. Those who support this movement (e.g. the president of the General Union of Egyptian Women) feel that it gives Egyptian women an opportunity to emancipate themselves from the overbearing control of the brotherhood and the Salafists. As for opponents, they argue that women ought to be free to wear the *hijab* if they so choose, and that wearing it is a religious duty. They also see the initiative of Sharif Choubani as an infringement on the moral standards of the country, as defined by religious guidelines. Both parties to this debate ignore the sociological dimension of the issue, which is that women are not really free to wear or not to wear the *hijab* and that they often do it not out of personal choice or as a fashion statement but rather under the weight of social or familial pressures.

The situation in Libya is far worse than in Egypt or Tunisia because in addition to the conservative social norms that Libyan women have to contend with, they also have to live under the rule of extremist religious groups, whose legitimacy is derived from the barrel of their guns, and who apply arbitrary forms of austere religious practice. These groups have typically imposed on women strict rules in terms of dress code, and the requirement that they be accompanied by a male minder whenever they are in public spaces. These measures are typically enforced under penalty of corporal punishment for the perpetrator and her male minder.

6.7 Participation in Political Life

In an effort to encourage women's participation in the political process, the Electoral Commission that organized the legislative elections of 2011 in Tunisia resolved to impose parity standards that all candidate parties must abide by. To this effect, the commission included an article that mandates that all candidate lists that are submitted by political parties must alternate between men and women. This resolution enabled no fewer than 5000 women to be candidates in the constitutional elections of 2011, though they were usually in second position. But while it mandated the principle of parity within each list, it did not mandate this principle between lists. Thus, in practice, most electoral lists were headed by men, not by women; only 7 % of electoral lists were headed by women. The party that was most scrupulous in dispatching an equal number of lists presided by women and men is the Democratic Modern Pole, which formed 17 lists headed by women out of a total of 33 lists. By contrast, Ennahdha formed only one list presided over by a women.

Since each list wins a number of seats in proportion to the number of votes it gets, two interesting phenomena occurred in the elections of 2011:

- Even though there was parity in the number of candidates in these elections, there was no parity in the number of candidates who were actually elected. The reason was that most lists had only enough votes to earn one seat, which normally went to the head of the list. Given that most lists were headed by men, most seats ended up being occupied by men.
- Paradoxically, the party that was most successful in getting women elected to the National Constitutional Assembly was Ennahdha. Indeed, while secular parties were widely fragmented, all the religious forces of the country coalesced around the Ennahdha party. Consequently it was Ennahdha that was most successful in gaining more than one seat per list, thereby diversifying the gender of its elected representatives. By contrast, the smaller secular parties typically collected only enough votes per list to earn one seat, which went to the head of the list, usually a man.

The issue of parity arose in the deliberations of the assembly (in 2012/2013), and arose again during the preparation of the election of the legislative body mandated by the 2014 constitution (Fall 2014). Progressives were again successful in imposing a standard of parity in political representation. Article 46 of the 2014 constitution provides: "The state must endeavor to achieve gender parity in elected bodies." This consolidates Article 34, which provides: "The state must endeavor to secure adequate representation of women in elected bodies." So the constitution imposes on the state the responsibility of supporting women's representation in political institutions. Note, however, that in both articles the constitution dictates what the state must do, rather than what result the state must achieve.

As for Egypt, the representation of women in the parliament is very small because it falls below the 2 % mark. Religious parties as well as secular parties opposed projects that would mandate specific quotas for women in parliament on the grounds that such a quota system might be artificial, impractical, and ultimately counter-productive.

Likewise, the representation of women in Libya's constitutional assembly did not exceed the 10 % mark. In a report published in May 2013, Human Rights Watch warns that the role of Libyan women in political institutions is rapidly shrinking, to the extent that it is at risk of subsiding completely. Most observers trace this phenomenon to the rise of Islamists to power in Libya. Also, Libyan women are under pressure to renounce gender activism, and many fear for their lives if they were to continue.

6.8 Conclusion

Arab women have participated actively in the political struggles that arose in Arab Spring countries, and they have transitioned seamlessly from fighting for democratic rights for all citizens against repressive regimes to fighting for women's rights when the overthrow of autocratic rule has inadvertently and unexpectedly produced gender-hostile religious rule.

Tunisia was a pioneer in enacting revolutionary gender legislation in the middle of the twentieth century; was a pioneer in starting the democratic transitions that came to be known under the collective name of the Arab Spring; and is a pioneer in a successful and relatively smooth transfer of power from the old autocratic regime to a transitional government, then to a new government formed according to the new constitution. Through all these transitions, the country has successfully used advanced political standards to further gender standards, and used advanced gender standards to further political standards.

But it would be ill advised for Tunisia to congratulate itself too soon and to rest on its laurels because it must remain vigilant to preserve its gains and consolidate them. For example, the declaration in the constitution of 2014 that Islam is the official religion of Tunisia can conceivably be used by ill-intentioned legislators to impose Sharia law as a constitutionally sanctioned measure. Also, the same article can be used to invoke a cultural exemption to the adoption of the CEDAW and thereby renege on many of the universal protections that women would otherwise enjoy.

Another privilege that is enshrined in CEDAW but could be challenged on the grounds of cultural exemption is the freedom of choosing one's life partner. Tunisian law does not treat men and women symmetrically with respect to marrying non-Muslims.

While the situation of women in majority Arab/Muslim countries varies from one country to another, they all suffer from the burden of cultural exceptions that stem from a restrictive reading of the religious guidelines, owing to archaic traditions of societies that are prone to conservative social norms.

Bibliography

Benkorich, N. 2011. L'islamisme à l'heure des printemps égyptien et tunisien. *Esprit* Mai (5): 162–166.

Bouachrine, I. 2012. R*jal* et leurs reines: le printemps arabe et le discours sur la masculinité et la féminité. *NAQD* 29 (1): 75–86.

Charrad, M. 2011. Tunisia at the Forefront of the Arab World: Two Waves of Gender Legislation. In *Women in the Middle East and North Africa: Agents of Change*, ed. F. Sadiqi and M. Ennaji, 105–113. New York: Routledge.

El Sadda, H. 2015. Article 11: Feminists Negotiating Power in Egypt. *Open Democracy*, January 5. http://www.opendemocracy.net/5050/hoda-elsadda/article-11-feminists-negotiating-power-in-egypt

El Tibi, Z. 2014. La place de la femme dans l'islam. *Société, droit et religion* 1 (Numéro 4): 59–64.

Fathally, J. 2012. Les droits des femmes à l'aube du printemps arabe: de "ne pas oublier les femmes" au "Femmes: n'oubliez pas !". *Études internationales* 43 (2): 213–230.

Gaté, J. 2014. Droits des femmes et révolutions arabes. *La Revue des droits de l'homme* [En ligne], 6| 2014, mis en ligne le 01 décembre.

Hafidha, C. 2014. Le combat pour les droits des femmes dans le monde arabe. FMSH-WP-2014-70.

Khosrokhavar, F. 2011. Les révolutions arabes: révolutions de justice sociale et de liberté. *Cultures & Conflicts* 83 (automne): 108–111.

Lamloum, O. 2006. Les femmes dans le discours islamiste. *Confluences Méditerranée* 59: 89–96.
Marks, M. 2013. Women's Right Before and After the Revolution. In *The Making of the Tunisian Revolution: Contexts, Architects, Prospects*, ed. N. Gana, 224–251. Edinburgh: Edinburgh University Press.
Monjid, M. 2013. *L'Islam et la modernité dans le droit de la famille au Maghreb: étude comparative: Maroc, Algérie, Tunisie*. Paris: L'Harmattan.
Mvogo, F. 2012. *Le Printemps arabe: Prémisses et autopsie littéraires*. Paris: L'Harmattan.
Roy, O. 2013. Le printemps arabe et le mythe de la nécessaire sécularisation. *Socio* 2: 25–36.

CHAPTER 7

"I Am Untouchable!" Egyptian Women's War Against Sexual Harassment

Nahed Eltantawy

The active participation of women in the political protests during Egypt's January 25 revolution of 2011 sparked hopes of a new era in Egypt—an era characterized by democracy, freedom, justice, gender equality, and women's empowerment. While thousands of Egyptian women stood side by side with men, demanding their political rights, there was another growing movement where women demonstrated their power. This was Egyptian women's battle to communicate anger about and intolerance of sexual harassment and violence against women.

This chapter demonstrates Egyptian women's empowerment and resourcefulness in their struggle against the long-ignored epidemic of sexual harassment. Drawing on empowerment and culture-jamming literature, I argue that Egyptian women's active political participation during the revolution enabled them to realize their hidden potential; increased their "power within"; boosted their self-confidence; and enhanced their ability to attract attention and enforce changes to their social tribulations. I explore how the women harness various media platforms to create online and offline communities to protest against sexual harassment and raise social awareness of this epidemic. Using examples such as HarassMap,

N. Eltantawy (✉)
High Point University, High Point, NC, USA

© The Author(s) 2018
S. Khamis, A. Mili (eds.), *Arab Women's Activism and Socio-Political Transformation*, DOI 10.1007/978-3-319-60735-1_7

Shoft Taharosh (I saw harassment) Facebook, and graffiti art, I demonstrate how Egyptian women are causing disruption and "noise" in the public sphere by creating open and public discussions about sexual harassment. I also demonstrate how online activism participation and engagement can transfer to the offline domain.

The chapter also highlights how women's battle against sexual harassment reflects broader gender struggles within society, such as existing power arrangements and issues of patriarchy. Such struggles reflect the greater shifts in women's status in the Middle East and North Africa (MENA). I attempt to illustrate how, slowly but surely, Arab societies are witnessing a gradual shift in mindset and, empowered by social media and by the Arab Spring, are moving further away from traditional patriarchal attitudes. Whether it is through innovative reporting tools, Facebook, Twitter, peaceful protests, or graffiti, Egyptian women's voices are being heard, and women's campaign to end sexual harassment demonstrates the empowerment that women in the MENA region are gradually benefiting from.

7.1 Methodology and Theoretical Framework

In this study I apply content analysis to describe and synthesize the content of textual and visual discourse that includes Facebook posts, blogs, graffiti art, and other online and offline initiatives to demonstrate Egyptian female activists' efforts to protest against sexual harassment, and communicate to harassers and to society in general that such abuses are no longer acceptable, nor will they be tolerated. I rely on theories of empowerment and culture jamming to argue that Egyptian women post-January 25 are fearless and empowered by their significant role in the Arab Spring, and ready to combat social epidemics and societal habits that degrade and humiliate women. These women seek innovative ways to interrupt the status quo and disrupt social channels to impose their concerns and attempt to correct society's attitudes towards women and sexual harassment.

According to Naila Kabeer (1994), the concept of empowerment is rooted in the idea of power and powerlessness. This concept relates to the interests of the grassroots or underprivileged groups in society (Kabeer 1994). Batliwala (1994) contends that empowerment was born out of discussions and debates, mostly by Third World feminists: "The process of challenging existing power relations, and of gaining greater control over the sources of power, may be termed empowerment" (1994, 130). Ediais (2003) adds that, while empowerment definitions in women's literature are ample and diverse, all generally agree on four general aspects: (1) For a woman to become empowered, she first has to have been powerless or disempowered compared with men. (2) Empowerment cannot be granted to women; women must claim their own empowerment. (3) Empowerment usually involves people making decisions or taking actions on essential issues that impact their lives. Such decisions can be made on an individual level or as a collective. (4) Empowerment does not lead to a final product or goal; it is an ongoing process (3).

Culture jamming is the second theory applied in this study. It is described by media activist Kalle Lasn (1999) as an allegory for interjecting media saturated by a consumer culture. In her definition of "culture jamming," Harold (2004) explains that the term refers to the disruption, interruption, sabotage, or blocking of existing transmissions controlled by the dominating powers of cultural life. She adds that it is the " 'glutting' of the system; it is an amping up of contradictory rhetorical messages in an effort to engender a qualitative change" (192). Hence, according to Harold (2004), cultural jamming should not be viewed as merely stopping corporate media. "Rather, it may be more useful to consider jamming as an artful proliferation of messages, a rhetorical process of intervention and invention, which challenges the ability of corporate discourses to make meaning in predictable ways" (192). Culture jammers utilize diverse tactics to interrupt and stop consumer-saturated messages spread by dominant multinational corporations (Warner 2007).

Although the theory of culture jamming focuses on consumerism, one can extend the concept to analyze other important issues. In his analysis of *The Daily Show*, Warner (2007) stipulates that Jon Stewart's news parody show, along with show writers and comedians, are political culture jammers who

> disseminate dissident interpretations of current political events, potentially jamming the transmission of the dominant political brand message. Like other culture jammers, The Daily Show subversively employs emotional and aesthetic modalities similar to those employed by political branding itself, thus interrupting it from within. (19)

In this chapter I extend Warner's analysis to argue that Egyptian women fighting sexual harassment are social and political culture jammers who employ innovative and visually appealing tactics to interrupt dominant social attitudes and public policies on harassment.

7.2 The Sexual Harassment Epidemic

One of the heated topics in Egypt, especially following the January 25, 2011 revolution, is that of sexual harassment. This is a problem experienced by the majority of women in Egypt of all ages, social classes, religious backgrounds, and dress codes (Rogers 2010). Assaults can be involve "nasty words, groping, being followed or stalked, lewd, lascivious looks, and indecent exposure" (Rogers 2010). Shoukry and Hassan (2008) define sexual harassment as

> unwanted sexual conduct deliberately perpetrated by the harasser, resulting in sexual, physical, or psychological abuse of the victim regardless of location, whether in the workplace, the street, public transportation, educational institution, or even in private places such as home or in the company of others such as relatives or colleagues, etc. (13)

One of the notorious attacks on Egyptian women was the downtown mob assault during the 2006 Eid-al-Fitr celebrations (Radwan 2011). As the public media turned a blind eye, bloggers and activists posted reports and videos online of the assaults, where women, veiled and unveiled, were surrounded by hundreds of men, groped, assaulted, and their clothes torn off (Abdelhadi 2006). This incident, which was covered on the privately owned satellite channel Dream TV, shocked many Egyptians who were unaware of how serious the harassment epidemic was (Abdelhadi 2006). Additionally, under former president Hosni Mubarak, government forces employed harassment as a tool to terrorize women, especially in public protests (Amar 2011; Radwan 2011). This is what Amar (2011) refers to as "sexualized state terror," employed during the Mubarak era, the Egyptian revolution, and the Muslim Brotherhood rule in 2012 (Amar 2011, 301). This was the case in the May 25, 2005 protests against Article 76 of the constitution.[1] Many female lawyers, journalists, and activists complained that women in these protests were singularly targeted, sexually assaulted, and their clothes ripped off (Radwan 2011).

Possibly the first eye-opening research to bring mass local and international awareness of sexual harassment in Egypt is a study conducted by the Egyptian Center for Women's Rights, led by the center's chair, Nehad Abul Komsan. According to this 2008 report, which was based on a study conducted on more than 2000 local women and men and more than 100 foreign women, 83 % of Egyptian women and 93 % of foreign women admit to having been sexually assaulted (Shoukry and Hassan 2008).

In a conservative society such as Egypt, many women traditionally chose to remain silent and not report incidents of assault ("The Fight against Sexual Assault on Tahrir Square" 2013). Yet in recent years, this trend has changed and, as this social problem is increasingly gaining more attention from women's groups and human rights organizations, women are becoming more vocal. One of the first harassment incidents that brought media and public attention to this growing problem was in 2008. The date October 21, 2008 marked the first court sentencing of a harasser to three years in prison, after truck driver Sherif Gomaa Gibrial groped 27-year-old film director Noha Rushdie from the window of his truck. Rushdie and a male bystander stood with the harasser, while her friend Hind Mahmoud went to report the incident at the nearest police station. Yet instead of siding with Rushdie, the police officers at the station blamed Mahmoud for what she was wearing and refused to arrest Gibrial. Determined to seek justice for her assault, Rushdie, Mahmoud, and the male bystander transferred Gibrial in a private car to a public prosecutor's office where they filed a complaint ("A First in Egypt" 2008). One could argue that this incident is significant because it marks the first punishment of a harasser, bringing local and international attention and making more Egyptians aware of the widespread problem. It is also noteworthy in highlighting empowered and courageous women such as Rushdie and Mahmoud, who were determined to seek justice despite discouragement by local police forces.

7.3 Women Attract Attention to Sexual Harassment

Starting in 2010, more women began to open up about their harassment experiences. Whether to reporters, or via blogs or social networking sites, a common trend is candid reports where women detail their horrific assaults. Below, 39-year-old Egyptian singer Dalia Abdel Wahab recounts her sexual assault during a women's march on January 25, 2013:

> Millions of hands were violating me … In a second my jacket and bra were off, and my shirt and trousers were being pulled off, my spectacles were lost in the melee… They stepped on me, pulled my hair … I could no longer

see faces. I felt that I could no longer breathe, I was suffocating ... I felt paralyzed, my brain was blank and I thought I was going to die. ("The Fight against Sexual Assault on Tahrir Square" 2013)

The publicizing of accounts like Abdel Wahab's are now more common, thanks to various initiatives, such as HarassMap, Shoft Taharosh (I've seen harassment), and others.

7.3.1 HarassMap

Launched in December 2010 as the first Egyptian anti-sexual harassment initiative to rely on social media and technology, the HarassMap campaign relies on open-source software to allow witnesses to document sexual harassment incidents across Egypt (Mayault 2011) (Fig. 7.1).

HarassMap works on several fronts: mapping harassment incidents; community action; and research. Perhaps the most significant and innovative idea launched by HarassMap is a geographical map of Egypt that identifies areas of harassment nationwide. Victims and witnesses tweet or text the exact location and details of incidents, which HarassMap then adds to its map. The incidents are identified by a red dot on the map, which can be expanded to provide a detailed report. According to HarassMap

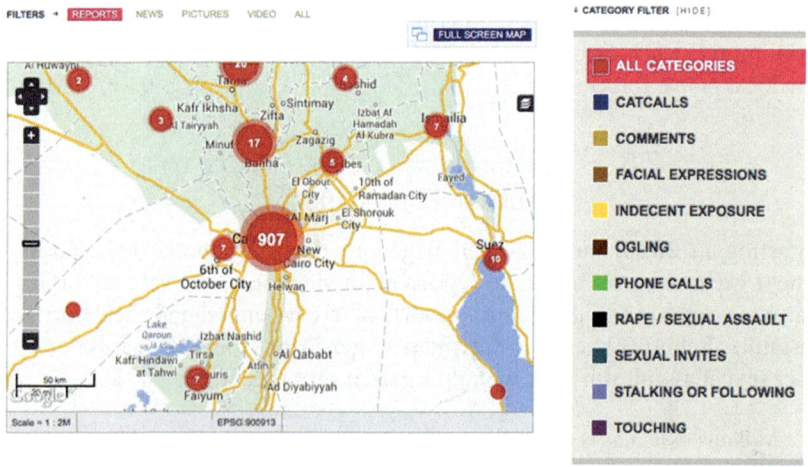

Fig. 7.1 A screenshot of the map from HarassMap

[the] map has many functions. It is a tool for victims and witnesses all over Egypt to anonymously share their experiences of harassment, and to report it. The map collects all reports, and each report appears on the map as a red dot. When you click on it, the full text of the report is displayed. Looking at the map gives you an overview of where harassment happens, as well as the opportunity to delve deeper and learn more about the individual stories. (HarassMap website 2013)

HarassMap not only aims to identify areas of harassment but also to give women a space to speak openly, and anonymously if they choose, about their experiences. The campaign seeks to correct stereotypes and make society aware of the widespread epidemic of sexual harassment (HarassMap website 2013). This is carried out through online and offline awareness campaigns, fundraisers, and community action. In one fundraising campaign, HarassMap posted a message on Indiegogo that reads:

HarassMap-donate & help end sexual harassment in Egypt
  To run a massive game-changing campaign in TV, print, online, on the ground, pop culture that will turn the tables on the sexual harassment epidemic. (Indiegogo 2013)

HarassMap trains volunteers and prepares them to approach people from all walks of life to discuss harassment and heighten public awareness of the problem. "Volunteers also use the information gathered on the map to dispel myths and stereotypes about harassment, to show that harassment is indeed a problem on that very street, and to start a discussion about how to intervene against it" (HarassMap website 2013) (Fig. 7.2).

The group relies on creative online and offline visuals to increase public awareness. Offline initiatives include the use of shopping bags carrying various messages about why diverse males engage in harassment. Among the questions posed on the bags are: If harassment is due to late marriage, then why does a father do it? If harassment is due to sexual oppression, then why does a seven-year-old boy do it? If harassment is due to a woman's clothing, then why is a *niqabi* woman harassed?[2] If harassment is due to ignorance, then why does a teacher do it? (HarassMap Facebook Page 2013).

Research is another significant area of activity for HarassMap members. From producing an annual HarassMap report to data collection on harassment incidents, the campaign stays active in its in-depth research on this social epidemic (HarassMap website 2013).

Fig. 7.2 HarassMap shopping bags campaign (Image courtesy of HarassMap)

HarassMap is a strong example of Egyptian female activists' empowerment via social media and technology. In their analysis of social media use in the Egyptian Arab Spring, Eltantawy and Wiest (2011) argue that most significant about the use of social media in the Egyptian revolution was how it changed social mobilization dynamics by infusing activism initiatives with speed and interactivity not witnessed in traditional mobilization. The same could be argued about Egyptian female activists who rely on social media and information technology to combat sexual harassment. These innovative tools enable sexual harassment activists to monitor developments in Egypt, join social networking groups, engage in discussions, and utilize technology to map harassers across the nation. Social media and communication technology are boosting women's confidence and empowering them with diverse tools that can assist them in turning their private problems into public ones.

7.3.2 Shoft Taharosh (I Saw Harassment)

In September 2012 the Facebook page for Shoft Taharosh (I saw harassment) was created by a group of activists who describe themselves as "a pressure group to end the crime of sexual harassment" (Shoft Taharosh Facebook Page 2013). The group aims to protect women against sexual harassment and raise awareness about the epidemic. According to these activists, their social pressure campaign involves various local nongovernmental organizations, plus human rights and women's groups, to monitor harassment and to execute means of fighting it on legal, social, and psychological fronts. The campaign works on three fundamental fronts: social media, volunteer work, and legal support. In terms of social media, the campaign relies on social networking sites such as Facebook and Twitter, where users can report detailed accounts of harassment incidents; and upload images, videos, and any other evidence (Shoft Taharosh Facebook Page). Shoft Taharosh also relies on volunteers to monitor the streets during major events or celebrations, to help women who are in danger of harassment, and to report harassment incidents. Finally, the campaign relies on volunteer lawyers, who are willing to provide legal assistance to female victims of harassment.

In an August 2013 campaign news release, the group warned against any sexual harassment during the religious Eid-Al-Fitr celebration. The release stated that I Saw Harassment volunteers would be present in downtown Cairo to protect women and report incidents of harassment. It continued:

> "I saw harassment" initiative consequently announces its presence in downtown Cairo during the days of the Eid El-Fitr holiday 2013 (3 days), particularly in the spots where high levels of sexual harassment where reported, as well as in front of cinema theatres. 'I saw harassment' initiative stresses the importance of all volunteers wearing the 'I saw harassment' T-Shirt, with the initiative's motto written on the front and on the back. (Shoft Taharosh Initiative press release 2013 Facebook)

Shoft Taharosh is unique in how it utilizes social networking sites to expose harassers and to give women a space to speak frankly, via text or video, about their harassment experiences. This is quite significant because it has helped to turn harassment from a taboo issue not discussed in public to one discussed in graphic detail, with the intention of embarrassing and exposing harassers. Examples of such initiatives include posts with information about a harasser, such as his phone number or exact location, inviting users to call his number to verbally reprimand him for harassing women (Shoft Taharosh Facebook Page 2013). Other examples are Facebook posts that give women tips on how to protect themselves against harassment. One example is a post warning women who intend to join protests to wear two layers of clothing, and a swimsuit that is hard to rip off in case they are approached by a harassment mob (Shoft Taharosh Facebook Page 2013).

One might argue that the most significant Facebook posts by Shoft Taharosh are those by female victims who openly and candidly describe their experiences and their reactions to harassment. In a July 15, 2013 post by Lyla El-Gueretly, she describes how a religious, middle-aged man with a beard[3] was harassing her from the window of the microbus he was riding. When El-Gueretly became offended and yelled at him to stop, the man yelled back, using obscenities and claiming that he did not do anything to her:

> I was furious by his audacity and his response and I decided that I would not let it go this time and I would not be silent because he crossed all lines and was acting as if he had the right to violate my body and unleash his sick imagination simply because I am walking in front of him… (El-Gueretly 2013)

El-Gueretly said the man then came out of the microbus and slapped her on the face multiple times while yelling profanities at her. This only made her more determined to take him to a police station. She insisted and called on the men who had witnessed the incident to assist her, and she filed a police report against him.

Such incidents are significant on several fronts. On the one hand, these posts clearly demonstrate the change in attitude by Egyptian women, who have gone from shame and silence to candid posts and a willingness to share their experience with everyone following the Shoft Taharosh page. The incident also reflects the women's new and empowered attitude and courage in the face of audacious and brazen harassers who think they can scare women into silence by screaming profanities and using violence.

Finally, these posts reflect the changing attitude of witnesses, who have gone from looking the other way or blaming the victim, to being willing to help and defend them. Loubna Skalli (2006) argues that female journalists in the Middle East are increasingly more aggressive and open, reporting on issues once deemed as taboo, which include sexual harassment. I would extend Skalli's statement to claim that women in the Middle East in general are increasingly more open to discussing these once-taboo issues, thus joining courageous female reporters in "breaking the culture of silence surrounding women's reality" (Skalli 2006, 40).

7.3.3 Resistance via Graffiti

A wall close to Tahrir Square displays a mural titled "The Circle of Hell," where a woman stands terrified, surrounded by a mob of men with hungry eyes who loom around her, yelling out remarks about her appearance. Artists Mira Shihadeh and Zeft drew this graffiti to denounce the growing trend of violent mob attacks on women in Tahrir and elsewhere, where girls are "encircled in mobs of 200 to 300 men who fight, pull, shove, beat and strip them" (Patry 2013) (Fig. 7.3).

Fig. 7.3 "The Circle of Hell" graffiti (Image courtesy of Melody Patry)

Graffiti has slowly emerged as an innovative and non-violent means of resistance employed by Egyptian women and men in their battle against sexual harassment. As part of the anti-harassment campaign in Egypt, artists are also working to bring public attention and awareness to this epidemic. Initiatives by local women's groups such as Noon el Neswa and the Mona Lisa Brigades,[4] as well as many independent female and male artists, aim to bring social awareness to sexual harassment and other injustices against women. Elnabawi (2013) explains that "a new wave of gender-sensitive street art and visual campaigns seeks to challenge the low status of Egyptian women by painting them in a positive light" (Paragraph 6). One example is graffiti by Mira Shihadeh of a woman, who stands strong and defiant, spraying men who approach her. The caption reads: "No to harassment" (Fig. 7.4).

Egyptian graffiti artists promoting female graffiti also include many men. One such artist, who goes by the name Zeft, created a stencil of Queen Nefertiti wearing a gas mask. The caption reads: "A woman's voice is revolution." This is in response to a common saying by Muslim conservatives that "A woman's voice is indecent/improper." Zeft circu-

Fig. 7.4 "No to harassment" graffiti (Image courtesy of Melody Patry)

lated his graffiti via social media, inviting the free download and use of his stencil as long as it was not for profit (El Zeft Facebook Page 2012) (Fig. 7.5).

Fig. 7.5 Queen Nefertiti graffiti (Image courtesy of Zeft)

Zeft's stencil graffiti was later endorsed by an Egyptian anti-sexual harassment campaign and appeared in several pro-Egypt rallies in various countries (Reade 2013). In a recent interview, Egyptian journalist and blogger Soraya Morayef said that the fact that male artists are advocating and supporting women's rights demonstrates a "significant shift in awareness" (as quoted in Reade 2013).

In his analysis of street art in Hispanic countries, Chaffee (1993) argues that it is characterized by its universal reach and is a significant medium of communication, given its ability to inform and persuade publics. He defines street art as including diverse forms of political communication, including graffiti, murals, wall paintings, and posters. Chaffee argues that such art gives voice to the voiceless; it can impact the public's emotions and political beliefs and it also "breaks the conspiracy of silence" (4). Truman (2010) extends this argument, saying that the essential purpose of graffiti is to "disrupt [the] public visual sphere and draw our attention to the ways in which public space is constructed and controlled" (3). In the case of Egyptian women, these artists successfully broke the silence and disrupted the public sphere to remind us of their revolutionary role and to bring public attention to long-ignored problems, such as sexual harassment. Women's graffiti and strong messages have forced the public to pay attention and acknowledge women's tribulations. Female street artists largely rely on paint and stencil portraits of women, combined with strong messages, as a way to communicate with the public and allow women to "reclaim public space," according to graffiti artist Nawara Belal (Fecteau 2012). The activists utilize visual media in the streets and social media to spread awareness of their campaigns and circulate their graffiti to reach out to audiences beyond their cities. In summarizing the significant role of graffiti in Egypt post January 25, journalist Morayef (2013) states:

> Here graffiti provides an alternative platform, not only to speak on behalf of those who are ignored, but also to speak directly to the state, to the people on the street, to embarrass us out of our nonchalance and amnesia, and force us to focus on the bigger picture... (Reade 2013)

Egyptian women are increasingly aware of and empowered by the influential role of graffiti and are expending this art to raise public awareness of patriarchal injustice and the marginalization of women, and to shame the political leaders who have long ignored their problems.

7.4 Analysis and Conclusion

It is difficult to measure the effectiveness or success of such initiatives, yet there is no doubt that these campaigns are creating societal change. In one post on Shoft Taharosh's Facebook Page, a campaign member writes "I saw a group of ladies who approached me and said we are in the streets and not afraid because we know that the Shoft Taharosh team is there to protect us" (Shoft Taharosh Facebook Page). Women's activism is encouraging more women to join the battle and break their silence regarding the sexual harassment epidemic. Activism is also empowering women to face their harassers and go out in public instead of hiding at home.

In terms of empowerment, Egyptian women's anti-harassment campaigns demonstrate women's development from powerless to empowered, thanks to social media, information technology, and visual art. Such initiatives are examples of what Skalli (2007) describes as the "emergence of empowering spaces and practices that result from the interactions between new communication technologies, resourceful young citizens, and dynamic contexts in the Middle East" (Skalli 2007, 9). Going back to Ediais's (2003) four criteria for empowerment, we find that Egyptian female activists meet all four conditions: (1) These women were once powerless in the face of harassment, in a male-dominated society that accepted this epidemic as part of the norm, and very few got involved to aid a victim of harassment. (2) Egyptian female activists claimed their own empowerment via social media, art, and information technology. Empowerment was not bestowed on these women; they had to fight and struggle to gradually claim their space in the public sphere and force sexual harassment onto the political agenda. (3) Obviously women are taking decisions on an issue that is very personal to almost every woman in Egypt. As mentioned earlier, this is a problem that impacts the majority of women in the country, so it is an issue that has a significant impact on women's lives. (4) Finally, whereas activists argue that they hope to raise awareness of sexual harassment, change attitudes, and eventually end this societal epidemic, there is no single goal or final product. These women's struggle is ongoing, and it may take years for them to achieve satisfactory results on a cultural and political level. Hence, based on these four criteria, it is fair to claim that Egyptian female activists fighting sexual harassment are indeed empowered women.

In terms of culture jamming, one could argue that Egyptian women are culture jammers in a social and political sense. These women, whom we can term "sociopolitical culture jammers," are indeed "glutting" the system with a diverse supply of non-violent visual means. They are disrupting the airwaves and "amping up" rhetorical messages of women's empowerment and women's resistance to sexual harassment to interrupt the dominant patriarchal rhetoric and culture passivity towards harassment.

There is no doubt that January 25 empowered women in their years of struggle against patriarchy and injustice. The revolution infused women with courage and gave them a voice. Women are no longer afraid to tackle taboo issues openly. Whether it is their uncensored exposure of scandalous military virginity tests, detailed accounts of sexual harassment, or blunt graffiti demands of freedom and equality, women can no longer be silenced. "Women have grown aware of the power they can wield; they can no longer be relegated to their homes and to traditional roles" (Esfandiari 2012, 4). In sum, women have realized their potential as empowered sociopolitical culture jammers and will continue to amp up their long-muted voices via innovative peaceful activism to reclaim social and political gains reaped during January 25.

Notes

1. The protests were against Mubarak's referendum on Article 76 of the constitution, which limited competition against him in the presidential elections.
2. *Niqabis* are conservative Muslim women who cover their face and wear long dresses.
3. The victim emphasized the beard to denote the harasser's conservatism, as many conservative Muslim men grow beards.
4. These are gender-sensitive Egyptian street artists.

Bibliography

A first in Egypt: Court sentences sexual assault. *WikiLeaks*. http://wikileaks.org/cable/2008/10/08CAIRO2251.html#help_2. Accessed Aug 13 2013.

Abdelhadi, M. 2006. Cairo Street Crowds Target Women. *BBC News*, November 1, 2006. http://news.bbc.co.uk/2/hi/6106500.stm?lsm

Amar, P. 2011. Turning the Gendered Politics of the Security State Inside Out? Charging the Police with Sexual Harassment in Egypt. *International Feminist Journal of Politics* 13 (3): 299–328.

Batliwala, S. 1994. The Meaning of Women's Empowerment: New Concepts from Action. In *Population Policies Reconsidered: Health, Empowerment, and Rights*, ed. G. Sen, A. Germain, and L.C. Chen, 127–138. New York: Harvard University Press.

Chaffee, L.G. 1993. *Political Protest and Street Art: Popular Tools for Democratization in Hispanic Countries*. Westport: Greenwood Press.

Ediais, S.M. 2003. Towards a Framework for Assessing Empowerment. Working Paper Series, International Conference, New Directions in Impact Assessment for Development: Methods and Practice. Manchester, UK. http://www.sed.manchester.ac.uk/research/iarc/pdfs/iarc_wp03.pdf

El-Gueretly, L. 2013. My Personal Account on a Harassment Incident. Shoft Taharosh Facebook Page, July 15, 2013. https://www.facebook.com/notes/lyla-el-gueretly/%D8%B4%D9%87%D8%A7%D8%AF%D8%AA%D9%89-%D8%B9%D9%84%D9%89-%D9%88%D8%A7%D9%82%D8%B9%D8%A9-%D8%A7%D9%84%D8%AA%D8%AD%D8%B1%D8%B4/10151662604422147

Elnabawi, M. 2013. Graffiti Campaigns Bring Women and Children into Street Art. *Egypt Independent*, February 18, 2013. http://www.egyptindependent.com/news/graffiti-campaigns-bring-women-and-children-street-art

Eltantawy, N., and J. Wiest. 2011. Social Media in the Egyptian Revolution: Reconsidering Resource Mobilization Theory. *International Journal of Communication* 5: 1207–1224.

El Zeft. 2012. *Nefertiti*, September 23. Retrieved from https://www.facebook.com/el.zeft.7/photos/a.219336521741985.1073741829.219336465075324/219339378408366/?type=3&theater

Esfandiari, H. 2012. Is the Arab Awakening Marginalizing Women? *Wilson Center Middle East Program Occasional Paper Series*. http://www.wilsoncenter.org/event/the-arab-awakening-marginalizing-women

Fecteau, A. 2012. A Graffiti Campaign Brings Strong Female Voices to the Street. *Egypt Independent*, March 10, 2012. http://www.egyptindependent.com/news/graffiti-campaign-brings-strong-female-voices-streets

HarassMap. 2013. HarassMap—Donate & Help End Sexual Harassment in Egypt. *Indiegogo*, July 15, 2013. https://www.indiegogo.com/projects/harassmap-donate-help-end-sexual-harassment-in-egypt--3#/

HarassMap. 2013. *#WhyDoesHeHarass*, December 29. Retrieved from https://www.facebook.com/HarassMapEgypt/photos/a.134106173328031.30432.125494177522564/627711773967466/?type=3&theatre

HarassMap website. http://harassmap.org/en/. Accessed 3 Aug 2013.

Harold, C. 2004. Pranking Rhetoric: 'Culture Jamming' as Media Activism. *Critical Studies in Media Communication* 21 (3): 189–211.

Kabeer, N. 1994. *Reversed Realities: Gender Hierarchies in Development Thought*. London: Verso.

Lasn, K. 1999. *Culture Jam: How to Reverse America's Suicidal Consumer Binge—And Why We Must*. New York: HarperCollins.

Mayault, I. 2011. HarassMap, the Pink Mafia. *Mashallah News*, November 28. Retrieved from https://www.mashallahnews.com/harassmap-pink-mafia/

Morayef, S. 2013. Women in Egypt Through the Narrative of Graffiti. *Egypt Source*, March 5, 2013. http://www.acus.org/egyptsource/women-egypt-through-narrative-graffiti

Patry, M. 2013. Egyptian Artists Declare War on Sexual Harassment. *Index on censorship*, May 15, 2013. http://www.indexoncensorship.org/2013/05/egyptian-artists-declare-war-on-sexual-harassment/

Radwan, N. 2011. How Egyptian Women Took Back the Street Between Two 'Black Wednesdays': A First Person Account. *Jadaliyya*. http://www.jadaliyya.com/pages/index/694/how-egyptian-women-took-back-the-street-between-tw

Reade, O. 2013. Egyptian Graffiti and Gender Politics: An Interview with Soraya Morayef. *Africa Is a Country*, March 28, 2013. http://africasacountry.com/2013/03/28/egyptian-graffiti-and-gender-politics-an-interview-with-soraya-morayef/comment-page-1/

Rogers, M. 2010. Why Is Sexual Harassment in Egypt so Rampant? *CNN*, November 1, 2010. http://insidethemiddleeast.blogs.cnn.com/2010/11/01/why-is-sexual-harassment-in-egypt-so-rampant/

Shoft Taharosh Facebook Page Comment. Facebook.com, July 3, 2012. https://www.facebook.com/photo.php?fbid=370091069780880&set=a.254556291334359.56991.253938978062757&type=1&theater

Shoft Taharosh Facebook Page Post. Facebook.com, August 4, 2013. Retrieved from https://www.facebook.com/messages/HarassMapEgypt

Shoft Taharosh Initiative press release. 2013. https://www.facebook.com/photo.php?fbid=384195608370426&set=np.218889024.663185080&type=1&theater&notif_t=notify_me

Shoukry, A., and R.M. Hassan. 2008. Clouds in Egypt's Sky: Sexual Harassment: From Verbal Harassment to Rape. *The Egyptian Center for Women's Rights*. http://egypt.unfpa.org/Images/Publication/2010_03/6eeeb05a-3040-42d2-9e1c-2bd2e1ac8cac.pdf

Skalli, L.H. 2006. Communicating Gender in the Public Sphere: Women and Information Technologies in the MENA. *Journal of Middle East Women's Studies* 2 (2): 35–59.

Skalli, L.H. 2007. New Modes of Communication: Web Representations and Blogs: North Africa. In *Encyclopedia of Women & Islamic Cultures Online*. Herndon: Brill.

The fight against sexual assault on Tahrir Square. *Your Middle East*, February 21, 2013. http://www.yourmiddleeast.com/columns/article/the-fight-against-sexual-assault-on-tahrir-square_13150

Truman, E. 2010. The (In)Visible Artist: Stencil Graffiti, Activist Art, and the Value of Visual Public Space. *Queen's Journal of Visual & Material Culture* 3: 1–15.

Warner, J. 2007. Political Culture Jamming: The Dissident Humor of 'The Daily Show With Jon Stewart'. *Popular Communication: The International Journal of Media and Culture* 1: 17–36.

CHAPTER 8

Stealth Revolution: Saudi Women's Ongoing Social Battles

Namie Tsujigami

Saudi Arabia is one of few cases where the Arab Spring had a positive impact on women's rights and social status. This was partly because of the Saudi government's swift response to the people's demands when the Arab Spring movements spread and reached the country. In addition to spending as much as $130 billion on building houses, providing bonuses, and expanding scholarship for students studying abroad, the government quickly implemented sociopolitical and socioeconomic reforms to create jobs for young men and women, as well as to include women in political decision-making processes for the first time in its history. This study explores Saudi women's agency and their attempts to maximize their rights and options through researching on both activist and non-activist women, as well as the Saudi government's measures to provide women with new labor and political opportunities. Based on these explorations, this chapter also explains why the ban on women driving remains.

This study combines the two concepts of Judith Butler's performative agency and Deniz Kandiyoti's patriarchal bargaining as its theoretical framework. Butler highlights the performative characteristics of gender,

N. Tsujigami (✉)
Centre for Middle Eastern Studies, Graduate School of Arts and Sciences, University of Tokyo, Tokyo, Japan

whereby performance constantly renews a set of relations and practices. In her words, "performativity starts to describe a set of processes that produce ontological effects, that is, that work to bring into being certain kinds of realities."[1] Performative power may be exercised to achieve equality with men. However, Saudi women may also strategically bargain their power and space within patriarchy to maximize their security and optimize their life options. They may even strengthen patriarchal relations in order to enjoy the benefits given to women. This is consistent with what Deniz Kandiyoti identified in her thought-provoking paper on patriarchal bargaining.[2]

8.1 Women: The Driving Force Behind the Arab Spring Protests in Saudi Arabia

It is said to be an unknown woman who for the first time shouted her demand to the government on a street in Jeddah, the main western port city in Saudi Arabia, when many neighboring Arab countries were experiencing unprecedented sizes and levels of protests and revolutions in what is now commonly known as the "Arab Spring." The woman took to the street on January 28, 2011 to advocate for an improvement to the crumbling infrastructure that had led to spates of dangerous floods. Some groups of bystanding men responded to her by shouting "Allah Akbar [God is great]."[3] Although many Saudi men were also inspired to protest in different cities after this incident, women played prominent roles in various kinds of protest and (walking and driving) rally. It was another group of women who protested in front of the Ministry of the Interior the following month to free the alleged members of Al-Qaeda cells who had been held in custody for almost a decade without a transparent criminal investigation or trial. Within a couple of months, a women's driving movement resurfaced. The online campaign, titled Women2Drive, called for Saudi women to drive on June 17, 2011. This driving campaign became the most significant among those that took place in the context of the Arab Spring in Saudi Arabia as it swept across Western media and social networking services.[4]

However, it was not the first time that Saudi women had protested against the ban on women driving. They expressed their desire to drive during the 1990–1991 Gulf Crisis. In November 1990, as many as 47 women took to their cars to protest against the country's ban on women driving. The female protesters decided to drive because, "in time of war mobilization and national emergency, we need to drive for the safety of our families."[5] According to the author's interview with one of the protesters, the group included 14 women with doctoral degrees, as well as several university administrators, who alerted the office of the governor of Riyadh in advance about their intent to protest.[6] The 14-car motorcade, which initially proceeded without any problems, was stopped within 30 minutes by the *muṭaw'in'* (members of the Committee for the Promotion of Virtue and Prevention of Vice), who surrounded the women. The women were taken into police custody, and their male relatives, or 'guardians,' were summoned and forced to sign documents agreeing that the women would never drive again. In the eyes of the state, the guardians, not the women, were accountable for preventing any future violation of the law.

Soon after the incident, criticism of the protesters spread rapidly. The following day, accusatory leaflets were scattered throughout Riyadh listing the women's names, addresses, and phone numbers to insult the female protesters. People took to the street in anger at the women who had protested and, in so doing, violated the law. More than 20,000 people gathered outside the governor's palace, enraged that the government was not able to prevent the women's driving protest. In light of this intense public pressure, the Ministry of the Interior issued a statement warning against future protests, based on a *fatwā* (a religio-legal opinion) by the then-grand mufti, Sheikh 'Abd al-'Azīz bin Bāz. As an additional punitive measure, the government prohibited female protesters from resuming their position as lecturers at universities and confiscated their passports for two years.

In contrast to the Gulf Crisis-era protests, participants in the driving campaign in 2011 did not drive together from a single gathering point. Rather, using the broadcast power of social media, they called for tens of thousands of supporters to drive by themselves in whichever direction they chose. Manāl Al-Sharīf, then information technology specialist with the state-owned oil company ARAMCO, took initiative. She decided to drive before the designated date, and Wajiha Al Huwaider, an activist who had organized an earlier driving campaign in 2008, uploaded onto YouTube a video clip of Al-Sharīf's driving.[7] After the authorities became aware of the video, they arrested Al-Sharīf and held her in jail for nine days. This deterred those who were planning to join the driving campaign on June 17. Some women drove that day, but the numbers did not reach a level that would have an impact on Saudi society. None of the women were arrested on June 17 for driving.

The outcome of the Women2Drive campaign was relatively disappointing for the protesters. Although there is no reliable figure available for the number of women who drove that day, the lack of arrests might suggest that there were very few. On the other hand, it might indicate that the police and other authorities had decided not to pay much attention to the driving campaign in the hope of weakening or undermining it. Indeed, some reports claim that the police deliberately ignored the driving women.[8]

However, two weeks later, five women were detained for defying the ban on women driving. Another woman was sentenced to ten lashes for her participation in Women2Drive. The punishment was pronounced only two days after King Abdullah's announcement incorporating women as full members of the Consultative Council and permitting their voting in future municipal elections. The king's announcement was presumably timed to compensate for the exclusion of women from the second municipal elections, which were planned for the week after. The King promised women participation in the Consultative Council from 2013 and the municipal elections scheduled in 2015. Likely concerned at seeming hypocritical, the King hurriedly pardoned the woman who had been sentenced to ten lashes, although he refrained from making any statements on the issue of women driving.

Other attempts to defy the driving ban did not work. Two Saudi women including Lujain Al-Hathlūl were arrested and detained for more than two months when they tried to drive into Saudi Arabia from the United Arab Emirates in December 2014. According to reports, they were subsequently transferred to a special tribunal, being treated as if they had committed "terrorism."[9] Al-Hathlūl was disqualified when she filed for candidacy in the 2015 municipal polls.[10] This suggests that the state intended not just to exclude women who were involved in the driving campaign from being active in the electoral process but to subject them to a deeper stigmatization for defying the norm.

8.2   A Driving Campaign for Whom?

Any woman in Saudi Arabia who wants to drive and who makes the decision to become involved in a driving campaign is likely to suffer for doing so. Some have been detained; one, as noted, was sentenced to corporal punishment, although she was subsequently pardoned by the king. The question arises as to why women still campaign at such cost and risk. In the video clip uploaded on YouTube, Manāl Al-Sharīf says that the campaign is for the women who cannot afford the foreign drivers that they would otherwise need, as well as for single mothers like herself.[11] She refers to women in lower-income strata who need to commute to work but cannot pay for a driver because of their low salary. Generally speaking, employers of Saudi women do not pay transport costs for female employees. Al-Sharif also highlighted that divorced mothers like her may have to drive to the hospital or other places in an emergency.

Important here is that the campaigners themselves are not always the ones most needing to drive. A general assumption is that women in Saudi Arabia are on the whole acutely deprived of freedom of movement, and that the advocates of driving are the ones who suffer heavily from the lack of freedom of movement. However, this is not always the case. During fieldwork, I had an opportunity to visit one of the campaigners at home. It coincided with the day when she and other campaigners got together to study how driving is legitimized in Islam, and they invited a Moroccan lecturer to speak to them. Her house was large enough to accommodate more than 20 people in one of many rooms. In a conversation with her husband, it was apparent that he was cooperative and understanding, and supportive of her work on the driving campaign. Afterwards, when she kindly offered transport back to the hotel, I rode in a luxury car driven by one of her foreign drivers. He was not the only driver for her household and he commented that his working conditions were very good compared with other chauffeurs. Unlike most ordinary foreign chauffeurs in Saudi Arabia, he had a day off and enjoyed reasonable working hours.[12]

Many of the driving campaigners from 1990, as well as this one, are from wealthy and well-educated families. Therefore, they do not necessarily suffer from lack of mobility. Just like many other feminist movements around the world that have been led by educated women from wealthier families, it is the more affluent and better-educated women who can afford to have the private chauffeurs that are needed to lead a driving campaign in Saudi Arabia. They are not only struggling for themselves but also for those who cannot afford chauffeurs.

8.3 Red Light to Women's Driving; Green Light to Women's Participation

The ban on women driving remains in place in Saudi Arabia and is unlikely to be lifted any time soon. Nonetheless, the government has found it difficult to ignore activists pushing for women's empowerment. In response to women's dissent, the then King Abdullah appointed 30 women to the

Consultative Council, and he decreed that women must comprise 20 % of the council's total membership. Although the announcement was given without prior notice, clearly the Baladi Campaign, through which female advocates pushed for women's participation in municipal elections, had an effect on the King's decision. Importantly, the speech did not simply end in a promise but substantive changes have been realized. In January 2013, as many as 30 women became full-time members of the 150-member Consultative Council. The other promise was realized after King Abdullah's death, when in December 2015 women cast their first vote in municipal elections, and as many as 21 women won seats in the poll. Although the outcome of the municipal election reflects strong male dominance—women won only 1% of the seats—it was nonetheless a considerable step forward that they were elected at all, and both in big cities and small towns.

It was not only in political spheres that women suddenly benefited from inclusion after some 80 years of Saudi history. The government accelerated efforts to include women in employment after the Arab Spring. In a program called *nitaqat*, a Saudization scheme started in 2011, the government set obligations to private enterprises to hire a certain percentage of Saudi men and women, according to the size of the company. Women started to work at female lingerie shops, perfume shops, and supermarkets, as well as being permitted to work at commercial pharmacies in addition to their previously permitted employment in hospital pharmacies.[13]

The question arises as to why the Saudi government conducted these reforms so suddenly, especially bringing women into decision-making processes and the labor market more prominently. From a short-term perspective, the second nationwide municipal elections had been planned in 2011, and thus the government might have sought to compensate for not including women in that poll.

The Saudi government had been criticized strongly for not allowing women to vote or to run for office in the first elections in 2005. The reason it gave was that women's polling stations could not be provided. After that, however, the Baladi campaigners demanded that the government include women in these elections as well as in the Consultative Council.

However, the decision was not simply made reactively to these campaigns. From a longer-term perspective, it should be understood as a continuation of Saudi Arabia's efforts at "'demystifying' and 'normalising' the lives of Saudi women."[14] As Madawi Al-Rasheed correctly puts it, Saudi Arabia began to exhibit greater transparency and to pay attention to highly educated Saudi women after the September 11, 2001 terrorist attacks, when the country drew international attention, partly due to its treatment of women. In the meantime, the Saudi government not only appealed to elite women but expanded educational opportunities to broader social classes. There are over 25 public universities in the kingdom compared with only eight in the 1990s. According to Saudi Arabia's Central Department of Statistics and Information (CDSI), more women in the country are advancing to higher education than men, with 432,000 female students enrolled at the university in 2007 compared to 309,000 male students.[15] When it comes to the number of the graduates, women overwhelmingly outnumber their male counterparts. Female graduates exceed men by more than 50 %. It was as a corollary that increasing numbers of women began to look for a job. This effort indicates Saudi Arabia's determination to holistically change the image of Saudi women's education and readiness to work. With these changes, women became increasingly substantive members of society, and very importantly the government perceived the need to include women in decision-making processes, the labor market, and other public activities.[16]

These changes have improved Saudi Arabia's notoriously low rankings in various international organizations' indices, such as the *World Economic Forum's Global Gender Gap Report*. The *Global Gender Gap Report 2015* highly elevated Saudi Arabia, as a country which attained one of the highest improvements in terms of women's labor participation as well as political participation over the eight years between 2006 and 2015. Saudi Arabia ranked 134th out of 145 countries in 2015, whereas it used to be 129th out of 134 countries in 2006.[17] Although the ranking does not demonstrate a big difference, elevation in scores in the field of education, economy and politics contributed to the higher recognition.

More importantly, although the current Consultative Council appointees are all highly educated elite women, this political shift may finally enable women who have remained politically ignored and unaccounted for to formally participate in civic processes. This progress will help women to perform agency as official council members who can suggest bills and participate in substantial processes of policy making.

8.4 Why the Driving Ban Remains

Women are now on the Consultative Council and the Municipal Council, and they are increasingly active in the labor market, yet the ban on driving remains. Thus the question arises as to whether women driving is really so abhorrent to the Saudis. The answer appears, overall, to be in the affirmative. There emerged a fierce debate about women driving after the June 17 driving campaign in 2011. In December 2011 the debate was reignited when a male Saudi academic submitted a report to the Consultative Council warning against the danger of increased prostitution, pornography, homosexuality, and divorce should women be allowed to drive.[18] The argument is totally groundless but the tactic was that any accusations that damaged the image of women driving would diminish the momentum of the campaign.

In the heat of these accusations, the driving campaign was revived. After the appointment of the female members of the Consultative Council, another online driving campaign was launched that called for women to drive on October 26, 2013. Following the campaign's inception, more than 11,000 women signed the declaration on the campaign website, www.oct26driving.com.[19] Like previous protests, organizers and participants faced a backlash. The website was hacked and temporarily modified by a detractor, who replaced the site's text with the message: "this page was hacked because I am against women driving in the country of two holy mosques" (see Fig. 8.1).

A critical difference between the Oct26Driving and the Women2Drive campaigns was that three female Consultative Council members backed up the protesters. They filed a recommendation to the council on October 8, 2013 to lift the ban on women's driving, and they asked the council to

Fig. 8.1 Hacked website of http://www.oct26driving.com (www.oct26driving.com/?page_id=13www.oct26driving.com/?page_id=13)

"recognise the rights of women to drive a car in accordance with the principles of Sharīaʿ (Islamic law) and traffic rules."[20] However, the council rejected the request on the grounds that it was irrelevant to the current transportation ministry discussion.[21]

For the Oct26Driving campaign, Sheikh Sālih al-Luḥaidān, a cleric, and a judicial and psychological consultant to the Gulf Psychological Association, opposed the idea on the grounds of 'scientific' evidence, claiming that driving "automatically affects ovaries and rolls up the pelvis."[22] By virtue of his authority as a cleric, this 'scientific' argument may have made a powerful impression on some. As a result, the second driving campaign ended in failure. On October 23 the Ministry of Interior delivered a statement condemning it. At least 25 women drove on the day of the demonstration. Although police stopped five of them, none were taken into custody.[23]

8.5 Are Saudi Women in Favor of Driving?

My primary research in the kingdom demonstrates that women are not necessarily advocates of what is understood as the 'emancipation of women' by outsiders. The freedom of movement so common in Western values is not so much assumed in Saudi Arabia, where there are strong supporters of male dominance and of the restriction of women's freedom of movement. It is not only conservative male members of society but many women too who are reluctant to see the ban on driving lifted. Fieldwork conducted in December 2011 in Riyadh, in which 14 non-activist Saudi women were interviewed, reinforces this reality. Eight of the women supported women's right to drive while the remaining six did not. Those who supported the drive movement were mostly younger, ranging between their teens and their 40s. Three of these had supported the campaign led by Manāl Al-Sharīf, who was taken into the police custody following the uploading of her video. The other five women, although believing that women should have the right to drive, did not support Al-Sharīf's campaign because they thought it was scandalous. These women feared risking their personal safety or becoming associated with scandal. Among those who supported women's right to drive, some believed that the driving ban should be lifted only with conditions attached, such as a minimum age requirement and that women should only drive during the day.

The remaining six women opposed lifting the ban. All of them were working women in their 40s with daughters. Their opposition centered mainly on their daughters' potential driving experiences, citing concerns of possible traffic accidents, harassment from other drivers, and losing control of their daughters' movements. Among them, a female medical doctor retorted: "Driving is not the priority. We have many other issues and problems to be solved."[24] Being a home doctor for a community, she did not hire a driver because she said she didn't need one. Her husband who works for the government drops her at work in the morning and picks her up in the afternoon everyday. She insisted that all women should have good means of transportation, but that doesn't necessarily mean that they should have a driver's license. She thought that women-only buses or a metro with women-only cars should be organized so that any transportation problems are solved. For her, for women to drive would be dangerous because, she claimed, juvenile delinquents are ubiquitous. It is known that juvenile delinguents in Saudi Arabia do not care about regulations or speed limits, and they drive with music at full volume. Interestingly, the women who refused to prioritize the driving issue did not claim to oppose women's rights. That said, nor were they interested in gender equality. In contrast to the claims from defenders of the women's rights, they simply stated that they did not wish to be burdened by tasks such as driving.

Some respondents also expressed disappointment that foreigners focus excessively on the idea that Saudi women are discriminated against simply because they do not have the right to drive. Because the ban on driving has attracted intense attention from foreigners, for some Saudis the women's driving issue is fundamentally a Western, and thus a foreign, obsession.

That said, some respondents' opinions did change over the years. I first interviewed Amira (a pseudonym) in 2007. Then she was a married woman in her 40s working in school administration and with four children. As a woman with her father's big legacy, she proudly asked: "Why do I have to become a mere driver when I can afford a driver?" She felt driving would degrade her, adding: "I prefer to enjoy the status like a princess' who is chauffeured to/from the places she wishes, leaving the driving burden to someone else."[25]

When I interviewed her in 2011, she seemed to have changed her mind. By then she was managing her own pastry manufacturing and sales business. As her commitments increased, she became more frustrated with the slow and unskilled drivers she hired. She mentioned that her driver once hit her parked car with her other car, forcing her to cover the repair costs for both. She also complained about the waiting time:

I am busy taking care of children. In addition, I have a job at school in the morning and turn to my own business in the afternoon and evening, but I sometimes lose time waiting for the driver to pick me up. The waiting time sometimes exceeds one hour. The driver makes excuses such as traffic jams, but I am fed up. I feel tempted to drive a car by myself, so that I don't have to be involved in troubles caused by the driver or to lose time waiting.[26]

Several interviews yielded similar results, both in 2007 and 2011. Although there are no statistics on how many Saudi women support or oppose women driving, subjective evidence from my two sets of qualitative interviews is that a considerable number of women oppose women driving if doing so is more strategically beneficial for them than the right to drive. This is a reflection of Deniz Kandiyoti's patriarchal bargaining, in which women attempt to strategize within social constraints. In choosing not to drive, women think that they can maximize their security and life options within the Saudi patriarchy. Women who support the ban believe that driving is a burden more than a freedom; some even enjoy being chauffeured by a driver or a male relative. Traffic congestion is one of the reasons they do not show an interest in driving. They prefer to stay at home, relax, or do other tasks rather than waste their time driving.

Additionally, mothers worry that if their daughters can drive, there is a greater risk of their sexual contact with strangers, which, given the cultural significance of virginity in the region, could put the entire family's honor at risk. In contrast, the teenage women interviewed could not cite specific reasons for supporting female driving but they seemed intuitively interested in it. As these girls can assure that their parents carefully protect their sexuality, they may place less importance on virginity or family honor.

Amira's case is particularly meaningful given the fact that more Saudi women are entering the job market, motivated by both increased educational attainment and, importantly, rapid inflation that can easily put their household under pressure. Increased drivers' wages are also affecting households, in addition to more and more women in need of transportation, due to their changed lifestyles. As has been discussed earlier, what Natasha Ridge calls a "reverse gender divide" is the case in Saudi Arabia.[27] Paradoxically, women are less likely to be employed than men despite their higher achievements in education:[28] the CDSI estimates the overall unemployment rate for Saudi women in the first quarter of 2013 at 34.8 %,[29] while the USA's Central Intelligence Agency estimates that the unemployment rate for women aged 15–24 exceeds 55.3 %.[30] Simultaneously, continuous inflation has put households under pressure. According to the CDSI, the 2014 inflation rate was 2.7 %.[31] This apparently influenced the domestic worker's wage rise, including that of the chauffeurs.

Given the combined impact of high unemployment rate and continuous inflation, increasing numbers of educated Saudi women are entering the workforce and have a greater need for mobility. Since the introduction of *Nitaqat*, most of the lingerie stores have started to put 'family only' stickers in front of the shop so that a man without female family members or a male-only group cannot enter. To my knowledge, women working in sales in perfume shops or as cashiers at supermarkets were not separated: they work in the same environment as male foreign salespeople. According to a report in the Saudi Gazette, as many as 180,000 Saudi women had been employed in full-time jobs in the private sector as of 2012.[32] In light of these changes, the issue of women's freedom of movement has become paramount. The appointment of female Consultative Council members had a huge impact on Saudi political decision-making. Women's issues are no longer a family-only concern but are institutionalized into public, political and social matters. Although the driving ban remains, it has now been elevated to an issue for the Consultative Council by some female council members. It is a proof that the appointment of female council members created a synergetic impact in which women are not just participating in politics, rather, they have also brought women's issues into the political arena.

8.6 Conclusion

Despite repeated campaigns, the ban on women driving remains in place. Women continue to negotiate power and space in the face of fierce opposition. That said, it is also the case that a considerable number of women support the ban on driving. Some fear for their daughters' safety and honor; others consider driving to be a burden. Many of these women are attempting to negotiate power and space in their own way by bargaining with and strategizing within the patriarchal structure. For them, driving does not necessarily mean freedom of movement, but it can be a burden. Even if it gives women freedom, women can face troubles that could seriously put them and their family's honor in crisis. This is why they try to deny the importance of women driving. Also, because of the excessive attention paid by outsiders to the issues associated with women driving, it is seen as foreign, thus irrelevant, by some Saudis.

Yet the social structure in Saudi Arabia is changing as more women join the workforce and, in turn, require convenient, reliable, and affordable transportation. Although a metro is under construction in Riyadh, it will not be completed until at least 2018. Even then, it won't provide transportation for women in other cities.

While drivers' wages are a negligible expense for high-income households, they are a costly indulgence for many others. It is particularly difficult for those in lower-income brackets to afford drivers. Coupled with the rapid population growth, this social stratification is expected to become more marked. In this context, hiring a chauffeur may become an item of conspicuous consumption and, for many women, an unaffordable extravagance.

Regardless, the appointment of 30 women as full members to the Consultative Council is a significant development towards involving Saudi women in formal decision-making processes. These female council members can now exercise their power to expand women's participatory space in society, either within the patriarchy (i.e. the establishment of women's-only public transportation) or in opposition to it (i.e. lifting the driving ban).

Challenges regarding power and space in Saudi Arabia are still to be negotiated. However, women's issues are no longer a family-only matter that politicians say nothing about. They are institutionalized in the decision-making processes along with the appointment of female Consultative Council members who may advocate for female agency.

Acknowledgment I am indebted to the interviewees in Saudi Arabia and King Faisal Center for Research and Islamic Studies who provided insight and expertise that greatly assisted the research. This study was enabled with a Grant-in-Aid for Scientific Research, 26703003, 24730148, 24310177, 24251008, 23401014, 25284176 and a grant provided by the KDDI Foundation.

Notes

1. Judith Butler. "Performative Agency." *Journal of Cultural Economy*, Vol. 3 No. 2. (2010): 147.
2. Deniz Kandiyoti. "Bargaining with Patriarchy." *Gender and Society*, Vol. 2 No. 3. (1988): 274–290.

3. For a protest in Jeddah, see "Rare: Protest in Jeddah, Saudi Arabia against Government Corruption", *YouTube*, accessed February 4, 2016, https://www.youtube.com/watch?v=dSZJt1ytmL4
4. For example, their facebook page enjoys as many as 17,998 likes as of February 6, 2016. "Support #Women2Drive", accessed on February 6, 2016, https://www.facebook.com/Women2Drive
5. Peter Wilson and Douglas Graham. *Saudi Arabia: The Coming Storm* (New York: M. E. Sharp, 1994).
6. My interview with a protester who participated in a driving protest in 1990. The interview was conducted on March 9, 2013 in Riyadh, mainly in English.
7. For Wajiha Al-Huwaider's video clip, see "English: Wajeha Al-Huwaider", accessed on February 6, 2016, https://www.youtube.com/watch?v=q8GiTnb33wE
8. "Saudi Arabia Women Test Driving Ban", *The Guardian*, June 17, 2011, accessed on February 7, 2016, http://www.theguardian.com/world/2011/jun/17/saudi-arabia-women-drivers-protest
9. "Saudi Women Driving Activists Freed from Prison", *AlJazeera*, February 14, 2015, accessed on February 9, 2016, http://www.aljazeera.com/news/2015/02/saudi-women-driving-activists-released-prison-150213075642894.html
10. "Saudi Women Begin Campaigning in Polls for First Time", *AlJazeera*, November 29, 2015, accessed on February 9, 2016, http://www.aljazeera.com/news/2015/11/saudi-women-campaigning-polls-time-151129160214419.html
11. "Manal AlSharif Driving in Saudi Arabia", YouTube, accessed on February 7, 2016, https://www.youtube.com/watch?v=sowNSH_W2r0
12. My interview with a Women2Drive protester, 2012, Riyadh. The interview was conducted mainly in English.
13. "Pharmacies Opened Up to Working Saudi Women", *Arabian Business*, February 4, 2013, accessed on February 7, 2016, http://www.arabianbusiness.com/pharmacies-opened-up-working-saudi-women-488187.html
14. Madawi Al-Rasheed, *A Most Masculine State: Gender, Politics, and Religion in Saudi Arabia* (New York: Cambridge University Press, 2013), 140.
15. Central Department of Statistics and Information, *Highlights: Demographic Survey 1428H (2007)*, 2007, 100–101, http://www.cdsi.gov.sa/english/index.php?option=com_docman&task=cat_view&gid=43&Itemid=113
16. Tsujigami, Namie. "Higher Education and Changing Aspirations of Women in Saudi Arabia", Dale Eickelman and Rogaia Abu Sharaf (eds), *Higher Education Investment in the Arab States of the Gulf: Strategies for Excellence and Diversity* (Berlin: Gerlach Press, 2017) PP. 42–54.

17. World Economic Forum, *The Global Gender Gap Report 2015* (Geneva: World Economic Forum, 2015), accessed on February 7, 2016, http://www3.weforum.org/docs/GGGR2015/cover.pdf
18. Sebastian Usher, "'End of Virginity' If Women Drive, Saudi Cleric Warns." *BBC*, December 2, 2011, accessed October 27, 2013, http://www.bbc.co.uk/news/world-middle-east-16011926
19. "Driving Affects Ovaries and Pelvis, Saudi Sheikh Warns Women," *Al Arabiya*, 29 September 2013, http://english.alarabiya.net/en/variety/2013/09/28/Driving-affects-ovary-and-pelvis-Saudi-sheikh-warns-women.html
20. "Saudi Shura Members Urge Lifting of Female Driving Ban," *Gulf News*, 8 October 2013, http://gulfnews.com/news/gulf/saudi-arabia/saudi-shura-members-urge-lifting-of-female-driving-ban-1.1240974
21. "Saudi Shura Rejects Women Driving Ban Move", *Al Jazeera*, 10 October 2013, http://www.aljazeera.com/news/middleeast/2013/10/saudi-shura-rejects-women-driving-ban-move-20131010164741609260.html
22. "Driving affects ovaries and pelvis, Saudi sheikh warns women," *Al Arabiya*, 28 September 2013, http://english.alarabiya.net/en/variety/2013/09/28/Driving-affects-ovary-and-pelvis-Saudi-sheikh-warns-women.html
23. Mohammed Jamjoom and Laura Smith-Spark. "Saudi Arabia Women Defy Authorities over Female Driving Ban", *CNN*, October 27, 2013, accessed October 27, 2013 http://edition.cnn.com/2013/10/26/world/meast/saudi-arabia-women-drivers/
24. My interview with a medical doctor, 28 December 2011, Riyadh.
25. My interview with Amira. 13th February, 2007 in Riyadh.
26. My interview with Amira. 27 December, 2011 in Riyadh.
27. Natasha Ridge, *Education and the Reverse Gender Divide in the Gulf States: Embracing the Global, Ignoring the Local* (Amsterdam: Teachers College Press, 2014), 63.
28. Diane Zovighian argues that women's access to the labor market is limited because their access to education is restricted in terms of study fields despite their high levels of educational attainment. Diane Zovighian, "Gulf Women's Participation in the Labor Market: Paid Labor, Care and Social Protection in Patriarchal Systems," in *National Employment, Migration and Education in the GCC*, ed. Steffen Hertog (Berlin: Gerlach Press, 2012), 183–230. In the meantime, John Willoughby points out that "segmented feminization" is taking place, where highly educated women compete successfully for professional jobs while women of lower educational attainment have more difficulty in replacing male expatriate workers. John Willoughby, "Segmented Feminization and the Decline of Neopatriarchy in GCC Countries of the Persian Gulf," *Comparative Studies of South Asia, Africa and the Middle East* 28, no.1 (2008): 184–99.

29. Central Department of Statistics and Information, *Quarterly Unemployment Rates (15 Years and Above) by Sex*, 2013, http://www.cdsi.gov.sa/english/index.php
30. Central Intelligence Agency, "Saudi Arabia," *The World Factbook*, accessed on February 10, 2016, https://www.cia.gov/library/publications/the-world-factbook/geos/sa.html
31. Central Department of Statistics and Information. *Change in the Cost of Living (Inflation) for* 2014, accessed on February 10, 2016, http://www.cdsi.gov.sa/english/index.php
32. Saudi Gazette, "Nitaqat paying off: Fakieh," *Saudi Gazette*, 13 June 2013, http://www.saudigazette.com.sa/index.cfm?method=home.regcon&contentid=20130613169702

Bibliography

Abukhalil, A. 2004. *The Battle for Saudi Arabia: Royalty, Fundamentalism, and Global Power*. New York: Seven Stories Press.
Al-Rasheed, M. 2013. *A Most Masculine State: Gender, Politics, and Religion in Saudi Arabia*. New York: Cambridge University Press.
Butler, J. 2010. Performative Agency. *Journal of Cultural Economy* 3 (2): 147–161.
Commins, D. 2015. *Islam in Saudi Arabia*. Ithaca: Cornell University Press.
Jerichow, A. 1998. *The Saudi File: People, Power, Politics*. New York: St. Martin's Press.
Kandiyoti, D. 1988. Bargaining with Patriarchy. *Gender and Society* 2 (3): 274–290.
Ridge, N. 2014. *Education and the Reverse Gender Divide in the Gulf States: Embracing the Global, Ignoring the Local*. Amsterdam: Teachers College Press.
Tsujigami, N. 2012. Sauji Arabia no Taiseinai Kenryoku (The Establishment of Power Relations in Saudi Arabia). In *Chuto Seijigaku (Analysing the Middle East: Bridging Comparative Politics and Area Studies)*, ed. K. Sakai, 49–62. Tokyo: Yuhikaku.
Willoughby, J. 2008. Segmented Feminization and the Decline of Neopatriarchy in GCC Countries of the Persian Gulf. *Comparative Studies of South Asia, Africa and the Middle East* 28 (1): 184–199.
Wilson, P., and D. Graham. 1994. *Saudi Arabia: The Coming Storm*. New York: M. E. Sharp.
World Economic Forum. 2015. *The Global Gender Gap Report 2015*. Geneva. World Economic Forum. http://www3.weforum.org/docs/GGGR2015/cover.pdf. Accessed 7 Feb 2016.
Zovighian, D. 2012. Gulf Women's Participation in the Labor Market: Paid Labor, Care and Social Protection in Patriarchal Systems. In *National Employment, Migration and Education in the GCC*, ed. S. Hertog, 183–230. Berlin: Gerlach Press.

Websites

Al Arabiya. 2013. Driving Affects Ovaries and Pelvis, Saudi Sheikh Warns Women. *Al-Arabiya*, September 28. http://english.alarabiya.net/en/variety/2013/09/28/Driving-affects-ovary-and-pelvis-Saudi-sheikh-warns-women.html. Accessed 4 Feb 2015.

Al Jazeera. 2013. Saudi Shura Rejects Women Driving Ban Move. *Al-Jazeera*, October 10. http://www.aljazeera.com/news/middleeast/2013/10/saudi-shura-rejects-women-driving-ban-move-20131010164741609260.html. Accessed 27 Oct 2013.

Central Department of Statistics and Information. 2007. *Highlights: Demographic Survey 1428H*. http://www.cdsi.gov.sa/english/index.php?option=com_docman&task=cat_view&gid=43&Itemid=113. Accessed 10 Feb 2016.

———. 2013. *Quarterly Unemployment Rates (15 Years and Above) by Sex*. http://www.cdsi.gov.sa/english/index.php. Accessed 10 Feb 2016.

———. 2014. Change in the Cost of Living (Inflation) for 2014. Central Department of Statistics and Information. http://www.cdsi.gov.sa/english/index.php. Accessed 10 Feb 2016.

Central Intelligence Agency. 2016. Saudi Arabia. *The World Factbook*. https://www.cia.gov/library/publications/the-world-factbook/geos/sa.html. Accessed 10 Feb 2016.

Gulf News. 2013. Saudi Shura Members Urge Lifting of Female Driving Ban. *Gulf News*, October 8. http://gulfnews.com/news/gulf/saudi-arabia/saudi-shura-members-urge-lifting-of-female-driving-ban-1.1240974. Accessed 27 Oct 2013.

Hussain, L. 2011. Saudi Woman Driver Spared 10 Lashes after King Intervenes. *The Independent*, September 30. http://www.independent.co.uk/news/world/middle-east/saudi-woman-driver-spared-10-lashes-after-king-intervenes-2363197.html. Accessed 10 Feb 2016.

Jamjoom, M., and L. Smith-Spark. 2013. Saudi Arabia Women Defy Authorities Over Female Driving Ban. *CNN*, October 27. http://edition.cnn.com/2013/10/26/world/meast/saudi-arabia-women-drivers/. Accessed 27 Oct 2013.

Majlis Al-Shura. 2013a. Shura Council Law. *Majlis Al-Shura*. http://www.shura.gov.sa/wps/wcm/connect/ShuraEn/internet/Laws+and+Regulations/The+Shura+Council+and+the+rules+and+regulations+job/Shura+Council+Law/. Accessed 30 Oct 2013.

———. 2013b. Members' CVs. *Majlis Al-Shura*. http://www.shura.gov.sa/wps/wcm/connect/ShuraArabic/internet/cv. Accessed 27 Oct 2013.

Saudi Gazette. 2013. Nitaqat Paying Off: Fakieh. *Saudi Gazette*, June 13. http://www.saudigazette.com.sa/index.cfm?method=home.regcon&contentid=20130613169702. Accessed 9 Nov 2013.

TEDTalks. 2013. Manal Al Sharif: A Woman Who Dared to Drive'. *YouTube*. http://www.youtube.com/watch?v=vNpmq6Ok-QQ. Accessed 28 Oct 2013.

The Associated Press. 2011. Five Saudi Women Drivers Arrested, Says Activist. *The Guardian*. http://www.theguardian.com/world/2011/jun/29/saudi-women-drivers-arrested-Jiddah. Accessed 9 Nov 2013.

Usher, S. 2011. 'End of Virginity' If Women Drive, Saudi Cleric Warns. *BBC*, December 2. http://www.bbc.co.uk/news/world-middle-east-16011926

Women2drive. 2015. *YouTube*. Accessed 5 Feb 2015. http://www.youtube.com/watch?v=akQ4ftcvO3M. Accessed 27 Oct 2013.

CHAPTER 9

Social Media, Social Learning Systems, and the Women's Movement in Tunisia After the Jasmine Revolution

Sana Jelassi

9.1 Introduction

This chapter is based on research undertaken in 2013 in which the use of social media (specifically Facebook) by the Tunisian social movements (with a focus on the women's movement) was examined. The aim is to examine the possible role of Facebook as a social learning tool, and based on the findings to shed light on new ways for its use by social movements in their strategies for outreach, mobilization, advocacy, and lobbying.

For many experts, social media shaped the wave of revolutionary movements known as the "Arab Spring" that started with the Tunisian uprising. This link between social and political movements and the use of social media started with the Ukrainian Orange Revolution in 2004 and was recently confirmed in the different Occupy Movements, including the (2013) Occupy Gezi Movement. Many enthusiasts regarding the role of social media claim that we are now in an era of a "social media fuelled type of protest," as named by Tukefci (2013). For Ghanem (2011), "Facebook

S. Jelassi (✉)
Amman, Jordan

and other social media platforms had begun to define the way in which information is discovered and shared, opinion is shaped and interactions take place among people."

For Jamil Wyne (2012), one of the effects of the Arab Spring was the acceleration of the internet penetration in the Middle East and North Africa (MENA) region and the increase in the use of social media. The first 11 months of 2011 witnessed a 68 % increase in Facebook users in the region. Furthermore, the use of social media witnessed a transformation. In a study by the Dubai School of Government, Fadi Salem and Racha Mourtada (2011) showed that by the end of 2011 the use of social media in the Arab World changed drastically. It had begun to include interventions to support social and political change as well as civic and political engagement.

On the other hand, others are skeptics when it comes to social media's role in bringing political change, among them Malcolm Gladwell, mentioned by Joseph (2011), who talks of "slacktivism," which is defined as low-risk activism without the commitment that makes a difference and brings effective change. For Goldsborough (2011), slacktivism suggests a lack of effort and effect in its concept. Furthermore, an increasing number of voices reported by Joseph (2011) are highlighting the role of social media in spreading rumors, propaganda, and hatred, but the author concludes that social media can be a neutral tool and states that "that in the free market of ideas, "bad" speech can be drowned out by "good" speech."

The political transition in Tunisia (2011–2014) was marked by the battle between modernists and Islamists to win political space, and Facebook was one of the many fields where this battle was fought. The complete antagonistic vision of society between the two groups, coupled with the lack of confidence in traditional Tunisian media, and the creativity and freedom enabled online, contributed to the enthusiasm witnessed on Facebook.

The Tunisian Jasmine Revolution freed the political and social space, and there is a continuing increase in the number of non-governmental organizations (NGOs) and social movements that are using social media for communication, outreach, lobbying, and mobilization. A Dubai School survey cited by Joseph (2011), distributed to Tunisian and Egyptian Facebook users in early 2011, found that their use of Facebook was to

- organize actions and manage activists: 29.55 % of Egyptians and 22.31 % of Tunisians;
- spread information about civil movements: 24.05 % of Egyptians and 33.06 % of Tunisians;
- raise awareness inside the country about movements: 30.93 % of Egyptians and 31.4 % of Tunisians;
- provide entertainment and other uses: 15.46 % of Egyptians and 13.22 % of Tunisians.

In the heated debate between Islamists and modernists, gender equality is a core issue, and social media is used to discuss and to organize by supporters of both movements. Social media is also facilitating new regional links for both sides, and ideas are circulating between the Arab countries in flows that did not exist before. This is facilitated by the climate of freedom generated by the Arab Spring and the easy access to social media. Facebook (specifically) is allowing through pages, groups, and subscriptions an exchange of ideas that are available to different audiences depending on their interests, and this is leading us to reflect about the links between social media and social learning tools, considering, for example, Facebook groups as communities of practice. We expect forms of social organization to be shaped by new technologies, and we consider the possibilities of acceleration of social learning with emerging new forms, inhabiting new spaces.

Looking particularly to the transition period in Tunisia (from January 14, 2011 till the finalization of the constitution in 2014), the research examined the identification of social learning emerging from the use of social media. The main focus was individuals and informal groups getting together virtually to shape and improve the outreach strategies of the Tunisian social movement but with a specific focus on gender equality. The research concentrated on gender equality because women's rights crystallized the debate between secularists and Islamists and was shaping emerging social movements. "In Tunisia, we had a lot of advantages under the rule of the last two presidents, but since the revolution we are worried about our rights ... Things can change very fast but we will not give up what we already fought for," said Sinda Garziz to Louise Sherwood from Inter Press Service in an article on Tunisian women's efforts to monitor the drafting of the constitution and to ensure that their rights are not weakened.

9.2 Methodology

Framed by social learning and specifically by Wenger's (2000) approach to communities of practice, their forms of belonging, their community dimensions, their boundary dimensions, and their identity dimensions, the research attempted to

- identify the contribution of Facebook, if any, to social learning;
- assess the development of new ideas (or their lack) and change in the Tunisian women's movement's forms of activism and its strategies, and how the latter are shaping and being shaped by the questions of values and ethics;
- make recommendations to improve outreach, mobilization, and lobbying strategies, as well as foster learning and knowledge-sharing.

The data for the research was collected through a literature review, including grey literature, and through participant observation.

9.3 Background Information

In the aftermath of the Arab Spring and with the Islamists' access to power in Tunisia, Egypt, and Morocco, concerns were raised about the change they would bring to different policies, including the issue of women's rights. The concerns were raised by academics looking into the social change generated by the "revolution," by economic partners, by multilateral organizations scrutinizing liberalism and moderation among the new Islamists masters, and most importantly by nationals of these countries and particularly women. In Tunisia, women's concerns and fears about their rights generated an important mobilization.[1] At the same time the Arab Spring was linked to emerging "social change" facilitated by social media. The latter created, among others, new links between individuals, groups, and countries that affect the dynamic of the social movements in the region and their practice.

9.3.1 Women and Transition in Tunisia

9.3.1.1 A Scrutinized Political Transition in Tunisia

Political transition in Tunisia started when the former president fled the country on January 14, 2011 after weeks of unrest, known as the Jasmine Revolution, and culminated with the adoption of a new constitution in

January 2014. Arieff (2012) wrote for the US Congress: "Tunisia's transition raises a wide range of questions for the future of the country and the region." He enumerated the elements shaping this process, including the upcoming reform of the political system, the influence of political Islam on institutions and society after the Islamists' success, and the transformation of formerly repressive machinery. He stressed the attributes that make Tunisia "a potential test case" for democratic transitions in the region. These are its middle class and its level of education, the small size of the country and the homogenous population, and the level of emancipation of Tunisian women. Deane Shelly (2012) praises the role of civil society organizations in shaping the Tunisian transition: "New Tunisian civil society is characterized by the fast-moving, collaborative way Arab citizens influence institutional changes by creating newly institutionalized frameworks for public participation" and recommends, among other things, working on the "twin tolerances" between the religious and political spheres, and the need to integrate all actors in the transition process and "navigate the differences between secular and religious Tunisians."

9.3.1.2 Cyberactivism in Tunisia
Belkaid (2013), introducing Yves Gonzalez-Quijano's book[2] on what he calls the spring of the "Arab Web," refers to the emergence of cyberactivism in Tunisia in 2000, corroborated by Kubler (2011). Cyberactivism changed the political activism landscape with the appearance of new actors, new issues, and new forms of resistance but it was also marked by repression, failure, and anonymity during the decade. During the Arab Spring, the experience in Tunisia and Egypt showed the three-fold freeing impact of new technologies: freedom of speech and mobilization, then coordination and organization, and eventually documentation and promotion. Quijano, as reported by Belkaid (2013), places the Arab Spring in the wider context of changes appearing in the region. He confirms the accelerated pace of internet penetration in the Arab world and the progression of the Arabic language in the new technology sector. He links this to wider societal change as shown by the appearance of "Arabizi."[3] These changes translate into a "renaissance" in the Arab world where the internet and new technologies allow intertwining political activism, arts, poetry, and a questioning of identity and social relations.

Cyberactivism in the Tunisian transition period is changing and reflects the dichotomy between Islamists and modernists. B'chir (2013) alleges that Ennahdha[4] has electronic militias that are pushing the government's agenda. The youth are supposedly recruited and trained, then tasked with crushing opposition leaders and groups using propaganda tools. These include the manipulation of press releases and photos, and digging in the past of opposition leaders and publishing all results on social media. Even if Bchir's article is not very clear and mixes data and information from an Egyptian journalistic investigation on the practice of the Islamist Brotherhood transposing facts to Tunisian Islamists, the suspicions continue from both sides as manipulative campaigns against politicians and civil society leaders are frequent, with peaks before the 2011 and the 2014 elections.

9.3.1.3 Women's Rights and the Women's Movement in Tunisia
"The reality is that women's rights have been a fact of life in Tunisia for decades," states Coleman (2011). She cites the Tunisian Code of Personal Status Code (CPS) adopted by Bourguiba,[5] the first Tunisian president, in 1956. The CPS abolished polygamy, granted divorce rights to women, and fixed the marriage age for both sexes, thereby limiting early marriage. Ben Ali, the ousted Tunisian president, also reinforced women's rights with the establishment of laws protecting women from gender-based violence, reinforcing women's custody rights, and promoting their political participation. The state leadership on women's rights made scholars talk of state feminism that uses "women as markers of Modernity" (Hawkins 2011). For many of Tunisia's feminists, women's emancipation is linked to the reformist movement in the country. For Skandrani[6] (2012), the adoption of the Tunisian CPS was possible because reformists such as Khair-Eddine[7] promoted girls' access to education in 1856. She refers to existing debate over the twentieth century with the "battle for the veil" started by early feminists that called for the abolition of the veil in 1924, and the abolition of polygamy in 1929. Another landmark is Tahar Haddad's book *Our Women in the Shariaa and in the Society*, which advocates for women's rights and which generated huge debate in Tunisian society (Churchill 2013).

Returning to the issue of state feminism, Krifa (2012) states that women's rights in Tunisia were paternalistically taken control of until the 1980s, when the Tunisian Autonomous Women's Movement emerged. This comprised middle-class women who benefited from the policy of free access to university. They had a history of activism with student leftist structures and used to gather in the cultural club Tahar Haddad in Tunis to discuss discriminations against women, the roots of these discriminations, and strategies to address them. This informal movement gave birth in 1989[8] to the Tunisian Association of Democratic Women (ATFD)[8] and the Tunisian Women's Association for Research and Development

(AFTURD).[9] The former works on the issue of women's rights and has a political analytical framework, while the latter focuses on research on women's rights and gender issues. However, their outreach was limited during the Ben Ali era because both organizations formed with three others (human rights organizations), the only autonomous organizations that stood for democracy and human rights in the country.

9.3.1.4 The Emerging Women's Movement After the Uprising
Dubruelh (2011) reports the emergence of a new women's movement in Tunisia following the 2011 elections and the Islamists' victory. Calls for demonstration were coming from women involved in the new organizations[10] that were set up after the uprising, but they feared for their rights. Various media voiced these fears, such as an article by Nasr (2013), which stated that Tunisian women are the biggest losers following the revolution. These fears and threats in fact galvanized Tunisian women and created an important movement for change in the society. Women were becoming involved in politics,[11] and were organizing, creating, and joining structures to fight for their rights. In an assessment of Tunisian Civil Society, Slovak Aid (2012) reckons that the role of emerging women's organizations is to be "rapidly pioneering in activities to empower women in all realms: economic, political and social."

9.3.1.5 Islamic Feminism
In an article, Latte Abdallah (2012) examines the role that can be played by Islamic feminism in the transition after the Arab Spring and the rise of political Islam. She highlights the rise of the movement in 2000 and the creation of new networks and groups supporting gender equality and gay rights, such as Musawah[12] (Equality), the Global Women's Shura Council,[13] and the International Group for Studying and Reflecting on Women's Situation in Islam (Groupe International d'Etude et de Reflexion sur la Femme en Islam).[14] However, these ideas and movements were not rooted in Tunisia in the time of the study and were not part of the public debate.

9.3.2 Social Media and Social Movements

As mentioned earlier, the role of social media was deemed to be crucial during the Arab Spring, and interest is increasing in documenting and analyzing how Facebook, YouTube, and Twitter were consecutively used to "organize the protest, to share information, and to let the world know." Questions are also being raised about the influence of social media on shaping social movements and political change. Sarah Anne Rennick (2013) writes: "For social scientists, these events (Arab Spring) challenge our notions of popular mobilization and social movement theory, of the sources of political change and democratic transition theory, and of agency of what constitutes the political more generally."

9.3.2.1 "Slacktivism" vs. Activism

Following the trend initiated by the 2004 Ukrainian Revolution and the 2009 Iranian Green Movement, the discussion about the link between social media and the protest movement continued in the aftermath of the Arab Spring. Comunello and Anzera (2012) oppose the "digital evangelists," who consider technology apps to be essential tools in uprisings, vs. the "techno-realists," who see these as irrelevant gadgets. Enthusiasts have defended the role played by social media in the success of the Arab Spring and in shaping the uprisings. Rennick (2013), after an analysis of the 2011 Egyptian Revolution, concludes that the role of social media was evident in two phases: it enlarged the movement to new actors, not necessarily activists in a premobilization phase; and then it supported the building of a common understanding within the movement during a collective action phase. This suggestion is supported by data on the acceleration of internet penetration and the increase in the use of social media in the MENA region, as reported by Wyne (2012), who mentions that in the first 11 months of 2011 there was a 68 % increase in Facebook users in the region. Links between social media and social movements continued during the 2013 Turkish demonstrations, leading the then Turkish prime minister to call social media "the worst menace to society." Tufekci (2013) talks about a "social media fueled type of protest" defined by eight common elements:

- a lack of organized institutional leadership;
- a feeling of lack of an institutional outlet;
- non-activist participation;
- breaking of pluralistic ignorance;
- organized around a "no" not a "go";
- external attention;
- social media as structuring the narrative;
- not easily steerable towards political action.

On the other hand, some authors continue to be skeptical when it comes to social media's role in bringing political change, among them Gladwell (2010), who refutes effective change made through "slacktivism," which he defines as an effortless activism where participation is increased by lowering expectations, sacrifices to be made, ties between fellow activists, and hierarchical structure and leadership. Aday et al. (2013) studied a constructed set of Arab Spring-related data from archived Twitter content with metadata from the URL shortening service Bit.ly. They concluded that the interest and consumption of data came from outside the region and that it was mass media rather than citizen media that held the interest of the world.

Two campaigns from the United Nations (UN) system show that the controversy about slacktivism continues. On the one hand, the United Nations Children's Fund (Sweden) launched a campaign stressing the inefficiency of slacktivism, "Slacktivists Take Note: We Don't Like Your Likes,"[15] while the World Food Programme (WFP) developed a campaign to collect likes on Facebook.[16] The campaign[17] claims that by liking the WFP you will not feed a child but WFP's partner will. These two campaigns illustrate the difference in expectations regarding social media's use even when it concerns an aspect as specific as fundraising.

Social media, as shown by the data from the Dubai School of Governance (see Introduction to this chapter), is contributing to new forms of activism, and what Tukefci calls "social media fueled protest" is definitely different forms of protest from the example of activism related to the Civil Rights Movement of the 1960s mentioned by Gladwell (2010), suggesting different forms of protest for different eras.

Comunello and Anzera (2012) offer a more nuanced view, limiting the role of social media to organizing protesters and sharing information. They see a clear role for social media in developing political consciousness in the transitional period following the uprisings. Furthermore, they refer to the change in society where organization is moving from communities to networks, and they cite Rainie and Wellman (2012), who refer to "networked individualism" as "the main operating system in contemporary societies."

For Castells (2000), a "new society" is emerging based on a new social structure and is concomitant with the deployment of new information technology. The latter is generating new forms of social interaction through networks. Castells argues that networks are old organizational forms known for their flexibility and adaptability, but also for their lack of performance, which is currently corrected through technological connections. Communities in sociology are social units where people are linked by territoriality, interests, and values.[18] Wenger (2000) defines communities of practice as the basic building blocks of social learning, which he defines through dimensions, boundaries, and identities.

9.3.2.2 Changing Societal Structures with New Technology?
Cohen (2012) offers an interesting reflection on the meaning of social action, and links social media to social energy. He uses Burke's definition of rhetoric as "the manipulation of men's beliefs for political ends," and he looks into the organization of social media (friends for Facebook and followers for Twitter) and how these constitute platforms for activism. Furthermore, Aouragh (2012) looks into social movement theories of collective action and analyzes the role of new technologies through the prism of mediation. She cites Bimber et al. (2005), who highlight the challenges posed by participation classically relying on strong ties and vanguards on the one hand and organization with defined leadership and chains of command on the other hand, defined by Gladwell (2000) as characteristics of effective activism. The latter element feeds the technorealists' skepticism about change brought through social media.

9.3.2.3 Knowledge Management and Social Networking
The role of communities of practice is emerging in building organizational learning with institutions creating opportunities to bring together practitioners who will share experiences and lessons learned. Knowledge management is achieved through networks and communities using Web 2.0 technology, as in the United Nations Development Programme's professional social networking platforms.[19] Elaine Garcia et al. (2011), discussing the usefulness of social networking sites, suggest that their use would capture both explicit and tacit knowledge, "hence knowledge sharing would occur both vertically and horizontally in the organization and, therefore, provide the desired impact of creating new knowledge and innovation." Harrysson et al. (2012) suggest that companies could use social media in their intelligence-gathering to inform strategic their

decision-making. They give various examples of information gathered through social media and networking tools that supported successes and could have avoided losses.

It is interesting to see how social networking is articulated with informal and lifelong learning. For example, Chatti et al. (2010), in introducing the 3P Learning Model, highlight the speed of change in the world and the decrease in the half-life of knowledge.[20] They associate personalization, participation, and knowledge pull in a new model that allows lifelong learning to adapt to a fast-changing environment.

9.4 Framing the Research Findings Through Social Learning Systems

Is Facebook a system that allows learning? Wenger (2000) defines a social learning system through community of practice, boundaries processes and identities. For Bawden (2010), a system is a group of interacting components where the principles of diversity are crucial for a chaotic transformation with emergent properties. Both of these authors' definitions qualify Facebook as a system—one that offers a multitude of spaces for interactions and for sharing. These are delimited by community dimensions, identities, and forms of belonging with blurring and changing boundaries. The system also offers Bawden's "requisite diversity" and chaotic transformation with emerging properties. What gives coherence to the multitude of ideas shared and what makes them emerge as "ideas in good currency" on Facebook? For Schon (1973), "ideas in good currency" are those existing in the periphery that are moved to the center when disruptions bring them to public attention. He states that the vanguard plays an important role in bringing these ideas to the attention and in defending them, changing them into good currency. The Tunisian uprising is clearly a disruptive change in the political and social context. It was generated by various elements that changed mainly the people's mindset, and the latter is generating more change in all spheres. It interconnects systems that were not connected; redefines, among others, social classes' boundaries; and questions the role of the vanguard.

Is the Tunisian women's movement part of the vanguard, is it succeeding in bringing ideas into good currency? How social movements influenced or failed to influence public opinion, and how Facebook is used by social movements for this purpose? These are some of the questions that the research looked into, identifying links between social learning and the use of social media.

Jim Woodhill's (2002) article "Sustainability, Social Learning and the Democratic Imperative" highlights the importance of conscious design and facilitation in the design of social learning and management of change. He deems three elements necessary: philosophical reflection, methodological pluralism, and institutional design. All three are lacking on Facebook. The research is an opportunity to reflect on the need for facilitation and design for creativity, and the emergence of new patterns and change, mainly in a context of disruptive change. Ray (2011) mentions that the role of social media is currently overwhelming the Habermas model (1964) of public opinion emerging through rational critical debate in the public sphere mediated by mass media. In Tunisia, all media were controlled by the state before the 2011 uprising, and were therefore subsequently discredited and disregarded. Furthermore, there is an acknowledged contribution of social media and citizen journalism to the occurrence of the revolution. Therefore information on Facebook is currently shaping the public debate and shaping the emerging public opinion. However, Facebook is not supposed to replace traditional media and is definitely lacking a framework for responsibility and accountability, as highlighted by Sarah Joseph (2012), whose article stresses, for example, issues of privacy and the use of false identities on Facebook.

Richard Bawden's (2010) article entitled "The Community Challenge" raises the questions of values and ethics in his critical social learning systems. He develops the inspirational learning and experiential learning models based on spiritual, conceptual, and concrete worlds. The two learning models frame the emerging ideas and discourses on Facebook and the mobilization that follows. There are emerging forms of activisms from Facebook groups with ideas copied, changed, and adapted, as shown, for example, in the similarities between the campaigns of the Uprising of the Arab Women and the "Yezzi Fock" (It's Enough) against Ben Ali. The research will look at whether issues like shared values are influencing the ideas or practice that are copied and whether they are defining elements in what will become "ideas in good currency."

9.5 ANALYSIS OF THE RESEARCH FINDINGS

The analysis was carried out using Wenger's (2000) tables on community, boundary and, identity dimensions (Tables 9.1, 9.2 and 9.3).

Table 9.1 Community dimensions

Community	Enterprise	Mutuality	Repertoire
Engagement	Discussions in the groups specifically are not about strategy-building but around advocacy and campaigning	The uprising initially created strong ties between people but then cleavage appeared around the elections when political manipulation through Facebook arose. However, links between individuals are being created and could be seen as contributing to social capital (e.g. Le Pacte Tunisien[a] and Time Citizen[b])	A pride of being Tunisian and revolutionary appeared and is new in the country. It is facilitated by Facebook (e.g. a traffic policeman was professionally rewarded after a video of him shared and his efforts praised in Facebook)
Imagination	There are differences between pages and groups but, interestingly, some of them are strictly managed and have a clear rule for what is published, including comments	Facebook after the revolution allowed the emergence of new leaders in the political arena but also in the civic arena. At the same time there are groups and pages supporting divergent interests, including those of the Ben Ali's era. Many pages are managed by individuals and groups using a nickname, and they are building legitimacy to various ideas, including controversial ones	Various pages, groups, and comments show that the perception that Tunisians have of themselves has changed a lot. What is remarkable is the appearance of nationalism: examples include the use of the national anthem and the flag
Alignment	There is no accountability on Facebook. Clearly some pages are better known than others and it depends on their purpose and activity. Individuals have pages with clear leadership and purpose. These are recognized through mechanisms such as the awards for social media (Tunisiana Web Awards 2012)	The communities are very loose but the commitment to "the cause" defended by the pages/groups makes a difference with more determined contributors in certain cases	There are no defined norms as the practice is emerging. However, informal codification based on mutual knowledge between, for example, known bloggers and cartoonists is emerging and is in contrast with anonymous pages that are campaigning for a political group or party

[a] http://pactetunisien.com/: contributing to "building a democratic, inclusive Tunisia where all citizens are equal" is the pact signed by 7429 Tunisians

[b] http://timecitizen.org/ is a website created and managed by a Tunisian where people seeking and offering help are registered

Table 9.2 Boundary dimensions

Boundary	Coordination	Transparency	Negotiability
Engagement	The Tunisian activity in support of the Occupy Gezi Park Movement in Istanbul shows how Facebook allowed the establishment of contacts between Turkish and Tunisian activists and the organization of an activity in support of the Turkish movement	Again the support for the Occupy Gezi Park Movement shows different examples of joined-up activities and mixing practice	It is not clear if joint activity allows for different perspectives. However, the new freedom of association and expression is generating divergence at all levels, mainly at the political level
Imagination	In the majority of cases there is no understanding of the different perspectives within the same page or group	Currently the groups' practice when it comes to activism is self-absorbed: organize, document, and publish. Practice is copied. On the other hand, some groups and individuals that used to publish on Facebook every single activity moved to active fieldwork	Pages and groups have members and followers who are supporters but also detractors. Then it depends on how far the comments are managed or not and the tolerance of different points of view and controversy
Alignment	Accountability and alignment are difficult to assess on Facebook. We can see from the event organized to support the Turkish Occupy Movement (1700 signed to attend and 35 went) that there is no real alignment	In some cases, intentions, commitments, norms, and traditions are made clear, but this is not always the case, and people are not necessarily interested or following the "agreed" or "established" norms	The administrators of pages and groups define "contracts" and "compromises." These are not necessarily followed. The differences in the pages come from the practice of the administrator, and the number of followers and their interests

Table 9.3 Identity dimensions

Identity	Connectedness	Expansiveness	Effectiveness
Engagement	Not all the pages and groups represent a community to engage with. It depends on administrators. There are differences between individual or organizations pages and Facebook groups, but there is no clear line because it depends on the administrators The pages are more open and participation is more diverse than the groups. The Uprising of Women in the Arab World gained huge regional visibility through it campaign on Facebook. Based on this success and for International Women Day (IWD) 2013 it organized a media campaign partnering with local NGOs featuring posters in various Arab cities There are clear communities on Tunisian Facebook. We could classify successful pages and groups as • professionals: for example, journalists; • pages with anonymous administrators but with a political or social aim; • pages and groups with clear objectives.	Expansiveness is one of the characteristics of Facebook, and new links are created between people (e.g. Tunisian and Turkish activists)	The success of pages and groups comes from the social competencies of their administrators

(continued)

Table 9.3 (continued)

Identity	Connectedness	Expansiveness	Effectiveness
Imagination	Conversations happen on few pages, where administrators are dedicating time and focus on specific issues	Members are defining themselves in wider regional and global communities, and they share references and a motto	Various reflections started on Facebook on what being Tunisian means in terms of cultural identity. However, there is no mechanism to make ideas converge
Alignment	Commitment to the community comes from the administrators. Mostly when principles are made clear, they are followed by the main participants On a page it is difficult to define what is shared by the followers but there is a common understanding of the page owner's views	The interests of participants and followers are difficult to establish but the page's administrators have wide interests	Accountability is not clear. Convincing others is possible and depends on affiliation to political ideas

9.6 INTERPRETATION OF THE RESEARCH FINDINGS

9.6.1 Facebook's Contribution to Social Learning

For Wenger (2000), "in a social learning system, competence is historically and socially defined…Knowing, therefore, is a matter of displaying competences defined in social communities." He defines three forms of belonging to social learning systems: engagement, imagination, and alignment. The data collected shows that Facebook allows a range of forms of engagement. It goes from discussing the political events in the country, the reforms that should be developed, to mobilizing for an event. It also allows imagination, and constructing an image of people, mainly through groups, pages liked, and persons followed. Alignment is also possible, and we observed national, regional, and international links created between groups and individuals based on perspectives and shared values.

9.6.2 Development of New Ideas in the Tunisian Women's Movement's Forms of Activism

The Jasmine Revolution in Tunisia and the "transition" created a new "nationalism" and "national pride," both alimenting civil and political interest and engagement. The initiatives multiplied and were reflected on Facebook. New civil society organizations were created and these set up Facebook pages and profiles. Individuals and small groups created groups discussing issues relevant to the transition, including gender equality. This is in contrast with the period before the revolution when civil society organizations were limited in numbers, depoliticized if not created to defend the government. Only five NGOs,[21] among them two women's organizations, were independent and faced huge restrictions, limiting the visibility of their work at the national level. The data shows that the two women's organizations, the ATFD and the AFTURD, did not use Facebook consistently, while new groups and organizations were more visible, more aggressive, and more innovative in defending gender equality on Facebook, as is the case with the newly created organization Equality and Parity, which led the campaign on women's political representation and participation.

The groups and pages created on Facebook by Tunisian groups and individuals translate the enthusiasm created by the Jasmine Revolution. This made the Tunisian people realize that everything is possible. New ideas were pouring into groups and pages, as shown by the number of emerging Tunisian cartoonists[22] on Facebook. However, as shown by the analysis, while imagination and engagement were predominant forms of interacting on Facebook, alignment was more problematic. The disruption created by the revolution shook traditional structures and allowed the emergence of a new vanguard. This started to organize itself and make connections through Facebook. The analysis of the data shows that groups and individuals are getting connected depending on their identities and values. This is the case for "new journalists"[23] using social media for their work, bloggers, public figures, and administrators of pages with thousands of followers. In fact, these new profiles and new vanguard were quicker in integrating the possibilities provided by Facebook. Until the end of August 2013, the Tunisian women's groups and organizations struggled to use Facebook consistently, and their profiles and pages were unevenly updated and their visibility and outreach limited. Communications regarding the events organized by the Tunisian women's movement for International Women's Day (March 8) or for the commemoration of the CPS (August 13) were led by coalitions in which women's organizations participated: the Tunisian General Labour Union[24] and the Union for Tunisia, respectively.[25]

9.6.3 A Framework for Social Learning for the Tunisian Women's Movement: The Issues of Values and Ethics

The data showed with Femen Tunisia, an International Women's Rights activists group, how the issues of values and ethics are treated and linked to public opinion through Facebook. The ATFD[26] was the first to announce its support of the group after the arrest of one of its member. For many others it took several days and various press articles and notes shared on Facebook to create a wider solidarity movement. Other issues of ethics and values are related, for example, to the blurring boundaries of the dimensions of Facebook's communities. As seen in the data analysis, Facebook is too loose to allow accountability. In the transition period in Tunisia, one of the emergent sectors is the increasing number of news websites and electronic media that are not bound to professionalism and ethics. Facebook users are sharing in their hunger for news that confirm their convictions, so in some cases a Facebook page will publish news, which is then published elsewhere without the sources being checked. We also noticed in the participatory observation, which is part of the methodology used for the research, that even well-established media do not always publish contradictory information, even when it is available.

9.6.4 Facebook and Outreach, Mobilization, and Lobbying Strategies

The data showed that in the events organized through Facebook there was a huge difference between the number of persons showing interest and committing to attend and the numbers of attendees. It also showed that organizations, activists, political leaders, and cartoonists used Facebook to increase their visibility and make their vision known, and then they moved to fieldwork. Therefore we can say that Facebook offers tools that enable and strengthen activism, such as outreach, advocacy, lobbying, and improving visibility. Other forms of activism cannot happen on Facebook, so clearly there is a need to combine approaches and methodologies to have more impact, and to increase the efficiency of interventions.

Facebook offers space and tools for social learning. Communities of practice, formed through pages, and groups with learning energy and self-awareness, are building social capital. Some of the pages and groups have a clear leadership structure with one or more administrators sharing tasks. The data showed that even if there were no rules about the role of a page's administrator, learning takes place through the evolution and change happening on certain pages and the non-evolution and "death" of others. The existence of vision on certain pages and defined ways for participation show leadership. Connectivity is achieved through discussions around the perspective and project of society defended by the pages, while membership includes both supporters of and opponents to the vision put forward by the page.

In terms of boundaries, the artifacts offered to the communities of practice created through Facebook are loose. Pages include all kinds of membership, while groups depend on the rules established by the administrator and therefore will have more or less limited participation. In most cases the rules established by administrators do not limit contradictory points of view but rather aggression. Coordination occurs in more homogeneous groups while transparency is variable. The administrators of some pages use nicknames but defend clear political and social perspectives and have to face rumors that they are on the pay roll of certain political parties. Negotiation is difficult because the divide is exacerbated by the perspective of elections, with two visions of the model of the society Tunisians aspire to, at least still in this stage.

The issue of the "model of society" that Tunisians aspire to, secular or Islamic, is linked to the issue of identities in communities on Facebook during the Tunisian transition. This is the main cause of cleavage in the society, as shown by the debates, groups, and pages. The question of identity and role of women in it is shaping connectedness and expansiveness with an increase of the links created at the regional level. The support from Tunisian secularists for the Turkish Occupy Gezi Movement is an example of these newly created regional, and wider, connections. Effectiveness is limited in a way by the cleavage between identities, which limits the focus on issues that would have been important in a transition period, such as accountability or reform of the security sector.

9.7 Recommendations Moving Forward

Facebook definitely offers useful tools for outreach, advocacy, lobbying, and visibility. Despite the debate about activism vs. slacktivism, it is clear that the former has different forms and that social media, and particularly

Facebook, can contribute to some forms and not others. The tools and artifacts observed in this research clearly do not contribute to fundraising but help to increase the visibility and profile of individuals, groups, and organizations.

> Recommendation 1: Women's organizations, and also social movements, should have clear strategies to be able to benefit from the opportunities for visibility, outreach, and impact on public opinion that are offered by Facebook, which are currently free. Visibility and outreach can easily be turned into opportunities for funding from others. Facebook also offers tools for networking and connectivity that did not exist in the past. These are also concomitant with a new mindset created by the revolution in Tunisia and probably by the new generation's familiarity with information technology. It is relevant to keep in mind, for example, that the Tunisian uprising was preceded by a campaign against internet censorship where new actors appeared. These were internet geeks who fought against censorship and were different from the human rights advocates and the generation of political activists that preceded them.
>
> Recommendation 2: Women's organizations need to integrate opportunities for connectivity and networking offered by Facebook into their work. There is a need to gather information and carry out analysis on these new tools and their users, and build evidence on how to make a difference, learning from the processes that are emerging from the change in the mindset particularly among Tunisian youth. Facebook offers platforms for learning, organizing, connecting, discussing, and building social movements. The Tunisian Revolution created the change in mindset that generated a huge interest in politics but much more in social solidarity, in citizenship movement, and in social movement. The gap between the rich and poor areas and the lack of democracy were acknowledged reasons for the uprising. Movements and groups were newly created to address these issues.
>
> Recommendation 3: Women's organizations, and social movements in general, can build spaces for learning where best practices are shared more systematically. This will maximize the impact and speed of learning, and will integrate more youth and probably new profiles into the movements. The Tunisian women's movement, and mainly the organizations that existed during the Ben Ali era, began the tran-

sition period with huge capital internationally and within the human rights and political elite. However, they failed to extend the visibility and use social media tools like Facebook once it was possible to do so and stayed within their known areas of expertise and their "traditional" operating practice.

Recommendation 4: Women's organizations should work systematically and strategically on their visibility and presence on social media. This should be done in a more professional way to ensure consistency, coherence, and alignment with their vision and strategy. The groups and pages with clear leaderships are the ones that make a difference and create interactions and interest on Facebook. These pages have rules and dynamic content. The question of ethics is also important and in many cases it is a factor in selection by followers and subscribers. Some of the leaders in the Tunisian women's movement surprisingly publish/share non-verified news on their own profiles but as public figures they should be much more selective.

Recommendation 5: Women's organizations and social movements should have clear "editorial" rules for their Facebook pages, and their leaders and members, as public figures, should even be careful about their personal pages. Questions of ethics and values should be addressed in a very consistent way.

9.8 Concluding Remarks

The Tunisian Revolution opened up the world of the possible to Tunisian people, who started dreaming about what their country could be. Facebook offered the opportunity for everybody to share ideas and discuss possibilities. These ideas are new and innovative in some cases but they are also widely scattered and not necessarily moving towards the center of any particular debate because of the effervescence generated by the uprising but with a lack of leadership and systems to channel this energy and possibilities. In fact the discussions and the different forums show the emergence of new actors that are disqualifying the vanguard and elite that existed in the country. The organizations of the women's movement and the members of the new groups were seen as elitist and were accused by Islamists of being complacent about the former regime. The organizations and individuals were not able till now to have a coherent strategy to give coherence and structure to their messages. However, there are signs that questions of values and ethics are emerging to structure the debates. There are two groups of values emerging and contrasting each other—one related to Islam and the second to human rights—and these are starting to give legitimacy to the persons and structures participating in the debate.

The ideological references and values are creating networks and opposing communities, where ideas are shared, discussed, and criticized, through participation with others. However, it is still individuals that are making a difference rather than organizations with structured and systematized strategies, at least in the case of the women's movement. The context as it is reflected in Facebook communities is volatile and changing at a quick pace, and social learning is accelerating.

Notes

1. The newly elected Tunisian president acknowledged that Tunisian women largely voted for him, amounting to 60 % of the voters.
2. Yves Gonzalez-Quijano, 2012, *Arabités Numériques: Le Printemps du Web Arabe*.
3. Written Arabic using Latin letters and numbers emerging from the use of mobile phone text messaging and social media.
4. Tunisian Islamist ruling party.
5. Bourguiba was known as the Tunisian women liberator and the builder of modern Tunisia, and many modernists today in their fight against a backlash, and the threat that the possible introduction of Sharia law might represent, refer to him. This article in *The Economist*, published when he died in 2000, summarizes his legacy, which is part of current debate. http://www.economist.com/node/303168
6. President of the association Equality and Parity.
7. Reformist Ottoman minister in Tunisia.
8. Tunisian Association of Democratic Women.
9. Association of Tunisian Women on Research and Development.
10. Some 17 organizations mainly created after the uprising signed a call for equality in August 2011 for the celebration of the CPS.
11. The coverage of the demonstration of April 9, 2013, commemorating the Tunisian martyrs, highlights the number of women who joined the demonstration of "the Union for Tunisia," a coalition of five modernist parties. http://jadal.tn/22580 published and accessed 09/04/2013
12. http://www.musawah.org/about-musawah
13. http://www.wisemuslimwomen.org/about/shuracouncil/
14. http://gierfi.org/
15. "Slacktivists Take Note: We Don't Like Your Likes", Brendan Rigby. Published July 15, 2013 and accessed July 21, 2013. http://www.whydev.org/slacktivists-take-note-we-dont-like-your-likes/

16. Why the World's Biggest Aid Agency Wants More Fans on Facebook by Justin Smith published 18/7/2013 and accessed 25/07/2013 http://www.huffingtonpost.com/justin-smith/world-food-programme_b_3584932.html
17. https://www.facebook.com/WorldFoodProgramme/app_624054217607158
18. http://en.wikipedia.org/wiki/Community (accessed 06/05/2013)
19. http://www.undp.org/content/undp/en/home/ourwork/womenempowerment/inside_undp/knowledge_management/
20. The half-life of knowledge is the amount of time that has to elapse before half of the knowledge in a particular area is superseded or shown to be untrue. https://en.wikipedia.org/wiki/Half-life_of_knowledge accessed 20/08/2013.
21. These are the Tunisian League of Human Rights, Amnesty International Tunisian section, the Association of Young Lawyers, the ATFD, and the AFTURD.
22. http://www.yakayaka.org/ is a website with a continuously growing community of Tunisian cartoonists.
23. For example, Emna Ben Jemma, who has a radio program on Express FM called *Hashtag*. She asks her page's followers for ideas and contributions to her program.
24. Union Générale Tunisienne du Travail,, the oldest, largest, and most respected workers' union in the country.
25. A five-party coalition representing the main opposition.
26. The ATFD.

BIBLIOGRAPHY

Aday, S., H. Farrel, D. Freelon, M. Lynch, J. Sides, and M. Dewar. 2013. Watching from Afar: Media Consumption Patterns Around the Arab Spring. *American Behavioral Scientist* 57 (7): 899–919.

Aid, S. 2012. Assessment of Tunisian Civil Society. http://www.pdcs.sk/files//file/Projekty/CSO%20Needs%20Assessment%20Tunisia%20Final%20PUBLIC.pdf. Published April 2012 and accessed April 4, 2013.

Al-Momani, M. 2011. The Arab "Youth Quake": Implications on Democratization and Stability. *Middle East and Governance* 3: 159–170.

Aouragh, M. 2012. Social Media, Mediation and the Arab Revolutions. *Triple C* 10 (N2): 518–536.

Arieff, A. 2012. Political Transition in Tunisia. http://www.fas.org/sgp/crs/row/RS21666.pdf. Published 18 June 2012 and accessed April 7, 2013.

Axford, B. 2011. Talk about a Revolution: Social Media and the MENA Uprisings. *Globalizations* 8 (5): 681–686.

B'chir, N. 2013. La guere sainte des milices electroniques d'Ennahdha. http://www.businessnews.com.tn/La-%C2%AB-guerre-sainte-%C2%BB-des-milices-%C3%A9lectroniques-d%E2%80%99Ennahdha,519,36653,3. Published March 1, 2013 and accessed March 3, 2013.

Bawden, R. 2010. The Community Challenge: The Learning Response. In *Social Learning Systems and Communities of Practice*, ed. C. Blackmore. London: The Open University.

Belkaid, A. 2013. Internet and the Arab Spring. http://akram-belkaid.blogspot.com/2013/01/internet-and-arab-spring.html. Published 26 January 2013 and Accessed 4 Nov 2013.

Bryant, E. 2012. Tunisians Worry About Loss of Freedoms Gained Under the Arab Spring. http://www.huffingtonpost.com/2012/10/06/tunisians-arab-spring-loss-of-freedom_n_1944218.html. Posted 10 June 2012 and Accessed 14 Jan 2013.

Castells, M. 2000. Toward a Sociology of the Network Society. *Contemporary Sociology* 29 (5): 693–699.

Charfi, F. 2013. La resistance des femmes tunisiennes face au projet hegemonique islamiste. http://www.leaders.com.tn/article/la-resistance-des-femmes-tunisiennes-un-combat-face-au-projet-hegemonique-islamiste?id=11083. Published 25 March 2013 and Accessed 2 Apr 2013.

Chatti, M.A., M. Jarke, and M. Specht. 2010. The 3 P Learning Model. *Educational Technology & Science*. 13 (4): 74–85.

Churchill, E. 2013. Tahar Haddad: A Towering Figure for Women's Rights in Tunisia. http://menablog.worldbank.org/tahar-haddad-towering-figure-women%E2%80%99s-rights-tunisia. Published 8 March 2013 and Accessed 3 Apr 2013.

Cohen, H. 2012. From Social Media to Social Energy: The Idea of the "Social" in "Social Media". http://www.commarts.uws.edu.au/gmjau/v6_2012_1/hart_cohen_ra.html. Accessed 11 Dec 2012.

Coleman, I. 2011. Women and the Arab Revolts. *Brown Journal of World Affairs* XVIII (1): 197–210.

Comunelo, F., and G. Anzera. 2012. Will the Revolution Be Tweeted? A Conceptual Framework for Understanding the Social Media and the Arab Spring. *Islam and Christian-Muslim Relations* 23 (4): 453–470.

Dahmani, F. 2012. Tunisia: Civil Society is Appearing. http://www.jeuneafrique.com/Article/JA2679p050-051.xml0/. Published 23 May 2012 and Accessed 15 Oct 12.

de Laat, M.F., and P.R.J. Simons. 2002. Collective Learning: Theoretical Perspectives and Ways to Support Networked Learning. *Vocational Training: European Journal* 27: 13–24.

Dhaouadi, M. 2013. Tunisia: The backlash in Women Rights Amid Rocky Political Transition. http://www.opendemocracy.net/meriem-dhaouadi/tunisia-backlash-in-women%E2%80%98s-rights-amid-rocky-political-transition. Published 12 March 2013 and Accessed 7 Apr 2013.

Dubruelh, C. 2011. Tunisie: Mystere autour de l'emergence d'un nouveau movementdefemmes. http://www.jeuneafrique.com/Article/ARTJAWEB2011110 5145033/. Published 5 November 2011 and Accessed 10 Mar 2013.

Garcia, E., F. Annansingh, and I. Elbeltagi. 2011. Management Perception of Introducing Social Networking Sites as a Knowledge Management Tool in Higher Education. *Multicultural Education & Technology Journal.* 5 (4): 258–273.

Gehrke, M. 2012. Arab Spring Revolutions Don't Reach Women. http://www.dw.de/arab-spring-revolutions-dont-reach-women/a-16403996. Published 25 November 2012 and Accessed 13 Jan 2013.

Ghanem, R. 2011. Arabizi is Destroying the Arabic Language. http://www.arabnews.com/node/374897. Published 19 April 2011 and Accessed 31 Mar 2013.

Giacomo, C. 2012. Women Fight to Define the Arab Spring. http://www.nytimes.com/2012/11/11/opinion/sunday/women-fight-to-define-the-arab-spring.html?_r=0. Published 10 November 2012 and Accessed 14 Jan 2013.

Gladwell, M. 2000. Small Change, Why the Revolution Will Not be Tweeted. http://www.newyorker.com/reporting/2010/10/04/101004fa_fact_gladwell?printable=true&currentPage=all. Published 4 October 2010 and Accessed 4 June 2013.

Goldsboroughs, R. 2011. Slacktivism is Becoming the New Activism. http://www.ccweek.com/news/templates/template.aspx?articleid=2296&zoneid=3. Published 10 January 2011 and Accessed 8 Jan 2013.

Harryson, M., E. Metayer, and H. Sarrazin. 2012. How Social Intelligence Can Guide Decisions. *McKinsey Quarterly* 4: 81–89.

Hawkins, S. 2011. Who Wears Hijab with the President: Constructing a Modern Islam in Tunisia. *Journal of Religion in Africa* 41: 35–58.

International Republican Institute. 2012. Tunisia: Overview. http://www.iri.org/sites/default/files/Tunisia%202-2012.pdf. Published 2012 and Accessed 7 Apr 2013.

Joseph, S. 2011. Social Media, Human Rights and Political Change. *Boston College International & Comparative Law Review* 35: 145.

Krifa, A. 2012. La question des Femmes en Tunisie: Droits, Luttes et Perspectives. Inter-peuples 204. http://www.ciip.fr/docum/docel/FTunisie.pdf. Published February 2012 and Accessed 1 Mar 2013.

Kubler, J. (2011). Les revolutions arabes et le web 2.0: Tunisie et Egypte Revue Averroes, Numero 4–5, Special "Printemps Arabe".

Latte Abdallah, S. 2012. Theologiennes feminists de l'Islam. http://www.lemonde.fr/idees/article/2013/02/18/theologiennes-feministes-de-l-islam_1834339_3232.html. Published in le Monde 18 February 2013 and Accessed 20 Feb 2013.

Leduc, S. 2012. The Unfinished Revolution of Tunisia's Women. http://www.france24.com/en/20120307-tunisia-unfinished-revolution-international-women-day-rights-islamist. Published 8 March 2012 and Accessed 14 Jan 2013.

Lee, K.N. 1993. *Compass and Gyroscope: Integrating Science and Politics for the Environment*. Washington, DC: Island Press.

Lewis, A. 2011. Tunisia protests: Cyber War Mirrors Unrest on Streets. http://www.bbc.co.uk/news/world-africa-12180954. Published 14 January 2011 and Accessed 15 Oct 2012.

Madrigal, A. 2011. The Inside Story of How Facebook Responded to Tunisian Hacks. http://www.theatlantic.com/technology/archive/2011/01/the-inside-story-of-how-facebook-responded-to-tunisian-hacks/70044/. Published 24 January 2011 and Accessed 19 Nov 2012.

Mandraud, I. 2012. Tunisia: Civil Society Resistance. http://www.lemonde.fr/international/article/2012/07/06/la-resistance-de-la-societe-civile_1730381_3210.html. Published 6 July 2012 and Accessed 15 Oct 2012.

McCafferty, D. 2011. Activism Vs. Slacktivism. *Communications of the ACM* 54 (12): 17–19.

Nasr, O. 2013. Post Revolution: Women Are Tunisia Biggest Losers. http://english.alarabiya.net/en/views/2013/04/09/Post-revolution-women-are-Tunisia-s-biggest-losers.html. Published 9 April 2013 and Accessed 9 Apr 2013.

Prince, R. 2011. Tunisia: Yezzi Fock (It's Enough). http://www.opendemocracy.net/rob-prince/tunisia-yezzi-fock-it%E2%80%99s-enough. Published 13 January 2011 and Accessed 19 Nov 2012.

Ray, T. 2011. The "Story" of Digital Media Excess in Revolutions of the Arab Spring. *Journal of Media Practice* 12 (2): 189–196.

Reardon, S. 2012. Social Revolution? It's a Myth. *New Scientist* 214 (2859): 24.

Rennick, S.A. 2013. Personal Grievance Sharing, Frame Alignment, and Hybrid Organizational Structures: The Role of Social Media in North Africa's 2011 Uprisings. *Journal of Contemporary African Studies* 31 (2): 156–174.

Salem, F., and R. Mourtada. 2011. The Role of Social Media in Arab's Women's Empowerment. Arab Social Media Report. Nov 2011. Vol 1. N3. Dubai School of Government.

Schön, D.A. 1973. Beyond the Stable State. New York: The Norton Library (first published in 1971).

Shelly, D. 2012. Transforming Tunisia: The Role of Civil Society in Tunisia's Transition. http://www.international-alert.org/sites/default/files/publications/Tunisia2013EN.pdf. Published February 2013 and Accessed 4 Apr 2013.

Skandrani, F. 2012. L'histoire du Mouvement Feministe Tunisien. http://journal.alternatives.ca/spip.php?article7056. Published 3 December 2013 and Accessed 20 Feb 2013.

Tukefci, Z. 2013. Is There a Social-Media Fueled Protest Style? An Analysis From #25Jan to #gezipark. http://technosociology.org/?p=1255. Published 1 June 2013 and Accessed 4 June 2013

Ulrich, W. 2005. A Brief Introduction to Critical Systems Heuristics (CSH). http://projects.kmi.open.ac.uk/ecosensus/publications/ulrich_csh_intro.pdf. Published 2005 and Accessed 14 Apr 2013.

Wenger, E. 2000. Communities of Practice and Social Learning Systems. *Organization* 7: 225.

Woodhill, J. 2002. Adapted from Woodhill (1999) Sustainability, Social Learning and the Democratic Imperative: Lessons from the Australian Landcare Movement. In *Social Learning Systems and Communities of Practice*, ed. C. Blackmore. London: The Open University, 2010.

Wyne, J. 2012. Arab Health Care and Online Development. http://www.ssireview.org/blog/entry/arab_health_care_and_online_development. Published 29 November 2012 and Accessed 6 Jan 2013.

Zuckerman, E. 2012. Cute Cats and the Arab Spring. http://www.scoop.it/t/mobilizing-knowledge-through-complex-networks. Published in April 2012 and Accessed 14 Apr 2013.

PART 3

Unfinished Legal Revolutions

CHAPTER 10

Gendering the Law in Egypt: A Tale of Two Constitutions

Lubna Fröhlich (Azzam)

10.1 Introduction: Women on the Way to Becoming Real Citizens?

The Arab Spring, and the current social movements with their transformative impulses, have grave consequences for women. I chose one country to illustrate this. It is the most populous Arab country and the one with a long history of women's activism dating back to the end of the nineteenth century (Al-Ali 2000; Badran 1995). Women[1] helped to spark the revolutions, beginning with a policewoman in Tunisia, being further enflamed in Egypt by a call for popular protest among young Egyptian women on the country's national police day. Asma Mahfouz, a young veiled woman who called for civil disobedience in January 2011 and helped to inspire the events around what is now termed the "Revolution",[2] contributed to Mubarak's ousting.

Women were visibly present in Egypt's Tahrir (Liberation) Square, demanding the right of democratic participation for Egyptians in their own society. Women and men felt so much a part of a larger common goal that they transcended gender and societal norms, sleeping next to each other, and sharing food. Even more remarkable was "the total absence of sexual

L. Fröhlich (Azzam) (✉)
Frankfurt, Germany

harassment and the acceptance of women as equals in the face of the autocracy that was about to be ruptured and decimated" (Sholkamy 2012, 155).

This in fact coincides with my research data, which I gathered in the period 2012–2015. One prominent female human rights activist and member of the Constituent Assembly (CA) in 2012, who very publically withdrew from the process before the drafting of the final 2012 document, stated: "So *all* the people have hope. Feeling like I have my country. *I am a citizen.*"[3]

Women's activism didn't start here; women also participated in the twentieth-century uprisings against British rule and have been intimately linked with national movements since the 1890s. Sexual harassment, which affects all women in Egypt, and which increased under Mubarak, is an ongoing challenge facing women upon entering the public sphere. It is used as a means of intimidating them and may be regarded as being structurally and institutionally condoned (by the Islamists, the military, and others), and it is the quintessential expression of the ruling patriarchal culture. This became painfully apparent on January 25, 2013 (the second anniversary of the revolution), when women were sexually assaulted publicly by groups of young men and the security forces failed to intervene.

Since 2011 there have been two constitutional referendums with two very different outcomes for women's codified rights—but also from the general tenor of the constitutional document itself. The 2012 constitution was passed with a majority of 66 %[4] but became redundant following the military coup of July 3, 2013. This led to the drafting of the current constitution, which represents an important step forward regarding normative gender equality in Egypt. This does not necessarily yet translate into real lived equality but it may be viewed both as a starting point and as the continuation of legislative change in the past.

10.2 Theoretical Background and Considerations

This chapter embraces Waylen's understanding of the kind of citizenship that such "liberalization" should achieve as one that is based on "full inclusion" (Waylen 2007). This is defined in the "broadest sense to include social and economic as well as civil and political rights" (16).

In this regard, the "full inclusion" of women's rights into the constitution of 2014 is an important criterion for equality. The approach of this chapter is from a universalist feminist human rights perspective, cognizant of the cultural specificities of the context.

This does not mean that the religious nature of Egyptian society is ignored but it is simply not given preferential treatment regarding women's equality. Analyzing gender law in Arab Spring countries requires an acknowledgment of the importance of religion in all aspects of society and for all religious communities. According to Donnelly, many cultural relativist arguments either ignore politics or confuse it with culture by confusing "what a people has been forced to tolerate with what it values" (Donnelly 2007, 296). Cultural relativism erroneously presupposes culture as a monolithic, homogenous, static and uncontested entity. On the contrary, he asserts, "Culture is not destiny—or, to the extent that it is, that is only because victorious elements in a particular society have used their power to make a particular, contingent destiny" (296).

Including women as full and equal citizens is a vital cornerstone regarding the ideational democratization of the country, and this was done in Article 11 of the 2014 Egyptian constitution. In this sense it may be asserted that the 2012 constitution excluded women, choosing to focus on the term "citizen" instead.

10.3 A Brief Look at the History of Women's Rights Activism in Egypt

An important watershed occurred in 1980 under Sadat with a constitutional amendment declaring Islam the religion of the state. This has grave implications for women to this day.

Looking at more recent history, on January 25, 2011, people gathered in Tahrir Square and demanded changes to the old Mubarak regime. They did this using the same slogans used during the "revolution"[5] of 1952 (Tadroz 2012). In the short term they were successful in these demands. Five years later, Egypt had witnessed two further regime shifts, democratic parliamentary and presidential elections, and two constitutional referendums. Democracy and freedom from authoritarian rule still appear to be far hopes, however.

In societies where religion defines identity, liberal democracy cannot be negotiated without reference to religious politics (Hashemi 2009). This is evident when one follows the debates surrounding women's constitutional rights. Ann Elisabeth Mayer (1995) makes the case that Middle Eastern governments use cultural relativism as a means to continue discrimination against women and deny them equal rights. Despite the fact that Egypt signed the Convention on the Elimination of All Forms of Discrimination Against Women (CEDAW), where signatories are required to comply with its provisions, it also signed the 1990 Cairo Declaration on Human Rights in Islam, which deems Islamic law as superior to human rights law, and thus it failed to change legislation in women's favor. This is still evident today in the retention of Article 2 of the constitution.

Women became visibly active in the 1919 rebellion against the British occupation, but their activism dates back even further, to the 1890s. The emergence of a nationalist movement and a women's movement coincided at that time, although it was no coincidence. According to Badran, the Egyptian women's movement and the nationalist movement became intertwined at this juncture and continued to be so for the rest of the century (Badran 1991). Women's liberation became closely linked with liberation from British rule, and women took to the streets demanding both personal freedom within the realm of the family and freedom from foreign rule (Stachursky 2013).

10.3.1 Egyptian Constitutions in the Past and Gender Law

The 1980 constitutional amendment, defining the Sharia not only as a main source of legislation, but as *the* main source of legislation (Dupret 2005, 163), was a turning point in Egyptian history. It came at an important moment for the entire region, following on the heels of the 1979 Islamic Revolution in Iran and "re-Islamization" across the region. From then on, Islam became the official state religion in Egypt. This was reflected in Article 2 of 1971 constitution: "Islam is the religion of the State and Arabic its official language. Islamic law (Sharia) is the principal source of legislation" (www.constitutionnet.org 2014).

This means that women's legal status must comply with "The principles of the Islamic Sharia" (www.sis.gov.eg 2014).

This vital article remains in place in the current constitution and reflects the ethos of this and previous constitution(s), hence as indicated by its prominent position. Ever since it was introduced, women activists have been trying in vain to get it removed. Legal change in women's favor is a slow process but has been taking place in Egypt since the foundation of the independent state (1952). It has to be asserted that the presence of this article is somewhat contradictory in relation to the new Article 11 of the

2014 constitution. This explicitly states women's equality with men and could be seen to be in conflict with "the principles of the Sharia," which emphasizes complimentary roles between women and men in the public and private spheres. Equality may not be confused with complementarity.

Despite what may perceived as a top-heavy state, Fahmy insists that it is in fact weak rather than strong. I would even claim that the strong use of force on the part of the security apparatus may be viewed as evidence of weakness. Here it demonstrates that it does not find it necessary to comply on the grounds of societal consensus but uses force to implement and protect its interests: "The weakness of the Egyptian state is manifested in its failure to penetrate society and transform it" (Fahmy 2002, 35).

This transformation has perhaps started to shift since January 25, 2011. It may still be too early to assess the situation but the wording of the 2014 constitution may be indicative of a watershed in Egyptian history.

Ostensively strong, the Egyptian state is as such weak. This was demonstrated by its lack of ability to transform independently and to represent all sections of society. This in turn has consequences for the structure of Egypt's civil society: because society and state are weak in Egypt, evolutionary trends did not develop. On the contrary, the weakness of the state equalled societal weakness and the system was preserved until January 25, 2011 and Mubarak's withdrawal. This was confounded by economic stagnation and a social status quo.

10.4 THE 1971 CONSTITUTION

In the past, some legal experts have claimed that women's rights were formally well codified in Egypt, while the main problem was with their implementation (Al-Gebali). In the 1971 constitution, Articles 8 and 40 stated that all citizens were equal and that "the state guarantees the equal opportunity of all citizens." In Article 40 there was an explicit ban on discrimination based on creed, race, or religion but without the mention of sex or gender. In the 2012 constitution there was no such article, one of various issues creating controversy among those trying to improve women's rights, and which also led to the withdrawal of prominent CA members.[6] By excluding this article, the 2012 constitution must be seen as negligent regarding the prohibition of discrimination against and protection of the individual. Its adoption in December 2012 was regarded as a severe blow to civic rights and freedoms which were no longer mentioned explicitly.

Beyond this, Article 5 of the 1971 constitution explicitly codified a weak commitment to non-discrimination, banning the founding of parties based on gender or racial discrimination. The relevant passage is: "It is prohibited, however, to exercise any political activity or to found any political party based on religious considerations or on discrimination on grounds of gender or race." This article was possibly aimed at the Muslim Brotherhood.

There was also a clear commitment on the part of the state concerning anti-discrimination and equality in Article 40. It was as follows: "All citizens are equal before the law. They have equal rights and duties without discrimination between them due to race, ethnic origin, language, religion or creed (Constitution of Egypt 1971).

It should be noted here that women and gender are not mentioned explicitly but the general term "citizen" is used to include both. Article 11 of the 2014 constitution may be regarded as an important improvement.

10.5 Women's Codified Rights Since 2011: The Story of Two Constitutions

It is important to note that what is excluded in a constitutional text is just as important as what is included. The 2012 constitutional process was an interesting one regarding gender relations and demonstrated a blatant disregard for women's rights. Not only was the process deeply flawed but so was the final document (which was ratified by popular referendum in December 2012), as stated by an activist and CA member of 2013.[7]

The previous constituent assembly (CA) had been disolved in March 2012 by the parliament because it was deemed unrepresentative. In the final sitting of the CA on November 29, 2012, there were only 85 delegates present, four of whom were women.

Prior to the establishment of the CA that eventually drew up the new constitution, there had been a predecessor established in March of 2012. It was dissolved by the Cairo Administrative Court in April 2012. The second CA was formed in June 2012 following negotiations between lawmakers and the Supreme Council of the Armed Forces, which ruled the country at that time. In addition to parliamentarians, seats were set aside for representatives of the Coptic Church, Al-Azhar, journalists, and military officers, among others. As the CA had been elected by parliament, and parliament was dissolved by court order in June 2012, the CA was again under threat to be dissolved by a court decision. In the final sitting of the CA on November 29, 2012 there were only 85 delegates present, four of them women (none of whom had a history of activism on women's human rights). This is important, it was the cause of much aggrievement amongst women's activists.

The CA was divided into the main parties and a number of their representatives. Of the 100 seats, the Muslim Brotherhood held 16, Salafi an-Nour 8, the New Wafd Party 5, the Egyptian Social Democratic Party 2, the Free Egyptians Party 2, the Building and Development Party 1, the Al-Wasat Party 1, the Reform and Development Misruna Party 1, the Socialist Popular Alliance Party 1, the Dignity Party 1 and independents 61. When the 2012 constitution was formulated during a 16-hour sitting on November 27, 2012, there were only four women present of the 85 members of the original 100-member CA. The women were not members of a civil society community, nor did they have a history of women's rights activism. Article 36, in favor of women's rights, was excluded entirely because despite attempts to find suitable wording, the different factions failed to reach an agreement.[8]

The CA was conservative and this was reflected in the constitutional draft it produced. It was also emphasized by one member of the 2013 CA that the group was vociferously against women's rights. One such woman was Azza Gharf one of the most prominent female members of the Muslim Brotherhood. There was a perception that a group of women who had no interest in improving women's human rights was included in the process. On the positive side, she said that following the efforts of women's rights advocates and activism to participate in the 2012 process, the subsequent complete exclusion of Article 36 created important momentum vis-à-vis the 2013 process.[9] Other factors such as the secular military economic complex also played a large role in this becoming a nominal success for women's postive legal rights. Members of civil society have thus criticized the composition of the CA. Despite promises to the contrary from the Muslim Brotherhood's side, 60 % of the CA was composed of representatives stemming from the Muslim Brotherhood and around 15 % were Salafis, adding up to an overwhelming three-quarters majority of Islamists. This left some observers from civil society and academia with "a very uneasy feeling."[10]

The National Council for Women had suggested several female members for the CA but none of these were selected to represent women's interests but rather simply because they were women and towed the party line. Among the seven women representatives, two were members of parliament from the Muslim Brotherhood-linked Freedom and Justice Party, one was a member of the International Islamic Committee for Women and Children, two were academics (one a liberal), one was a political activist and a member of the El-Wafd Party, and one was a representative of the non-governmental organization community with a liberal position. Thus women's interests were severely underrepresented in the CA, but it wasn't only about numbers, as I was made aware by one interviewee. It was more about the "group of women"[11] involved in the process, who were perceived as having very little interest in increasing women's rights and had little or no background/history of pro-women's activism. In addition, women's rights advocates favored women's nominal equality in the form of the term "equal citizen" in the constitution. This is a most nebulous term, meaning all and nothing at all. Of course women are citizens, no one would dispute this but what about the structural inequality they are faced with on a daily basis in Egypt? There was also a certain tension between the various factions within the assembly. Whereas some female members were perceived as being too adamant in their attempts to achieve their aims, others expressed a deep sense of betrayal from the liberal sections within the body because of their lack of support. This suggests a non-cohesive atmosphere among the members of the committee charged with formulating the constitution.[12]

The 2012 constitutional process was an interesting one in terms of gender relations and the protection of other "minorities." Women most certainly are not now and never have been a minority in Egypt, despite their structural disadvantages. Not only was the process somewhat problematic but the final document, which was ratified by popular referendum in December 2012, was left very open and general. According to lawyers and activists, it is a document that is not without controversy. The reasons for this are given below.

In addition to the constitution, women in Egypt are governed by personal status legislation, which specifies the treatment of women in family matters according to their own religious community, as each religion has its own personal status code. It must also be noted that women must belong to one of the three recognized religious communities[13] in Egypt (Muslim, Christian, or Jewish). There is no provision for those with no religion, from a religious minority, or even from other well-known religious communities, such as Buddhism or Hinduism.

10.6 Some Specificities of the 2012 Constitution

Regarding the 2012 constitutional document, the following is important. Articles 4 and 219 were added. Article 4 concerns Azhar, giving it a special position in the Egyptian constitution. Article 219 emphasized Sunni Islam and its special position and importance in Egyptian society, and makes it a point of reference for Egyptians. Furthermore, Article 11 (see below) places the state as guardian over public morality, which makes it relevant for women and their rights.

In fact, the wording used in the 2012 constitution asserting the equality of all citizens, without reference to specific societal groups, such as women or religious minorities, is significant. Women's rights did not feature explicitly in the document, as mentioned above. In an interview with a female Muslim Brotherhood member of the CA,[14] I was informed that the vagueness of the final text was intentional. According to this view, women should be regarded as equal citizens and not specifically as women.

Groups lobbying for women's rights tried to reach agreements between the more conservative sections of the CA—that is, the religious faction—in order to protect what they felt were women's interests. This was not possible, however, prompting them to withdraw from the process entirely.[15] Thus the conflict between the secular/liberal and Islamic factions overshadowed the negotiations. The inclusion of Articles 4, 219, and 198 is an indicator of this. Causing "harm to the armed forces" (Article 198, 2012) was now subject to sanction by military justice. It can also be claimed that allowing the military autonomy over its budget is proof of an agreement between the factions. One cannot claim that this directly hinders women's rights but it limits one's ability to protest to achieve them. Conversely, the explicit omission of women, their rights, and their obligations confronted women with practical disadvantages. In the 1971 constitution's Article 40, citizen's rights were defined explicitly.

Article 11 of the 2012 constitution on morality is worth mentioning specifically. Ambiguity surrounds the constitutional call on the state to protect "morality" in this article. It is not clear what an article awarding the state the privilege to oversee "public morality"[16] actually means. It was neither spelled out how that would be done (in the form of a "moral police," such as in religious/conservative systems such as Saudi Arabia or Iran?), nor what the relationship between the moral principles and universal human rights and equality between citizens would be. It was also questionable as to the justification of such an article in an ostensivley secular liberal and modern constitution. In Article 11 there is a guarantee that motherhood would be protected (as in all previous constitutions). Widows and divorced[17] women receive no explicit mention (see below for the contrast with the 2014 constitution). In this context, the charge may be levied against the CA that its members failed to comprehend the function of a constitution in protecting the individual citizens' rights and to frame their duties towards the state. This is something which is difficult to believe since the majority of the CA were legal experts. It is certain, however, that there were huge internal and external pressures to produce a document that could be put to a referendum.

As was demonstrated above, this version of the constitution was a departure from the constitution of 1971. There were several reasons for this. President Morsi (2012–2013) was adamant about holding the referendum in mid-December 2012 and to have a constitution which represented the interests of his party, the Muslim Brotherhood, but also fulfilled international expectations that such elections would take place.

Furthermore, Articles 40 and 8 of the 1971 constitution are no longer a component of the new constitution. Article 40 overtly forbids discrimination according to "creed, belief and religion." Article 8 forbids discrimination on the grounds of gender. These were vital, especially in light of Article 2. More importantly, Article 5 explicitly states:

> Citizens have the right to establish political parties according to the law and no political activity shall be exercised nor political parties established on a religious referential authority, on a religious basis or on discrimination on grounds of gender or origin. (The Constitution of the Arab Republic of Egypt 1971, 2014)

This is very important to note.

Although Muslim women's rights are central in the Egyptian context, the interests of women from other religious communities are not subordinate. It is important to acknowledge the importance of the role religion plays in all aspects of society, but also to contain this influence and acknowledge that Egyptian society does not exist in a vacuum divorced from tendencies in neighboring countries and societies, and on a global level. Including women as full and equal citizens is a vital cornerstone of gender equality. This also requires securing their rights by codifying them explicitly, as is the case in the 2014 document. In this sense it may be asserted that the 2012 constitution did not exclude women but it failed to recognize their special role and their need for constitutional protection.

10.7 THE 2014 CONSTITUTION

In the following sections I chose to highlight articles[18] which I deemed to be important in the 2014 constitution, but also those pointed out to me by my interviewees,[19] who were involved in the 2013 constitutional process (i.e. specifically members of the CA, such as the vice-president).

10.7.1 Article 6: The Egyptian Nationality

Women's ability to pass their nationality onto their (biological[20]) children, which was actually de jure the case since the amendment of the Nationality Law in 2004,[21] was codified into Article 6. This means that it is now not only regulated by ordinary legislation and ministerial decrees, but it is also a component of the highest law in the land. This right is unique in the Arab world. This could also be viewed as a way to change culture, specifically what I refer to as "a culture of equality" and of vital symbolic value, and creates a general base for broader societal equality. Although there have been problems with the implementation of this law, it was a milestone in confirming women's equality by enshrining it into the constitution. The vice-president of the 2013 CA, MZ, was also intrumental in having it included in the constitution because she was involved prior to 2004 in its inception and formulation. This article has yet to be tested but it gives Egyptians equal rights in passing on their nationality to their biological children, defining the Egyptians as the children of Egyptian men and Egyptian women. Previously, the passing on of nationality had been regulated by ordinary legislation and ministerial decrees, most notably an amendment to the Nationality Law in 2004. Therefore, the constitution provides a basis for the equal treatment of all Egyptians which creates a constitutional challenge to laws which discriminate against dual citizens (Badawy 2014).

10.7.2 Article 11: Women's Equality

This is arguably the most important new article concerning women's rights in the constitution. Indeed, it is so vital that I deem it necessary to cite it verbatim with my added emphases:

> The State shall ensure the achievement of equality between *women and men* in all civil, political, economic, social, and cultural rights in accordance with the provisions of this Constitution.
>
> The State shall take the necessary measures to ensure the *appropriate representation* of women in the houses of representatives, as specified by Law. The State shall also guarantee women's right of holding *public and senior* management offices in the State and their *appointment in judicial bodies* and authorities *without discrimination*.
>
> The State shall *protect women against all forms of violence* and ensure enabling women to strike a balance between family duties and work requirements.

The State shall provide care to and protection of motherhood and childhood, *female heads* of families, and elderly and neediest women.[22] (www.sis.gov.eg 2014)

It is important to note the exact wording, women being mentioned before men, emphasizing their special role and need for protection. Here the state makes a commitment to achieving equality between the sexes. Implicit is recognition of the current lack of equality. The commitment to ensuring appropriate representation is very important and specified further in Article 180, although it does not yet extend to the national parliament. It is left open whether to apply the article to the National Assembly (maglis as-shaab) but does not contain a prescription to do so. Women are underrepresented in the judiciary so it was necessary to codify their appointment to judicial bodies explicitly. It was also no coincidence that the vice-president of the 2013 assembly, Mona Zulfucar, is a woman, a jurist and a (women's) human rights activist with a long history in the field. As was emphasized by several of my interview partners,[23] the state commitment to protect women from "all forms of violence" is a vital novelty. The fact that this expression is not qualified leaves it open to interpretation on the part of the courts in a very broad sense. Should the court so decide, it could also include psychological violence, threat of physical violence and so forth. This is important to note. It was also vital to include "female heads of families,"[24] reflecting social reality in Egypt in which many women are divorced, effectively abandoned, and/or the sole breadwinner in the family. This was not mentioned in the 2012 constitution, nor indeed in previous ones.

Article 53:

All citizens are equal before the Law. They are equal in rights, freedoms and general duties, without discrimination based on religion, belief, *sex*,
[...]
Discrimination and incitement of hatred *is a crime punished by Law.*
The State shall take necessary measures for *eliminating all forms of discrimination*, and the Law shall regulate creating an independent commission for this purpose. (www.sis.gov.eg 2014)

The above wording is very strong and should lead to the codification of new laws, especially as a result of the commitment on the part of the state to establish an independent commission for this reason.

Article 93 deals with international treaties and conventions by expressing the binding nature of all international human rights agreements, covenants, and conventions following their ratification. This, of course, includes the CEDAW, which Egypt signed and ratifed in 1981. Prior to 2004, the country did not fully comply with this Article 9 of CEDAW, specifically paragraph 2.

Article 180 deals with appropriate representation in local councils (25 % women, 25 % youth less than 35 years of age). This means that a quarter of the seats are reserved for women and a quarter for youth, arguably confirming their importance in the January 25 revolution. It was also vital to have this included in the constitutional document because positive discrimination is part of the highest law in the land.

10.8 Gender Law in the Arab Spring Countries: Some Conclusions Drawn from the Egyptian Case

Formally regarding women's normative legal rights, the 2011 Revolution certainly brought advancements. It arguably even brought about the most radical amendment to constitutional law concerning women's positive legal rights. Women seized their opportunity in 2013 to radically renew the constitution, which was a direct result of the exclusion of their rights in the 2012 document (prompted by their frustration with and eventually their voluntary exclusion from the 2012 constitutional process). Nevertheless, this would not have been imaginable without the events following January 25, 2011.

The 2014 constitution is, at least in a nominal sense, a vast improvement on the 2012 document, and it even represents a further development of the 1971 document, especially concerning women's nominal positive legal rights. It is indeed an improvement on all previous versions. However, the laws which resulted from this document have yet to be formulated, ratified, and applied. It has also been noted that changing culture is even more challenging than amending laws in women's favor. Another important aspect is the implementation of law and the codification of laws resulting from the constitution. This is not, however, the subject of this chapter.

Now that the laws have been changed, society and culture in general have to catch up. The problematic articles will need to be contrasted with those described above. This is true across the Arab world. However, the rights codified herein could be seen as being exemplary for other Arab countries.

The arguments above have been made from a liberal feminist perspective. This is not, however, the current narrative nor the consensus in the dominant section of Egyptian society. Egyptians are conservative, religious, and bound to their historical roots. This is equally true for Christians, Jews, and Muslims. What this vital document really means for the majority of ordinary Egyptian women remains to be seen.

Notes

1. Asma Mahfouz.
2. I also term it a "revolution" is how because this Egyptians refer to it. I also use it to denote the beginning of my analysis and argue that it was indeed an important moment and change in paradigm in Egypt. As I am seeking to understand the country from within (albeit with an outside perspective), I use terms employed by indigenous Egyptians. I also chose to base my empirical analysis on those still living and working primarily in Egypt. Furthermore, I should like to note that the word for "revolution" is the same as the word for "revolt" or "uprising" in Arabic. If one looks at the origins of the word—that is, its three-letter root—it becomes evident that it is also synomyous with a bull or ox, indicating something which is strong, single-minded, and possessing somewhat brutish force. It has also been noted that these are both principally different words, but I find the methaphor of a revolution as an ox an interesting one because it is a slow rather than a quick process (animal), which once set in motion is difficult to stop.
3. Interview with AS in Cairo on February 22, 2015. My emphasis.
4. Per referendum in which only 33 % of the electorate participated.
5. Ironically, this was also a coup d'état instigated by the army or "Free Officers" under Nasser's command.
6. Manal al Tibi withdrew very publicly from the process with an open letter. For more information, see El-Tibi, Manal (translated by Bassem Sabry). www.jadaliyya.com. Text of Manal El-Tibi's Resignation Letter to Egypt's Constituent Assembly. October 10, 2012. http://www.jadaliyya.com/pages/index/7777/text-of-manal-el-tibis-resignation-letter-to-egypt (Accessed 18 October, 2012).
7. Personal interview with prominent female activist and lawyer MZ in Cairo in 2013. This view was also echoed by a prominent member of the NGO community in his personal interview with me. I have both interviews on file.
8. Personal interview in Cairo, May 29, 2014, with a member of the 2013 CA. I have the full interview on file.
9. This is from the same interview.

10. Personal interview with a prominant female women's rights activist in Cairo 2013. I have the full interview on file.
11. Literal citation from an interview carried out in Cairo on May 29, 2014 with a member of the 2013 CA HS. I have the full interview on file.
12. This is based on personal interviews and conversations carried out in Cairo in Feburary/ March 2013. I have the notes to the conversations on file.
13. Mentioned in the constitution in Article 3. See http://www.sis.gov.eg/Newvr/Dustor-en001.pdf
14. My emphasis.
15. This chapter is based entirely on interview data collected in Cairo in 2013, 2014, and 2015.
16. HS pointed out in her personal interview with me that this term is very nebulous and it was important to rid the 2014 constitution of such inclarity.
17. It is also ambiguous in that one may pose the question as to why widows are more important than women who have been deserted by their husbands.
18. I do not comment on all articles pertaining to women's rights, but the most important ones in my opinion.
19. In personal interviews carried out in Cairo in 2014–2015. I have the data on file.
20. Adoption is virtually impossible in Islam.
21. Decree No. 12025 of the Year 2004 Concerning Certain Provisions Enforcing Law No. 154 of the Year 2004 on Amendment of Certain Provisions of Law No. 26 of the Year 1975 Concerning the Egyptian Nationality. http://www.refworld.org/docid/432aaab74.html
22. My emphasis.
23. These were carried out in Cairo in February–April 2014. I have the original interviews on file.
24. See the discussion above.

Bibliography

Abdelrahman, M. 2004. *Civil Society Exposed: The Politics of Egypt*. London: Tauris Academic Studies.

Abdoul-Kasem Al-Allaghi, F. 2006. The Role of Arab Non-Governmental Organizations as a Development Vehicle. In *Arab Women and Economic Development*, ed. H. Handoussa, 75–98. Cairo: The American University in Cairo Press.

Abu-Lughod, L. 2010. The Active Social Life of "Muslim Women's Rights": A Plea for Ethnography, Not Polemic, with Cases form Egypt and Palestine. *Journal of Middle East Women's Studies* 6: 1–45.

Afshar, H. ed. 1996. *Women and Politics in the Third World*. London: Routledge.
Ahmed, A.S. 2008. *Islam Today. A Short Introduction to the Muslim World*. New York: I.B. Tauris.
Al-Ali, N. 1994. *Gender Writing/Writing Gender*. Cairo: The American University in Cairo Press.
———. 2000. *Secularism, Gender and the State in the Middle East: The Egyptian Women's Movement*. Cambridge UK: Cambridge University Press.
Al-Ali, N., and N. Pratt. 2009. *Women & War in the Middle East*. New York: Zed Books.
Al-Bazzaz, A.A.R. *Min wahy al-urubah*. Cairo.
An-Na'im, A. 2001. Human Rights in the Arab World. A Regional Perspective. *Human Rights Quarterly* 23 (3): 701–732.
Antes, P. 2007. *Religionen im Brennpunkt: religionswissenschaftliche Beiträge 1976–2007*. Stuttgart: Kohlhammer.
Arato, A., and J.L. Cohen. 2002. *Civil Society and Political Theory*. Cambridge, MA: MIT Press.
Badawy, T. 2014. Egyptian Citizenship Legislation, Private International Law, and Their Impact on Individual Rights. *Middle East law and governance (Brill)* 6: 272–295.
Badran, M. 1991. Competing Agenda: Feminists, Islam and the State in 19th and 20th Century Egypt. In *Women, Islam and the State*, ed. D. Kandiyoti. London: Macmillan.
———. 1995. *Feminists, Islam and Nation: Gender and the Making of Modern Egypt*. Princeton: Princeton University Press.
———. 2009. *Feminism in Islam. Secular and Religious Convergences*. Oxford: One World.
Banaszak, L.A. 2010. *The Women's Movement Inside and Outside the State*. New York: Cambridge University Press.
Banaszak, L.A., K. Rucht, and D. Beckwith. 2003. *Women's Movements Facing the Reconfigured State*. Cambridge, UK: Cambridge University Press.
Baran, Z. 2010. *The Other Muslims*. New York: Palgrave Macmillan.
Barnett, M.N. 2009. Sovereignty, Nationalism, and Regional Order in the Arab States System. In *Politics of the Modern Arab World: Critical Issues in Modern Politics*, ed. L. Khalili, 9–42. Cornwall: Routledge.
Baron, B. 2005. *Egypt as a Woman: Nationalism, Gender and Politics*. Berkeley: University of California Press.
Bayat, A. 2007. *Making Islam Democratic: Social Movements and the Post-Islamist Turn*. Stanford: Stanford University Press.
Berger, P.L. 1990. *The Sacred Canopy: Elements of a Sociological Theory of Religion Anchor Books*. London: Anchor Books.
Black, A. 2008. *The West and Islam. Religion and Political Thought in World History*. New York: Oxford University Press.

Bos, E. 1996. *Vergleichende Außenpolitik*. Wiesbaden: Verlag für Sozialwissenschaft.
Botman, S. 1999. *Engendering Citizenship in Egypt*. New York: Columbia University Press.
Brunngräber, A., ed. 2001. *NGOs als Legitimationsressource: zivilgesell schaftliche Partizipationsformen im Globalisierungsprozess*. Opladen: Leske und Budrich.
Butterwegge, C., B. Lösch, and P. Ralf. 2008. *Kritik des Neoliberalismus*. Wiesbaden: VS Verlag für Sozialwissenschaften.
Casanova, J. 1994. *Public Religions in the Modern World*. Chicago: University of Chicago Press.
Casanova, J. 2008. Public Religions Revisited. In *Religion: Beyond the Concept*, ed. H. de Vries, 101–119. London: Fordham University Press.
Christiano, K.J., et al. 2008. *Sociology of Religion: Contemporary Developments*. Lanham: Rowman & Littlefield Publishers.
Connell, R.W. 1990. The State, Gender and Sexual Politics: Theory and Appraisal. *Theory and Society* 5: 507–544.
Diamond, L.J. 1994. Rethinking Civil Society: Toward Democratic Consolidation. *Journal of Democracy* 5: 4–17.
Diamond, L.J., et al. 2003. *Islam and Democracy in the Middle East*. Baltimore, MD: Johns Hopkins University Press.
Diamond, L., and M.F. Plattner, eds. 2009. *Democracy: A Reader*. Baltimore: The Johns Hopkins University Press/National Endowment for Democracy.
Donnelly, J. 2007. The Relative Universality of Human Rights. *Human Rights Quarterly* 29 (2): 281–306.
Dupret, B. 2005. A Return to the Sharia? Egyptian Judges and the Reference to Islam. In *The Sharia in the Constitutions of Afghanistan, Iran and Egypt— Implications for Private Law*, ed. N. Yassari, 121–170. Berlin: Mohr Siebeck.
El Alami, D.S. 1992. *The Marriage Contract in Islamic Law in the Shari'ah and Personal Status Laws of Egypt and Morocco*. London: Graham & Trotman.
Elyachar, J. 2002. Empowerment Money. The World Bank, Non-governmental Organizations, and the Value of Culture in Egypt. *Public Culture* 14 (3): 493–513.
Enayat, H. 2004. *Modern Islamic Political Thought*. London: I.B. Tauris.
Fahmy, N.S. 2002. *The Politics of Egypt*. London: Routledge Curzon.
Fattah, M.A. 2006. *Democratic Values in the Muslim World*. Cairo: The American University in Cairo Press.
Fergany, N. 2005. The UNDP's Arab Human Development Reports and Their Findings. In *Demokratisation in the Middle East. Dilemmas and Perspectives*, ed. B. Rahbek, 20–47. Aarhus: Aarhus University Press.
Gerami, S., ed. 2001. *Women and Fudamentalism*. New York: Garland.
Gerlach, J., and M. Siegmund. 1995. *Nicht mit ihnen und nicht ohne sie: Die Rolle von Frauen in der Gesellschaft seit 1952*. Hamburg: Litverlag.

Goetz, A.M., and S. Hassim, eds. 2003. *No Shortcuts to Power: African Women in Politics and Policy Making*. London: Zed Books.
Habasch, R. 2008. *Political Participation of Women in the Arab World: An Overview*. New York: UNDP-POGAR.
Hall, S., and P. du Gay. 1996. *Questions of Cultural Identity*. London: Sage Publications.
Hamzawy, A., ed. 2003. *Civil Society in the Middle East*. Berlin: Schiler.
Handoussa, H., ed. 2006. *Arab Women and Economic Development*. Cairo: The American University in Cairo Press.
Harders, C. 1995. *Frauen und Politik in Ägypten: Untersuchung zur Situation ägyptischer Politikerinnen*. Münster: Opladen.
Hart, W.D. 2000. *Edward Said and the Religious Effects of Culture*. Cambridge, UK: Cambridge University Press.
Hashemi, N. 2009. *Islam, Secularism, and Liberal Democracy. Toward a Democratic Theory for Muslim Societies*. New York: Oxford University Press.
Hatem, M. 1992. Economic and Political Liberation in Egypt and the Demise of State Feminism. *International Journal of Middle East Studies* 24 (2): 231–251.
———. 1994. Egyptian Discourses on Gender and Political Liberalization: Do Secularist and Islamist Views Differ? *Middle East Journal* 48 (4): 661.
———. 2002. *The Nineteenth Century Discursive Roots of the Continuing Debate on the Social Contract in Today's Egypt*. San Domenico (I): EUI Working Paper RSC No. 2002/13, 2002.
Hausmann, M., and B. Sauer. 2007. *Gendering the State in the Age of Globalisation*. Plymouth: Rowman & Littlefield.
Herbert, D. 2003. *Religion and Civil Society: Rethinking Public Religion in the Contemporary World*. Aldershot: Ashgate Publishing Company.
Hill, E. 2010. *Women Make Leap in Egypt Parliament*. http://english.aljazeera.net/news/middleeast/2010/11/2010111813029420433.html. Accessed 15 Dec 2010.
Ibrahim, F., ed. 1995. *Staat und Zivilgesellschaft in Ägypten*. Hamburg: Universität Münster.
Ismael, T.T. 2001. *Middle East Politics Today: Government and Civil Society*. Gainesville: University Press of Florida.
Joseph, S. 1994. *Gender & Family in the Arab World*. Washington, DC: (A special) MERIP publication.
Kaldor, M. 2004. *Global Civil Society: An Answer to War*. Cambridge, UK: Polity Press.
Karam, A. 1998. *Women, Islamisms and the State: Contemporary Feminisms in Egypt*. London: Macmillan.
Keck, M.E., and K. Sikkink. 1998. *Activists Beyond Borders: Advocacy Networks in International Politics*. Cornell: Cornell University Press.
Keddie, N. 2003. Secularism and Its Discontents. *Daedalus*.

———. 1988. Ideologie, Society and the State in Post-Colonial Muslim Societies. In *State and Ideology in the Middle East and Pakistan*, ed. F. Halliday and H. Alavi. Basingstoke: Macmillan.
Khafagy. 2007. *Al Ahram Weekly Online*.
Khalili, L. 2009. *Politics of the Modern Arab World. Critical Issues in Modern Politics*. Oxon: Routledge.
Khan, M.W. 1995. *Women Between Islam and Western Society*. New Delhi: The Islamic Center (Publications Division).
Krüger, G. 2006. Islamismus und Frauenbild im Spiegel des ägyptischen Wochenmagazins. Doctoral Dissertation. Universität Hamburg, Hamburg.
Lovendurski, J. 2005. Introduction: State Feminism and the Political Representation of Women. In *State Feminism and Political Representation*, eds. J. Lovendurski, C. Baudino, M. Guadagnini, P. Meier, and D. Sainsbury, 1–19. Cambridge, UK: Cambridge University Press.
Lustick, I.S. 1997. The Absence of Middle Eastern Great Powers. Political "Backwardness" in Historical Perspective. *International Organization* 51: 653–683.
Martens, K. 2005. *NGOs and the United Nations. Institutionalization, Professionalization and Adaptation*. Basingstoke: Palgrave.
Mayer, A.E. 1995. Cultural Particularism as a Bar to Women's Rights. In *Women Living Under Muslim Laws, Dossier 16*, ed. A. Wolper and J.S. Peters, 21–32. New York: Routledge.
Mendieta, E., ed. 2005. *The Frankfurt School on Religion: Key Writings by the Major Thinkers*. New York: Routledge.
Mitchell, T. 1991. America's Egypt: Discourse of the Development Industry. *Middle East Report*. 18–34.
Mitchell, T. 2002. McJihad: Islam in the U.S. Global Order. *Social Text* 20: 1–18.
Moghadam, V.M. 1994. *Modernizing Women: Gender and Social Change in the Middle East*. Cairo: American University in Cairo Press.
Moghadam, V. 1998. *Women, Work, and Economic Reform in the Middle East and North Africa*. Boulder: Rienner.
Moghissi, H. 1994. *Populism and Feminism in Iran: Women's Struggle in a Male-Defined Revolutionary Movement*. London: Macmillan.
Mohanty, C. 1988. Under Western Eyes: Feminist Scholarship and Colonial Discourses. *Feminist Review* 30: 65–88.
Molyneux, M. 1998. Analysing Women's Movements. *Development and Change* 29 (2): 219–245.
Morton, A.D. 2007. *Unravelling Gramsci*. London: Pluto Press.
Naff, T. 1993. *Paths to the Middle East: Ten Scholars Look Back*. New York: New York University Press.
Nardulli, P.F., ed. 2008. *Domestic Perspectives on Contemporary Democracy*. Chicago: University of Illinois Press.

National Council for Women in Egypt. 2010a. http://www.ncwegypt.com/english/prog.jsp. Accessed 24 May 2010.

———. 2010b. *Women Empowerment Through Coalition Building with the Civil Society.* http://www.ncwegypt.com/english/prog.jsp. Accessed 3 Nov 2010.

Nazir, S., ed. 2005. *Women's Rights in the Middle East and North Africa.* New York: Freedom House.

Norton, A., ed. 1995. *Civil Society in the Middle East.* Leiden: Brill.

Nusair, I. 2009. Gender Mainstreaming and Feminist Organizing in the Middle East and North Africa. In *Women & War in the Middle East,* ed. N. Al-Ali and N. Pratt, 131–157. London: Zed Books.

O'Donnell, G., and P. Schmitter. 1986. *Transitions from Authoritarian Rule: Tentative Conclusions for Democracy.* Baltimore: Johns Hopkins University Press.

Pateman, C. 1988. *The Sexual Contract.* California: Stanford University Press.

Phillips, A. 2009. Religion: Ally, Threat, or Just Religion? In *Debate on the Public Role of Religion and Social and Gender Implications,* ed. J. Casanova and A. Phillips, 35–59. Geneva: United Nations Research Institute for Social Development.

Plattner, M. 2008. *Democracy Without Borders? Global Challenges to Liberal Democracy.* Lanham: Rowman & Littlefield.

Pollard, L. 2003. Egypt: Early 20th century to present. In *Encyclopedia of Women & Islamic Cultures. Methodologies, Paradigms and Sources,* ed. S. Joseph, vol. 1, 204–207. Leiden/Boston: Brill.

Posusney, M.P. 2003. Globalisation and Labor Protection in Oil-Poor Arab Countries: Racing to the Bottom? *Global Social Policy* 267–297.

Pratt, N. 2007. The Queen Boat Case in Egypt: Sexuality, National Security and State Sovereignty. *Review of International Studies* 44: 129–144.

Rattansi, A. 1997. Postcolonialism and Its Discontents. *Economy and Sociology* 26: 480–500.

Reilly, N. 2009. *Women's Human Rights.* Cambridge, UK: Polity Press.

Research Network on Gender, Politics and the State. 2010. http://libarts.wsu.edu/polisci/rngs/. Accessed 9 Nov 2010.

Richards, A., and J. Waterbury. 2008. *A Political Economy of the Middle East.* Boulder: Westview Press.

Roded, R. 1999. *Women in Islam and in the Middle East.* London: I.B. Taurus.

Sadowsky, Y. 1997. The New Orientalism and the Democratic Debate. In *Political Islam, Essays From Middle East Report,* ed. J. Stork and J. Benin, 33–50. California: University of California Press.

Said, E. 1993. *Orientalism.* London: Vintage.

Schlenker-Fischer, A. 2009. *Demokratische Gemeinschaft trotz ethnischer Differenz. Theorien, Institutionen und sozial Dynamiken.* Wiesbaden: VS Verlag für Sozialwissenschaften.

Sharabi, H. 1970. *Arab Intellectuals and the West*. London: The Johns Hopkins Press.
Sholkamy, H. 2012. Women Are Also Part of This Revolution. In *Arab Spring in Egypt: Revolution and Beyond*, ed. B. Korany and R. El-Mahdi, 153–174. Cairo: The American University in Cairo Press.
Shukri, S.J.A. 1999. *Social Changes and Women in the Middle East*. Aldershot: Ashgate.
Siapno, J.A. 2003. Political Science. In *Encyclopedia of Women & Islamic Cultures. Methodologies, Paradigms and Sources*, ed. S. Joseph, vol. 1, 404–411. Leiden/Boston: Brill.
Simma, B., ed. 2002. *The Charter of the United Nations*. Munich: Beck.
Stachursky, B. 2013. *The Promise and Perils of Transnationalizaton*. New York: Routledge.
Stetson, D.M., and A. Mazur. 1995. *Comparative State Feminism*. California: Sage Publications.
Tadroz, M. 2012. *The Muslim Brotherhood in Contemporary Egypt*. New York: Routledge.
Teixeira, N.S., ed. 2008. *The International Politics of Democratization. Comparative perspectives*. Cornwall: Routledge.
The Cairo Declaration of Human Rights in Islam. 1991. Cairo.
The Center for Development and Population. 2010. *Girls' Education and Youth Development*. Washington, DC: The Center for Development and Population Activities. 3 November 2010.
The Constitution of the Arab Republic of Egypt. 1971. http://www.constitutionnet.org/files/Egypt%20Constitution.pdf. Accessed 15 Feb 2016.
The Constitution of the Arab Republic of Egypt, 1971 (as Amended to 2007). 12 December 2014. http://www.constitutionnet.org/files/Egypt%20Constitution.pdf. Accessed 15 Jan 2016.
The Constitution of The Arab Republic of Egypt 2014: Unofficial Translation. 24 March 2014. www.sis.gov.eg/Newvr/Dustor-en001.pdf. Accessed 02 Feb 2016.
Tomppert, L., and S. Nazir. 2005. *Women's Rights in the Middle East and North Africa: Citizenship and Justice*. Maryland: Freedom House/Rowman and Littlefield.
UNDP. Arab Human Development Report. 2005. *Towards the Rise of Women*. New York: UNDP. 2006.
Waterbury, J., and A. Richards. 2008. *A Political Economy of the Middle East*. 3rd ed. Boulder: Pegasus Books Group.
Waylen, G. 2007. *Engendering Transitions: Women's Mobilization, Institutions, and Gender Outcomes*. Oxford: Oxford University Press.
Yount, K.M., and H. Rashad, eds. 2008. *Family in the Middle East: Ideational Change in Egypt, Iran and Tunisia*. Cornwall: Routledge.

Yuval-Davis, N. 1997. *Gender and Nation*. London: Sage.
Zubaida, S. 2005. *Law and Power in the Islamic World*. London: I.B. Tauris.
———. 2004. Islam and Nationalism. *Nations and Nationalism* 407–420.

CHAPTER 11

From Lalla Batoul to Oum Hamza: New Trends in Moroccan Women's Fight for Citizenship

Brahim El Guabli

11.1 INTRODUCTION

Moroccan postcolonial history will certainly remember July 1, 2011 as a historic moment that was shaped by the participation of Moroccan protesters. This date marks the first time the king initiated a constitutional reform in immediate response to a serious popular uprising. Even though most political actors in the country had consistently dismissed the urgency of any constitutional change, the formation of the nebulous February 20 Movement,[1] which is the Moroccan version of the Arab

---

This chapter is a version of a paper commissioned by the Tunisian branch of Heinrich Böll Stiftung Foundation in 2013. I hereby acknowledge their support and permission to publish this extended and more argued version of the article. I should also like to thank Charlie Huntington (Swarthmore College) who brought his strong editing skills to bear on the final version.

Unless the source is in English, all the translations from the Arabic and the French are mine.

B. El Guabli (✉)
Princeton University, Princeton, NJ, USA

uprisings, proved them wrong. When the makhzan state failed to market the idea of a Moroccan exceptionalism, in tandem with the eruption of the Arab uprisings, modifying the constitutional text was the only option available to the monarchy to stave off a revolution. Despite the maneuvering involved in the process, the significance of July 1 emanates from the fact that it was the first time a people-imposed constitutional change had been adopted in post-independence Morocco. The swiftness of the makhzan state's reaction and its unprecedented responsiveness to protesters' demands cannot, however, conceal the fact that it has monopolized the reform mechanisms and sidelined protesters' most immediate claims, such as sacking corrupt individuals from the royal entourage. The constitutionalization of Moroccan women's long-awaited parity with their male co-citizens finally crowned their century-long struggle for recognition and equality under the law. In this chapter I analyze four cases from three different historical moments to contextualize Moroccan women's struggle for equity from 1910 to 2011. For each period I investigate the nature of the struggle and how the monarchy responded to women's dissidence. Furthermore, I demonstrate how the emergence of what I call "deep-Morocco feminism" is taking shape in places where elitist discourses have failed to create a sustainable base. Finally, I draw critical attention to the politics underlying the nature of the reforms made to the constitution in 2011.

Despite Morocco's new constitution being the result of a hasty, vertically controlled process, many observers extolled what they thought were its merits.[2] Numerous international religious and political leaders, from Yusuf al-Qaradawy, the Qatar-based influential Egyptian cleric, to Nicolas Sarkozy, the former French president, invested heavily in toppling Muammar Qadhdhafi, and media outlets, both print and audiovisual, highlighted the significance of the new text. Most of them seemed to agree on the advanced nature of the reforms and on the fact that the constitutional document that resulted from them would thrust Moroccans into a new era of democracy and rule of law.[3] The constitutional reform seemed to meet, at least on paper, most demands the protesters put forward, including the ones that both legal and "illegal" opposition parties had been claiming for five decades.

11.2 From the Sultan's Jails to Deep Morocco: Four Moments in Moroccan Feminism

11.2.1 Lalla Batoul: A Feminist at the Turn of the Century

The credit for constitutional achievement belongs to Moroccan women alone. These women made tremendous sacrifices, including the loss of freedom and life, in order to reach this historic moment of the constitutional consecration of parity with their male compatriots. New archival research has made it possible to describe at least 100 years of feminist struggle extending from 1910 to 2011. Thanks to his work in the colonial archives in Nantes, renowned Moroccan historian Maati Monjib (2013) has uncovered the story of a hitherto unknown feminist symbol from the turn of the century.[4] His unearthing of Batoul Benaïssa's story carries the potential of establishing an older genealogy for Moroccan feminism, which starts with her political imprisonment in 1910. Lalla Batoul Benaïssa, whose tribulations were part of the general fight over the rule of Morocco between King Abdelaziz (1894–1908) and his brother Abdelḥafid (1908–1912), could be said to be the "first woman political prisoner" in the history of modern Morocco.[5] After King Abdelḥafid overthrew his brother, King Abdelaziz, he targeted the latter's aides in a witch-hunt campaign. The ordeals of El-Bacha Benaïssa,[6] Batoul Benaïssa's husband, and about two dozen of his immediate family members, emanated from his political position as one of Abdelaziz's closest aides.[7] Even though both El-Bacha Benaïssa and Batoul Benaïssa were arrested and tortured, Batoul's suffering was documented and widely circulated in the international press at the time.[8] King Adelḥafid not only imprisoned Batoul but also participated in her torture.[9] The documents that Monjib discovered describe how her torturers crucified her and did not spare her breasts during their cruel treatment inside her cell in the monarch's palace.[10]

Lalla Batoul was not only the spouse of a powerful political figure at a very critical moment in Moroccan history;[11] she also combined intelligence, beauty, and culture, as well as a great interest in international relations. According to the diplomatic documents that Monjib unearthed in the French archives, this Fassi (aristocratic woman) had a wide network of connections among the Europeans living in Morocco. She may also have mastered foreign languages at a time when Moroccan women were not even allowed to leave their houses. Moreover, everything about her friendships and lifestyle contradicted the conservative atmosphere of her time.[12] Her torture and ultimate jailing in the Sultan's harem could be equally attributed to her modernity as to her husband's affiliation with King Abdelaziz. Although Monjib has not proposed the existence of concrete evidence of Batoul's feminist agenda, her story illustrates the heavy toll that Moroccan women have paid since the turn of the century to achieve equity with men. Furthermore, Batoul's torture in the presence of the king testifies to the fact that the Moroccan monarchy played an active role in the repression of women when they displayed dissidence or did not fit the traditional roles assigned to them.[13] Batoul can therefore be considered to be the first known pioneer modern Moroccan feminist who paid dearly for her untimely independence, modernity, and resistance to *makhzani* authoritarianism.

11.2.2 The Left and the "Years of Lead" (1972–1999): Conquering the Public Space

Moroccan women's activism took other forms in both the colonial and postcolonial periods. Even though their struggle for genuine equality, partnership, and real representation in the political and social institutions in the country took shape under French colonization, these demands intensified in the postcolonial state (al-Fassi 1952).[14] Moroccan women in the colonial era addressed requests to the nationalist political leadership to eradicate polygamy and grant women the right to seek divorce through the court system (*divorce judiciaire*). They also contested Islamic jurisprudence's denial of women's equality with men. However, when Le Code du Statut Personnel (The Code of Personal Status) was written in 1957, the all-male committee deprived women of their basic rights and turned them into everlasting minors under the law. Thus, for many years, Moroccan women were not able to get married without a *walī* (a guardian). They could not seek divorce, or, if they did, the procedures were long, exhausting, and burdensome. Additionally, women married to foreign nationals were unable to pass down Moroccan citizenship to their children. Until the reform of the *mudawwana* (family code) in 2004, husbands had absolute sovereignty, at least theoretically, over the family. When women were granted custody over their children, alimony was usually not sufficient to support them after the breakdown of their marriage. Since the laws lacked the efficacy to coerce husbands to provide their divorcees and offspring with housing, divorced Moroccan women sought refuge in their parental homes in most cases. Exacerbating the situation, the spread of corruption and misogynistic attitudes among the family judges (*quḍāt al-usra*) made divorce all the more detrimental to women's rights. Despite the reform of the *mudawwana* in 2004, Human Rights Watch as recently as 2013 noted "discriminatory provisions in regards to inheritance and the right of husbands to unilaterally divorce their wives" in the new family code.[15]

Reversing Moroccan women's second-class citizen status required the use of various strategies, ranging from peaceful activism to radical action. The experience of women activists of March 23 and Ilā l-Amām (Let's Move Forward!) is of the utmost importance, since they succeeded in subverting the established gender roles in Moroccan society. Their enlistment in revolutionary activism, which attracted attention to their deprivation, shifted the spatial boundaries that confined women to the constrained and constraining spaces of private and family spheres. Saïda Menebhi, probably the first post-independence martyr of Moroccan feminism, Fatna El Bouih and Latifa Jbabdi and their comrades have grown in significance over the years, thanks to their political engagement during the "years of lead."

Saïda will be mostly remembered for dying in 1977 following a long hunger strike at the age of 25. As an unflinching Marxist-Leninist activist, she wedded open denunciation of injustice with covert political action to topple the monarchy (Daure-Serfaty and Serfaty 1993),[16] which Ilā al-Amām held responsible for all the ails of Moroccan society. Additionally, Saïda advocated for the self-determination of the inhabitants of formerly occupied Spanish Sahara. While the majority of Ilā al-Amām's former members, including Abraham Serfaty, its founder, have recanted their positions regarding the self-determination of the Sahrawi people after Saïda's death, her emphasis on this right should be understood as a demonstration of her staunch belief in the people's inalienable right to freedom of choice. Instead of forcing her to renounce her revolutionary convictions, the brutal torture she experienced in Derb Moulay Cherif only deepened her revolutionary political positions. Consequently, feminism and the fight against authoritarianism converged in this determined activist.

Disappearance and illegal detention did not deter Saïda from pursuing her activism by other means. Even the notorious Derb Moulay Cherif, with its myriad torture techniques and cacophony of suffering, failed to silence her poetic voice. In a poem from January 1977 "This Woman Is Not Alone," she sums up the tribulations of Moroccan women through the figurative story of the people's daughter who ended up in jail because of the empowered's machinations against her. Not only does Saïda (1978) depict how the patriarchy has tried to bilk the woman out of her rights, but she also manages to penetrate deeply inside her ebullient emotions to describe the anger simmering within her. "This Woman Is Not Alone" speaks the truth about the interconnectedness of the struggles in Morocco and the universal liberation of downtrodden people all over the world. Even if the woman is suffering in Morocco, she is the "Victim of New York's and Paris's Lackeys' abuse of power."[17] Saïda's poem cannot be clearer about her condemnation of the multiple injustices inflicted upon Moroccan women. They have suffocated under the weight of a double authoritarianism since 1956.[18] The new postcolonial state, which worsened under Hassan II's ascension to power in 1961, failed to live up to women's expectations. Consequently, Ilā al-Amām, Saïda's ideological family, which included women in its revolutionary underground cells, sought to overthrow Hassan II's dictatorship and liberate Moroccans from its grip. Ilā al-Amām waged a fierce discursive and ideological battle against Hassan II's brutal dictatorship from the early 1970s through to the end of the 1990s. Saïda Menebhi was one of this fight's beacons, an effort which eventually led to her demise owing to the effects of a 34-day spell in a jail in Casablanca.

Saïda's de facto assassination only strengthened Moroccan women's intent to liberate themselves. Saïda Menebhi and her comrades could be said without exaggeration to have conquered the public space through their suffering in disappearance and imprisonment. While in prison, they asserted their womanhood and sought the recognition of their status as female political detainees (El Bouih 2001),[19] even though the prison authorities slowly adjusted to the aberration of women political prisoners. It was a sea change for prison administration—whose personnel were hitherto only used to already stigmatized criminals (prostitutes, killers, drug addicts…)—to discipline women who shattered their horizon of expectation. This new brand of female prisoner was feisty, principled, and most of all valorous. Therefore their very presence in jail represented a threat to the incarcerating state and its security apparatus. The outcome of their activism, in jail and outside, is the development of the Moroccan liberal feminist movement in the broadest sense of the term (Salime 2011).[20]

Fatna El Bouih reports in her memoir, *Hadīth al-'atama* (2001), how policemen renamed each woman in her group with male names.[21] This symbolic masculinization of the detainees served two purposes. First, it put these women on a par with the exclusively male police officers, which legitimated their brutal torture. Second, it was the whole notion of being a woman in the minds of these guards that was being redefined; a woman ceases being one no sooner than she acts and behaves outside the circumscribed limits that the male institutions prescribed for her. Consequently, because political activism is an exclusively male domain, women political prisoners, in the minds of these prison guards, deserved whatever pain they inflicted on them. Since they posed a threat to the social hierarchy in which men occupy the center stage, punishment doubly excluded them from both society and womanhood. Fatna became Rachid, the tough guy, owing to her transgression of and encroachment on this men-only turf.[22] Nevertheless, the guards also realized the limits of their methods before a cluster of willful women who not only survived imprisonment but used their carceral experience to undermine misogyny and dictatorship.

Latifa Ajbabdi (2001), in the footsteps of Saïda Menebhi, heroically challenged her torturers and resisted their attempts to break her will. Her resistance, however, pushed her jailers to the brink of self-hatred. Having crossed the threshold of fear and intimidation, Latifa describes how she succeeded at turning the torturers' game against them:

> One day, I was surprised when they put a gun on my temporal bone. I was being interrogated at gunpoint. Fear did not infiltrate me at all. I rather felt that I had the upper hand despite the appearances. I felt an internal sublimation in front of them. My immense stubbornness during challenging times, my unflinching determination, my exceptional ability to persevere since my childhood, and my belief in my choices and convictions were consolidated by torture. Death was easier than giving in, not only because I am an activist who embraces a cause but also because I am a woman, and I had no right to be weak, to betray my womanhood.[23]

She went on to found l'Union de l'Action Féminine after her liberation from jail in 1983. The organization works to "abolish all forms of discrimination against women in all fields (social, juridical, economic and cultural), advocate for the integration of women in decision-making circles, fight violence against women and uproot illiteracy among women in particular."[24] The strong involvement of grassroots feminist organizations such as Ajbabdi's have been conducive to creating the climate which allowed the substantive reform of the *mudawwana* on October 4, 2004.[25] Owing to space constraints, I will not address all the reforms put forward by the new family law, but it is important to point out the essential changes that women have (de jure and de facto) enjoyed since then. Moroccan women have been able to marry whom they pleased without the approval of a guardian. They also obtained co-responsibility for their households. Moreover, the new *mudawwana* set 18 as the minimum age of marriage;[26] restricted polygamy and made it difficult sustain; and recognized civil marriage under Moroccan law.[27] Finally, as husbands lost the ability to repudiate their wives at will, women acquired the right to seek divorce through simplified procedures.[28]

In the wake of the Arab uprisings, a new generation of Moroccan women activists has assumed the mantle of their forerunners. They have taken the feminist ideas even deeper into sections of society where leftist activists failed to establish their presence. However, Saïda's generation, in addition to reappropriating the public space, established the indispensable legal and institutional framework needed for the protection of women. Their failure to enroot their movement in the "dregs" of society, where the quotidian culture and generalized perceptions about women are generated, will be explained in the following pages. Hassan II's death and the removal of many legal obstacles could not but foster the concretization of this shift.

11.2.3 Oum Hamza: New Voices from the Arab Uprisings

Oum Hamza, an ordinary mother of three, who hails from a popular neighborhood in Casablanca, is the iconic figure of the new brand of feminists who have emerged in Morocco since 2011. The failure of the first generation to convince this category of Moroccan women to join their societal project is mostly the result of both discursive and class-related divides separating them. Discursively, Moroccan feminists are mostly highly educated and their discourse, while entirely resonant with the educated people's aspirations, is not necessarily tailored to the marginalized sections of society. Additionally, class underlies the difference in concerns between large sections of Moroccan women and their wealthier and highly educated counterparts. This is in line with Khadija Riadi's controversial statement that some Moroccan feminist groups are disconnected from the daily concerns of Moroccan women (al-Massāe 2015). Therefore, when Oum Hamza and her kind use words such as "citizenship," "humiliation," "human rights," "long live the people," "activism," and "dignity" in their discourse, it is an indication of the deep change simmering in this other Morocco, which has been disenfranchised for a long time. Furthermore, the appropriation of these notions and their reconfiguration into ways that better represent the aspirations of popular women signals deep Morocco's proactive agency.

Oum Hamza's manifesto is simple, clear, and pragmatic. In a video interview posted on YouTube, she details her sociopolitical demands as follows:

> It is my right to be treated for free and with dignity. It is my right that the police respect my dignity. It is our right to benefit from the riches of our country regularly. It is our resources that you use to build (your houses) and invite Shakira and Nany to the Mawazin festival for which you pay billions. This money belongs to our children, to our people. The police and the regime need to know that we are the ones who are paying for their salaries … we are fighting and we will continue our struggle to build a better future for our grandchildren.[29]

Deep Morocco feminism is action driven and directly concerned with the urgent needs of women and girls whom social inequities afflict the most. Oum Hamza's improvised speech directly advocates a de facto, expeditious social justice program. Many other Moroccan women are challenging the authorities in countless acts of unheard-of resistance in domains where men usually act freely. The upsurge of this phenomenon can be witnessed on a quotidian basis throughout Moroccan urban and rural centers. Women's participation in deep Morocco feminism ranges from denouncing the poor quality of education available to their children to protesting against the expropriation of their ancestral lands. Thus, they have been spearheading a bottom-up movement in which women are leading and winning major battles against the very structures that have tried to subdue them. Regardless of its successes, this trend also has its share of tragedy. At the most extreme, helplessness pushed Fedoua Laroui to immolate herself in front of a public administration in Beni Mellal, and Amina Filali committed suicide in the aftermath of the legal failure to protect her rights as an underage victim of rape.

Oum Hamza's brand of feminism is also symptomatic of two important things. First is the existence of a transformative movement among women in the long-forgotten, impoverished and neglected sections of society. This grassroots movement, in which Oum Hamza is the tip of the iceberg, demonstrates failure of the state's intimidation efforts to repress these mostly illiterate women's outcry against marginalization and exclusion.

It also shows that illiteracy, which was intentionally imposed on them,[30] failed to prevent them from gaining awareness of their precarious condition. Second, it suggests the urgent need for more practical social policies to address the structural exclusion, which is the sad fate of most Moroccan women. Oum Hamza's fight attracts attention to poverty, illiteracy, street violence, rape, and the lack of opportunities for youth in a way that resonates with most Moroccans. Furthermore, Oum Hamza denounces the epidemic corruption in all aspects of Moroccan life.

Legislation alone cannot resolve these grievances, which require realpolitik and concrete action to provide tangible benefits to the people. Indeed, this evolution is natural in the course of Moroccan women's activism: a bottom-up movement is appropriating and turning into praxis the ideals of top-down feminism, which has long been at the helm of the achievements of Moroccan women. While top-down feminism set up the institutional structures for the protection of women's rights, the bottom-up movement works within these frameworks to launch subaltern action from the margins to put an end to their exclusion.

11.2.4 The sulāliyyāt: A Peasant Movement Refiguring Citizenship and Belonging

Deep Morocco feminism takes its most potent manifestation in the movement of *sulāliyyāt*. The *sulāliyyāt* movement started in 2007 when the Association Démocratique des Femmes du Maroc's took action to support the struggle of the women from the rural Commune of Haddada in the Governorate of Kénitra (Berriane and Ait Mous n.d.).[31] These *paysannes* from rural areas came together to denounce "the injustice that they have been undergoing for many years: each time they ceded land, their brothers received indemnities, while they were excluded."[32] What started as a localized issue, mostly thanks to the efforts of a retired public servant named Rqia Bellot, metamorphosed into a major national movement of subaltern women. This inspired scholars to work on the elaboration of "a critical conception of ideologies of patriarchy, property, modernism and problems of equality of sexes" in this context (Chalbi-Drissi 2012).[33] The *Sulāliyyāt*, therefore, morphed into a major national movement of subaltern peasant women against the residues of patriarchy, which works in cahoots with the state to preserve their subordinate status. According to Yasmine Beriane, "the initiative of the women of the region of Kénitra transformed into a national mobilization to claim the right of all women of Moroccan tribes to benefit from the repartition of collective lands."[34] Moroccan economist and sociologist Hassania Chalbi-Drissi (2012), in her detailed study titled *Le genre dans les nouvelles politiques foncières au Maroc*, rightly suggests that in the movement of *sulāliyyāt* "we are witnessing the gradual formation in these women of a radical realization of their oppressed condition which, in its recent consequences, may be 'revolutionary,' because by speaking they challenge the dominant order."[35]

The *sulāliyyāt* movement represents deep Morocco's subversion of patriarchy and state authority in the terrain of collective property of land. Having grown up in one of the rural communities that had *sulāli* lands, I have witnessed women's expropriation take place as a quotidian practice. The *nuwwāb* (all male), with the connivance of the state agents (all male as well), exploit the legal void in this field to disinherit the people who cannot fight this overly complicated system. The *nuwwāb al-arāḍi al-sulāliya* (village representatives in charge of collective lands) wield absolute power to distribute collective lands, denying or giving benefits to whomever they please. Thus the archaic Dahir of April 27, 1919, which was drafted and ratified under the French protectorate, has been continually deployed to institutionalize patriarchy and prevent women from benefiting from their right to collective lands in Morocco. Therefore the insurgency against it from mostly rural women and the strong mobilization their movement garnered throughout the country is another confirmation of the deep changes that have taken place among women in these usually overshadowed parts of the country. These developments also point to a cultural change that allows women to confront their male family members to assert their rights. *Sulāliyāt* is also *une affaire de famille*, which means that fettering, supposedly ancestral, customs are being toppled.

Land ownership in rural communities signifies wealth but also indicates rootedness. Being denied a share of the collective lands is tantamount to being stripped of citizenship owing to the connotations of expropriation, alienation, and rejection from the community of citizens embedded in the distinction between *amṣlī/aṣlī* (Berber/Arabic words meaning original in the land) and *imzzi/barrānī* (a Berber word meaning the one who arrived later/the stranger/the outsider). One can be born in a village and spend their entire life within the tribe, but can still have the *imzzi* status. Consequently, *imzzān/barraniyīn*, both men and women, have no rights to collective lands. *Sulāliyāt*'s actions therefore have a wider effect on the way citizenship is conceived and practiced in rural communities. Their activism is not solely redressing the wrongs done to women under the pretext of local customs, which disinherited them, but also refiguring the significance of community, which should be based on a system of duties and rights that govern the relationships within the community. When the Ministry of the Interior issued Directive No. 60 on October 25, 2010 in direct response to *sulāliyāt*'s demands, it not only addressed women's requests but also tried to provide a definition of *les ayant droit* (*dhawū al-ḥuqūq*). This magical category, which the Moroccan legislator did not bother defining for more than 80 years, has been employed to exclude powerless elements from the benefits that go with this classification. Therefore what started as a group of women seeking to claim their ancestral land carries the promise of clarifying an ambiguous *dahir* (royal decree) that has been used to discriminate against vulnerable groups, women included, in urban and rural Morocco for decades.

11.3 THE NEW CONSTITUTION BETWEEN CHANGE AND THE RHETORIC OF CHANGE[36]

The changes made to the constitution of Morocco show that the drafting commission clearly intended to constitutionalize specific, human rights-related demands. The new constitutional text recognized Amazigh as an official language besides Arabic (Article 5), established a de jure parity between men and women for the first time (Article 19), and consolidated individual liberties. Moreover, the text of the constitution outlaws all forms of discrimination, torture, and abuse of power (Articles 20, 21, 22, 23),[37] such that to Professor Omar Bendourou (2014) the new constitution "appears like a human rights constitution."[38] The National Human Rights Council, the official human rights watchdog, has also underlined that the new constitution "provides for the primacy of international convention [*sic*] ratified by Morocco and the domestication of their provisions." Morocco's paranoia about its image abroad may explain this focus. The drafters of the constitution have intentionally appropriated the language of human rights because it proved to be a successful strategy when the state used it to "turn" the page of the "years of lead," and it can serve as a marketing tool internationally as Morocco faces serious challenges on human rights grounds in resolving the protracted Western Sahara issue. Hence, a constitution that deftly redeploys the rhetoric of human rights is more likely to receive the blessings of the international community and give the regime a desperately needed positive image abroad. Furthermore, focusing on human rights in a period of strife may also betray the makhzen state's bid to gain time to better assess the situation when the protests subside. It is easier to incorporate reforms that will remain *lettre morte* for a long time before being turned into executive laws. As a result, while these reforms are commendable, they cannot make observers forget that the balance of power, which is essentially concentrated in the hands of the king, remains the same. The unfolding developments in the country, following the ratification of the constitution, are the litmus test that will confirm or invalidate the genuineness of the changes. As Moroccan historian Driss Maghraoui (2011) clearly states, "While the constitution speaks of human rights, as late as 15 August 2011 there are people from the February 20 movement who are being detained illegally."[39]

If government statistics are to be trusted, 98.49 % of the Moroccan electorate granted their approval of these changes. The share of Moroccan women in this constitutional reform is a legitimate celebration of the adoption of the principle of equity between men and women after a delay of more than 50 years. A few months after the adoption of the new constitution, Khadija Errabeh, a member of the Association démocratique des femmes du Maroc in Casablanca, declared that parity is "a big step."[40] However, while acknowledging the importance of this step, she underlines the necessity of taking urgent measures to resolve the many outstanding issues that hinder the Moroccan women's participation in the country's sociopolitical life as full citizens:

> This should allow progress on many issues, including the implementation of existing laws, compliance of our laws with major international declarations on human rights, and work on new laws which the feminist movement has been awaiting a long time. The fields of action are numerous: the law against domestic violence has not yet been adopted in Morocco, abortion, the reform of the legislation on inheritance, elimination of polygamy, the inclusion of gender dimension in governance and women's access to administration, and political parity.[41]

Errabah's statements, which were published in November 2011, reflect a societal wariness regarding the implementation of the principle of equality. While most of the reactions to the ratification of the new constitution were to the effect that women's problems were forever solved, her cautious comments have the merit of reminding us that what remains to be done is just as crucial as the constitutionalization of equality.

The UN Working Group on the issue of discrimination against women in law and in practice, in its January 2012 report dedicated to Morocco,

> recalls that the Convention on the Elimination of All Forms of Discrimination against Women requires States to achieve not only purely formal or de jure equality, that is equality between women and men in and before the law with respect to formal opportunities and treatment, but also de facto or substantive equality, whereby women enjoy equality with men in practice.[42]

The group clearly cautions Morocco against the potential discrepancy between the legal text and its implementation. However, it did not take a long time to witness this divide between rhetoric and practice in the political arena. When the Justice and Development Party's first government was appointed in January 2012, coinciding with the publication of the above-mentioned UN report, only one woman was appointed in a cabinet of 31 members. The irony, however, was that she was a member of the Islamist party, whereas all the putatively liberal parties nominated two women whose chances to be appointed in ministerial positions were practically nil.[43]

The makhzen state has a long history of using important and divisive issues to bolster its image and strengthen its grip on power. It is within this logic that Frédéric Vairel (2004) calls for a distinction between reform and its language in the Moroccan context. He also warns us about the fact that the "political adjustment of the Moroccan regime does not presume its democratization in any way."[44] Nevertheless, it is important to underline the disastrous consequences of manipulating women's legitimate right to equality rather than merely waiting to see what happens in the larger geopolitical context. In addition to continuing the fight for the implementation of complete equity, the makhzan state should be pressured to resolve Moroccan women's daily problems, which require effective and urgent solutions.[45] When we analyze the *makhzenian* policies regarding women, it becomes apparent that this call for wariness is not a trivialization of the stupendous societal achievement of equity in the text of the constitution. These caveats draw attention to the fact that the Moroccan regime can find ways to buy time when it comes to implementing these reforms in order to emerge victorious when life resumes its course. Wariness is even more critical when we take into consideration the situation of Moroccan women in the global context of human rights and economic development, according to the UN High Commissioner for Human Rights, in these fields Morocco leaves a lot to be desired.[46]

Moroccan women's battle for their rights has been an uphill one, but they fight with a steadfast belief in the righteousness of their demands. The milestone achievement of constitutional equality in the aftermath of the July 1 reforms is but another step in the long struggle for the liberation of women (and men) in a country whose constitution is adorned with beautiful ideas, most of which remain confined to paper. For the constitutional reform to be meaningful for women, it should be accompanied by efficient and serious policies to eradicate illiteracy (40 %), domestic violence (68 %), psychological abuse (48 %),[47] poverty, exclusion, and economic disparities (Skalli 2001).[48] Education and cultural change should be the cornerstone to any effort aimed at curbing the prevalent social misconceptions about women. A liberating educational system, which teaches people that they are equal, productive, intelligent, and independent, regardless of their sex or gender, is an urgent necessity. Overall, an emancipatory societal project is necessary to liberate Moroccan people, women and men, from political and economic subjugation. Only through "the action and reflection of men and women upon their world in order to transform it,"[49] in the words of Paulo Freire (1996), can Moroccans witness a true liberation.

11.4 Conclusion

This chapter has highlighted how equality between men and women is one of the most important changes the February 20 Movement managed to put on the official agenda in 2011. To understand the historical trajectory of the process of Moroccan women's textual equity, I have used four different moments in the development of the feminist movement in Morocco to highlight their enormous sacrifices in their arduous march towards equality and full citizenship. While the story of Batoul Benaïssa requires more research to examine her political agenda and the ways in which it fits within the feminist discourse of her time, the activists of the Marxist movements, both March 23 and Ilā al-Amām, have established the legal and institutional framework within which Moroccan women can work without fear. One of the limits of the Moroccan feminist movement is its inability to ingrain itself in the margins, which I have called deep Morocco feminism, but the distended political atmosphere in the wake of Hassan II's death and the dire economic needs and frustrations of this deep Morocco pushed women from these margins to the center stage. Oum Hamza and the *sulāliyāt* movement could rightfully be called the harbingers of profound transformation, an energy that has fermented in these sectors of society. I have also attempted to attract attention to the dangers latent in the uncritical acceptance of the rhetoric surrounding these changes. Any political reform, especially in a country such as Morocco where the state has a long tradition of using ad hoc committees to buy time, should only be measured by the degree of its implementation in reality.

The ongoing protests in the Rif demonstrate Moroccan women's success at proving inconsistencies between the state's discourse and its actual actions. The brutal pounding of a trash truck owned by a fish merchant named Muḥsin Fikirī as he was attempting to prevent the authorities from destroying his confiscated goods sparked a ḥirāk (Advocacy Movement) that is enmeshed in the unworked-through legacies of six decades of historical injustice in the Rif. Defying isolation, linguistic barriers and social conservatism, both married and single Riffian women have actively participated in an unprecedented political mobilization against generalized marginalization and disenfranchisement. Interwoven in Muḥammed Ibn Abdulkarīm al-Khaṭṭābī's repressed legacy, the unhealed wounds of the Rif War (1958–1959) and the local population's feeling of ḥogra (disempowerment), Riffian women's participation in ḥirāk al-Rīf is a powerful embodiment of the sociocultural revolution that has been in the working in deep Morocco. Nawāl Bin ʿAysa and Sīlyā al-Ziyānī are iconic figures whose harsh treatment by the state proves the failure of the 2011 Constitution to create a more progressive approach to women's rights. Whereas al-Ziyānī has been under arrest since early June, Bin ʿAysa was spared that fate most likely for the fear of aggravating the situation by jailing this mother of four small children. However, she continues to be summoned to the police station to intimidate her. Bin ʿAysa, who has replaced Nāsser al-Zafzāfi at the helm of the ḥirāk since the end of May, is a housewife with no political affiliation. In her latest video, she states that ḥirāk al-Rīf has "unmasked the state and removed all the makeup [from its face]. [The ḥirāk] proved that this is merely a state of slogans, where exist no freedoms, no law, nothing." This iconoclastic woman uses her leadership privilege to point the incoherence between the state's discourse and the reality of human development in Morocco. More importantly, however, Bin ʿAysa undermines this discursive strategy, which the state has successfully used to create the illusion of change while continuing the repression in covert ways.[50]

NOTES

1. Apart from the extreme left parties, such as the Parti Socialiste Unifié and the Parti de l'Avant-Garde Démocratique et Social, none of the traditional parties, including al-Ittiḥād al-Ishtirākī, deemed constitutional reforms necessary. Of course, in a political arena like Morocco's, parties are aware of the limitedness of their margin of maneuver, which makes them refrain from making demands that they have no clout to impose.
2. The pro-regime daily *Aujourd'hui le Maroc* presents statements by Hillary Clinton, Katherine Ashton, Rachida Dati, and a few others in which they eulogize Morocco's adoption of the new constitution and underline its importance. See *Aujourd'hui Le Maroc*. "Réactions internationals." *Aujourd'hui le Maroc*. July 4, 2011, accessed April 20, 2015. http://aujourdhui.ma/focus/reactions-internationales-77995
3. Ibid.
4. Maati Monjib,"Supplice de Lalla Batoul: Moulay Hafid au cœur du scandale," *Zamane*, February (2013): 6–9.
5. Ibid.
6. *El-Basha* is an important political position in Morocco. The most famous Basha in the modern history of the country is probably Thami El Glaoui, the Pasha of Marrakesh during the colonial period. El Glaoui's power was such that he played a major role in deposing King Mohamed V in 1953.
7. For more information about this important period of Moroccan history, see Miller, Susan Gilson. *A history of modern Morocco*. Cambridge: Cambridge University Press, 2013 and Bazzaz, Sahar. *Forgotten Saints: History, Power, and Politics in the Making of Modern Morocco*. Boston: Center for Middle Eastern Studies of Harvard University, 2010.
8. Monjib, "Supplice de Lalla Batoul," 7.
9. Ibid.
10. Ibid.
11. This was a critical moment for the Moroccan state. Between internal strife, owing to the Abdelaziz and Abdelhafid's fight over power, and external incursions on Morocco's sovereignty emanating from European powers, the Makhzan was facing serious challenges to keep its authority.
12. Monjib, "Supplice de Lalla Batoul," 6–9.
13. The Moroccan monarchy has developed its rhetoric regarding women's rights over the years. Because Hassan II understood that guaranteeing the sustainability of his authority hinged upon keeping women in their traditional roles, his discourse regarding women was consistently conservative. Despite the important changes that happened during the last years of his rule, he repressed women and refused them their right to participate in political life for various reasons.

14. al-Fassi, Allāl. *al-Naqd al-dhātī*. Cairo: al-Maṭbaʿet al.-ʿĀllamiya, 1952.
15. Human Rights Watch. "World Report 2013: Morocco/Western Sahara: Events of 2012." *Human Rights Watch*. Accessed May 4, 2014. http://www.hrw.org/world-report/2013/country-chapters/morocco/western-sahara?page=2
16. Daure-Serfaty, Christine, and Abraham Serfaty. *La mémoire de l'autre*. Paris: Au Vif Stock, 1993, 90.
17. See: Menebhi, Saïda. *Poèmes, lettres, écrits de prison*. Paris: Comités de lutte contre la répression au Maroc, 1978.
18. Allāl al-Fassi tries to distinguish between rural and urban Morocco regarding women's rights. While Berber customs, in his understanding, fettered women in rural areas, women's rights in the urban centers faced other challenges. See al-Fassi, "*al-Naqd al-dhātī*," 260–264.
19. El Bouih, Fatna. *Ḥadīth al-ʿatama*. Casablanca: Le Fennec, 2001, 44–45, 76.
20. Zakia Salime, "New Texts Out Now: Zakia Salime, Between Feminism and Islam: Human Rights and Sharia Law in Morocco." *Jadaliyya*. November 30, 2011, accessed 20 April 2013. http://www.jadaliyya.com/pages/index/3341/new-texts-out-now_zakia-salime-between-feminism-an%E2%80%A6
21. El Bouih, *Ḥadīth al-ʿatama*, 15.
22. Ibid.
23. Ibid, 128.
24. "Présentation L'Union de l'Action Féminine." *E-Joussour*. January 17, 2011, accessed April 5, 2013, http://www.e-joussour.net/node/7544
25. Leila Rwihi (1995) explained the importance of the socioeconomic initiatives taken by the Democratic Association of Moroccan Women: "we realized that direct action among women was important as well. Yet, there was another important work which was the pressure we were able to exert, as women, to change laws. This lobbying worked on the four levels of power: political, legislative, judiciary and the media is certainly primordial." Accessed on April 5, 2013, http://graduateinstitute.ch/files/live/sites/iheid/files/sites/genre/shared/Genre_docs/3535_Actes1997/08_leilarh.pdf
26. As late as December 23, 2015, the Moroccan parliament passed a law to extend the use of the proof of marriage to another five years. While the liberal parties and NGOs denounced this law as a way which helps families to bypass the 2004 family code, which set minimum marriage age at 18, the Islamists argue that this extension is necessary to document the many marriages that families conduct without any documentation. While the documentation of marriage is a real concern to protect women's and

children's rights, this loophole is also being used to conduct illegal marriages, which acquire legality through the proof of marriage exceptional laws. On July 9, 2014, *TelQuel* weekly magazine published a story in which it claimed that 35,000 marriages involving minors are conducted every year in Morocco despite Article 19 of the family code. Moreover, the magazine places the blame with family judges who validated 85 % of these marriages. See Chambost, Pauline. "Plus de 35, 000 mariages précoces par an." *TelQuel*. July 9, 2014, accessed February 28, 2016. http://telquel.ma/2014/07/09/35-000-mariages-precoces-an_1408599.

27. Most of these reforms were already contained as suggestions or *ijtihādāt* in Allāl al-Fāssi's *al-Naqd al-dhātī*, in which he formulates his vision of the changes that should happen to the Moroccan family and the place of women in them. Al-Fassi's reform is well known, but it is mind boggling to see how these changes took almost 50 years to be incorporated into the family code.
28. Joundy, Lamia. "L'évolution du statut de la femme au Maroc." N.d., accessed 5 April 2013. sociologos.insa-lyon.fr/.../FEMMESINGENIEURES/fr
29. "Mouvement du 20 Février Casablanca." December 2, 2012, accessed March 21, 2016. https://www.youtube.com/watch?v=FXdT19rXPos. My transcription of Oum Hamza's speech does not take into account the stops, breathing, and elisions that are normal in an improvised oral speech.
30. *Al-Naqd al-dhātī* does explicitly state that depriving women of their rights is also linked to their ignorance and illiteracy in places where the state can normally afford to bring education.
31. Berriane, Yasmine, and Fadma Ait Mous. "Terres collectives et inégalités: le combat des soulaliyates." *Economia*. N.d., accessed April 30, 2014. http://www.economia.ma/fr/numero-20/e-revue/terres-collectives-et-inegalites-le-combat-des-soulaliyates
32. Berriane and Ait Mous. "Terres collectives et inégalités: le combat des soulaliyates."
33. Chalbi-Drissi, Hassania. "Le genre dans les nouvelles politiques foncières au Maroc." *Codesria*. November 20, 2012, accessed April 15, 2014. http://www.codesria.org/IMG/pdf/2-Crises_agraires_Hassania_Chalbi.pdf
34. Berriane and Ait Mous. "Terres collectives et inégalités: le combat des soulaliyates."
35. Chalbi-Drissi Hassania. "Le genre dans les nouvelles politiques foncières au Maroc."
36. This subtitle was inspired by Vairel Frédéric's "Le Maroc des années de plomb: équité et réconciliation?" *Politique africaine* 96, no. 4 (2004): 181–195.

37. Royaume du Maroc. Secrétariat Général du Gouvernement. "La Constitution Edition 2011." *Royaume du Maroc. Secrétariat Général du Gouvernement.* N.d., accessed May 3, 2013. http://www.sgg.gov.ma/constitution_2011_Fr.pdf
38. Bendourou, Omar. 2014. "Les droits de l'homme dans la constitution marocaine de 2011: débats autour de certains droits et libertés." *La Revue des droits de l'homme. Revue du Centre de recherches et d'études sur les droits fondamentaux* 6 (2014). See also "La promotion des droits de l'Homme au Maroc." *Albayane.* December 19, 2012, accessed May 3, 2015. http://www.albayane.press.ma/index.php?option=com_content&view=article&id=15009:la-promotion-des-droits-de-lhomme-au-maroc&catid=44:actualites&Itemid=118
39. Maghraoui, Driss. "Constitutional reforms in Morocco: between consensus and subaltern politics." *Journal of North African Studies* 16, no. 4 (2011): 679–699.
40. Deffrennes, Marine. "Elections au Maroc: '15% de femmes, ce n'est. pas la parité.'" *Terrafemina.* November 25, 2011, accessed April 10, 2015. http://www.terrafemina.com/societe/international/articles/9011-elections-au-maroc-l-15-de-femmes-ce-nest-pas-la-parite-r.html
41. Ibid.
42. United Nations. "Report of the Working Group on the Issue of Discrimination Against Women in Law and in Practice." *United Nations.* June 19, 2012, accessed April 5, 2014. http://www.ohchr.org/Documents/HRBodies/HRCouncil/RegularSession/Session20/A-HRC-20-28-Add1_en.pdf
43. This shows the existence of a double-speak when it comes to women's rights in Morocco. Despite the draconian procedures that a cabinet formation has to go through before the appointment of the designation of the members of the government, no attention was paid to the gender disequilibrium in the nominations.
44. Vairel, Frédéric. "Le Maroc des années de plomb: équité et réconciliation?" *Politique africaine* 96, no. 4 (2004): 181–195.
45. An example of this is illustrated in a report by the Moroccan Ministry of Justice in 2010. According to this, the number of underage girls whom the courts allowed to proceed with their marriages increased from 29,847 to 41,098 between 2008 and 2010. Even though the new *mudawwana* made these marriages an exception, they seem to have become a rule in practice. It is clear that the family judges were misusing their discretionary authority to marry off underage girls (see *Aufaitmaroc*, 12 October 2012).
46. United Nations. "Concluding observations of the Committee Against Torture (Morocco)." December 21, 2011, accessed on April 5, 2014. http://www2.ohchr.org/english/bodies/cat/docs/CAT.C.MAR.CO.4_en.pdf

47. Basch-Harod, Heidi. "Uncertainty for the future of the Moroccan women's movement." *Open Democracy*. March 1, 2012, accessed on 10 April 2013. https://www.opendemocracy.net/5050/heidi-basch-harod/ uncertainty-for-future-of-moroccan-women%E2%80%99s-movement
48. See Skalli Loubna. "Women and poverty in Morocco: The many faces of social exclusion." *Feminist review* 69, no. 1 (2001): 73–89.
49. Freire, Paulo. *Pedagogy of the Oppressed*. Penguin Education Politics, 1996.
50. Nawāl Bin 'Aysa tu'abbi'u limasīrat 20 yulyūz bil-ḥusaima [Nawāl Bin 'Ayssa Mobilizing for July 20th March in Alhoceima]. July 13, 2017. Accessed 13 July 2017. https://www.youtube.com/watch?v=4bGw7Pwamt0.

BIBLIOGRAPHY

Aujourd'hui Le Maroc. 2011. Réactions internationals. *Aujourd'hui le Maroc*. http://aujourdhui.ma/focus/reactions-internationales-77995. Accessed 20 April 2015.

al-Fāssi, Allāl. 1952. *al-Naqd al-dhātī*. Cairo: al-Maṭba'at al-'Āllamiya.

Basch-Harod, H. 2012. Uncertainty for the Future of the Moroccan Women's movement. *Open Democracy*. https://www.opendemocracy.net/5050/heidi-basch-harod/uncertainty-for-future-of-moroccan-women%E2%80%99s-movement. Accessed 10 April 2013.

Bazzaz, S. 2010. *Forgotten Saints: History, Power, and Politics in the Making of Modern Morocco*. Boston: Center for Middle Eastern Studies of Harvard University.

Bendourou, O. 2014. Les droits de l'homme dans la constitution marocaine de 2011: débats autour de certains droits et libertés. *La Revue des droits de l'homme. Revue du Centre de recherches et d'études sur les droits fondamentaux* 6 (2014).

Berriane, Y., and F. Ait Mous. n.d. Terres collectives et inégalités: le combat des soulaliyates. *Economia*. http://www.economia.ma/fr/numero-20/e-revue/terres-collectives-et-inegalites-le-combat-des-soulaliyates. Accessed 30 April 2014.

Chalbi-Drissi, H. 2012. Le genre dans les nouvelles politiques foncières au Maroc. *Codesria*. http://www.codesria.org/IMG/pdf/2-Crises_agraires_Hassania_Chalbi.pdf. Accessed 15 April 2014.

Chambost, P. 2014. Plus de 35 000 mariages précoces par an. *TelQuel*, July 9. http://telquel.ma/2014/07/09/35-000-mariages-precoces-an_1408599. Accessed 28 February 2016.

Daure-Serfaty, C., and A. Serfaty. 1993. *La mémoire de l'autre*. Paris: Au Vif Stock.

Deffrennes, M. 2011. Elections au Maroc: '15% de femmes, ce n'est pas la parité.' *Terrafemina*. http://www.terrafemina.com/societe/international/articles/9011-elections-au-maroc-l-15-de-femmes-ce-nest-pas-la-parite-r.html. Accessed 10 April 2015.

El Bouih, F. 2001. *Hadīth al-ʿatama*. Casablanca: Le Fennec.
Freire, P. 1996. *Pedagogy of the Oppressed*. London: Penguin Education Politics.
Human Rights Watch. 2014. World Report 2013: Morocco/Western Sahara: *Events of 2012*. *Human Rights Watch*. http://www.hrw.org/world-report/2013/country-chapters/morocco/western-sahara?page=2. Accessed 4 May 2014.
Joundy, L. N.d.. L'évolution du statut de la femme au Maroc. sociologos.insalyon.fr/.../FEMMESINGENIEURES/fr. Accessed 5 April 2013.
La promotion des droits de l'Homme au Maroc. *Albayane*. December 19, 2012. http://www.albayane.press.ma/index.php?option=com_content&view=article&id=15009:la-promotion-des-droits-de-lhomme-au-maroc&catid=44:actualites&Itemid=118. Accessed 3 May 2015.
Maghraoui, D. 2011. Constitutional Reforms in Morocco: Between consensus and Subaltern Politics. *Journal of North African Studies* 16 (4): 679–699.
Menebhi, S. 1978. *Poèmes, lettres, écrits de prison*. Paris: Comités de lutte contre la répression au Maroc.
Miller, S.G. 2013. *A History of Modern Morocco*. Cambridge: Cambridge University Press.
Monjib, M. 2013. Supplice de Lalla Batoul: Moulay Hafid au cœur du scandale. *Zamane*, February 2013: 6–9.
Mouvement du 20 Février Casablanca. December 2, 2012. https://www.youtube.com/watch?v=FXdT19rXPos. Accessed 21 Mar 2016.
Présentation L'Union de l'Action Féminine. *E-Joussour*. January 17, 2011. http://www.e-joussour.net/node/7544. Accessed 5 April 2013.
Royaume du Maroc. N.d. Secrétariat Général du Gouvernement. "La Constitution Edition 2011." *Royaume du Maroc. Secrétariat Général du Gouvernement*. http://www.sgg.gov.ma/constitution_2011_Fr.pdf. Accessed 3 May 2013.
Salime, Z. 2011. New Texts Out Now: Zakia Salime, Between Feminism and Islam: Human Rights and Sharia Law in Morocco. *Jadaliyya*, November 30, 2011. http://www.jadaliyya.com/pages/index/3341/new-texts-out-now_zakia-salime-between-feminism- an%E2%80%A6. Accessed 20 April 2013.
Skalli, L. 2001. Women and Poverty in Morocco: The Many Faces of Social Exclusion. *Feminist Review* 69 (1): 73–89.
United Nations. 2011. Concluding Observations of the Committee Against Torture (Morocco). http://www2.ohchr.org/english/bodies/cat/docs/CAT.C.MAR.CO.4_en.pdf. Accessed 5 April 2014.
———. 2012. Report of the Working Group on the Issue of Discrimination Against Women in Law and in Practice. *United Nations*. http://www.ohchr.org/Documents/HRBodies/HRCouncil/RegularSession/Session20/A-HRC-20-28-Add1_en.pdf. Accessed 5 April 2014.
Vairel, F. 2004. Le Maroc des années de plomb: équité et réconciliation? *Politique Africaine* 96 (4): 181–195.

CHAPTER 12

Concluding Remarks: What's Next?

Sahar Khamis and Amel Mili

This volume provides the reader with a taste of various forms of gendered resistance and activism, stretching across different Arab counties, and through several phases. The purpose of this overview was to unpack the complexities of Arab women's multifaceted realities, identities, resistances, and struggles across different Arab countries, some of which were part of the so-called Arab Spring movements, and some of which were not, as well as across various settings, sites of struggle, contexts, and domains, including the political, social, and legal spheres.

In investigating Arab women's multiple roles as initiators and active agents of change, we have explored an array of feminisms, which manifested themselves in various forms, and developed through different phases, ranging from top-down state feminism to bottom-up women's grassroots movements, and stretching before, during, and after the so-called Arab Spring uprisings.

In revisiting the concept of gendered activism and its evolution and multiple manifestations, the chapters have covered an array of topics ranging from the legal aspect, such as exploring constitutional rights as a way to

S. Khamis (✉)
University of Maryland, College Park, MD, USA

A. Mili
University of Pennsylvania, Philadelphia, PA, USA

© The Author(s) 2018
S. Khamis, A. Mili (Eds.), *Arab Women's Activism and Socio-Political Transformation*, DOI 10.1007/978-3-319-60735-1_12

reshape the cultural understanding of the concept of gender; to the political aspect, such as unpacking the bravery and heroism of Arab women who used social media as effective tools to enact their political activism in the midst of the Arab Spring movements; to the social aspect, as exemplified in women who designed campaigns to resist all forms of social oppression, injustice, and discrimination, including sexual harassment.

Adopting a feminist standpoint, which acknowledges women's strengths, respects their subjectivities, and hails their voices, the case studies in this book revealed how Arab women interpreted their multifaceted realities and strived to change them by using their communicative skills, unlocking the emancipatory potential of their own empowerment and activism, and acting as agents of change in their own societies, through engaging in political, social, and legal transformations simultaneously.

We can argue that they were acting as "subaltern counterpublics" (Fraser 1992) who actively defied the hegemonic, dominant power structures in their societies, whether they were autocratic, dictatorial regimes, repressive social structures, or cultural modes of domination, by engaging in multiple forms of resistance to restructure the boundaries between public and private spheres, social and political domains, and online and offline activism (Radsch and Khamis 2013).

To fully grasp and analyze the different forms of activism, which exhibited themselves across different categories of Arab women, in different countries, and in varied domains, this volume relied on theoretical insights as well as empirical case studies, since it is only through this combination of empirical evidence and theoretical and conceptual interpretations that we can arrive at fully comprehensive and deeply nuanced understandings of the dynamics and mechanisms of interrelated, intertwined, and complex phenomena, such as women's gendered activisms, resistances, and struggles.

In exploring the relationship between political activism and gender equity movements, the contributors in this volume embarked on an exploration of these different types of movements, across different temporal, spatial, and topical boundaries and domains. In doing so, they tried to unpack the motivations and triggers behind these movements, and to assess their success in achieving their goals, by posing questions such as: How did women frame their demands within, and across, these movements? What were the most important goals and objectives they had? Were they effective or ineffective in achieving their set goals? What were the most effective tools and tactics they employed? How effective were these movements in terms of networking and expanding their outreach? Which segments and groups of society were closer to women and more sympathetic to their concerns and demands and why? And what were the institutional opportunities that became available through these movements, as well as the limitations and constraints they encountered?

In light of these investigated aspects, a number of other important questions emerged which need to be addressed moving forward:

- What lessons could be learned from the victories and setbacks of Arab women's movements, in general, and from the victories and setbacks of these movements, as they manifested themselves before, during, and after the Arab Spring uprisings, in particular?
- What could be some of the expected opportunities and potentials, as well as challenges and limitations, awaiting gender equality movements in the Arab region, moving forward?
- How can Arab women's rights groups negotiate the ongoing political and social transitions in this volatile region to both consolidate their existing gains and push for more gender-equitable reforms in the legal, political, and social domains, moving forward?

In answering questions about the lessons which could be learned for the future, and what can be predicted or expected moving forward, it is difficult to make specific or exact predictions owing to the transitional, transformative, and in flux nature of this region, which has undergone a lot of turmoil. However, we can attempt to give some broad guidelines and to come up with general directions based on what has been unfolding in this region, so far, in the context of political developments, as well as gendered struggles and resistances, and as revealed through the findings of the various case studies which are covered in this volume.

In exploring the creation of gendered activism at the intersection between politics, culture, and power, across political, social, and legal domains, in different historical phases, and between different Arab countries, it was mandatory to acknowledge how women activists in the Arab world "are redefining the boundaries of private and public spheres, linking political and social domains, connecting national and international audiences, and performing mainstream and citizen journalism" (Radsch and Khamis 2013, p. 881).

In other words, it could be said that Arab women played multiple roles and engaged in different levels and forms of activism and resistance before, during, and after the Arab Spring uprisings. For example, "In addition to influencing their fellow citizens to participate in the uprisings, many young women cyberactivists became influential as media outreach coordinators, citizen journalists, and translators or bridges to the international press" (Radsch and Khamis 2013, p. 885).

In engaging in all of these activities, Arab women were actually cutting across the boundaries between the political and social domains, as well as the public and private spheres, using new media technologies. In that sense, it could be said that "Citizen journalism was a particularly powerful form of cyberactivism because of its capacity to shape the public agenda and put traditionally hidden issues, like sexual harassment or human rights, on the agenda" (Radsch and Khamis 2013, p. 885).

In doing so, these women activists were, in fact, breaking new ground and taking their gender activism to the next level, by influencing the agenda of mainstream media and shaping their content, through a spillover from the realm of citizen journalism, which placed gender-related issues and concerns at the center stage of media coverage.

Arab women's engagement in these multiple forms of activism, both online and offline, in the virtual sphere and on the ground, resulted in multidimensional personal, legal, social, and political revolutions, which we argue, as the case studies have revealed, are far from simple, and far from finished, as they continue to transit and evolve.

Six years after the eruption of the so-called Arab Spring or Arab Awakening movements, it becomes mandatory to revisit the notions of gendered identities, activisms, and resistances, as they continue to constantly manifest themselves in multiple forms, on different levels, through various sites, and across several phases. In this regard, it is especially important to investigate how and why Arab women activists leveraged an array of tools and techniques, including, but not limited to, social media, on-the-street activism, and even artistic forms of expression, such as graffiti, to enact new forms of leadership, agency, and empowerment, in an effort to express themselves freely and to ensure that their voices are heard locally, regionally, and internationally.

In reassessing Arab women's multiple activisms, struggles, and resistances six years after the eruption of the Arab Spring uprisings, it is useful to remember that Arab women's multiple forms of activism and resistance were not born at the historic moment known as the Arab Spring. Rather, as some of the case studies in this book suggest, such as the chapters tackling the Cedar Revolution in Lebanon or the quest for women's rights in Saudi Arabia, there has been a tide that was rising and a wave that has been coming for a number of years before the eruption of these uprisings, and Arab women have been diligently searching for the relevant platforms to enact their activism, in addition to searching for relevant weapons to use in their struggles, such as social media.

Also, as mentioned earlier, we cannot assume a relationship of causality when it comes to exploring the connection between gender activism and sociopolitical transformation, or between Arab women's quest for equal rights and the eruption of the massive uprisings in 2011. Rather, we can only assume a relationship of correlation and association, whereby one acts as a catalyst for the other.

We have to bear in mind that the Arab Spring, as an important turning point, flows from its own historical context that provided it with a set of opportunities, as well as constraints and limitations. Likewise, we cannot detach or separate Arab women's gendered movements, with all their potentials and limitations, victories, and setbacks, from the realities which unfolded in the Arab region before, during, and after the Arab Spring.

In fact, we can confidently argue that just as the Arab Spring movements brought about a lot of promise and potential for Arab societies, but also had major setbacks, or even backlashes, owing to a number of complex factors, the same could be said in terms of its impact and effect on Arab women's movements and its multiple implications on them, which cannot be detached from the overall sociopolitical context in their respective countries, as reflected in these uprisings and their aftermath.

Politically and socially, the Arab Spring showcased Arab women's heroism, activism, and bravery in an unprecedented fashion. As previously mentioned, besides the political struggle that has been, and still is, taking place in many parts of the Arab world, there is an equally pressing, ongoing, gender-specific struggle—namely, women's struggle to secure political, legal, and social gains for themselves, despite many obstacles and challenges. In other words, although Arab women fought alongside men to overcome dictatorship and autocracy, "unlike men, women face two battles: the first for political change and the second to obtain a real change of their societal status to become fully equal to their male counterparts" (Alamm 2012, p. 14).

Yet the Arab Spring has also unveiled the vulnerability of women's rights' movements, and the difficulty of their undertaken mission, since Arab women had to fight and struggle in order to protect their already acquired rights, rather than seeking to develop and expand these rights further.

This could be best understood and interpreted within the context of the multiple constraints and challenges confronting Arab women, in the aftermath of the Arab Spring movements and the new realities they imposed throughout the region. These challenges include, but are not limited to, the difficulty of organizing effective sociopolitical reform movements in the midst of a highly turbulent political environment; the need to fight reactionary social forces and stagnant cultural mindsets and traditions, which are still alive and well in many parts of the Arab world; the rise of political Islam, as witnessed in the success of some religious groups and their rise to power, which could be an impediment to further gender equity; the continued imposition of a top-down, cosmetic feminism, which only serves the elites and those in power and does not take into account the best interests of the sweeping majority of women; and an unsafe public space, which poses the risk of rape, humiliation, and harassment, which are all shamefully exploited to deter women from full participation in the public sphere and to discourage them from continuing their activism and moving forward with their struggles.

One of the most important characteristics of the sociopolitical context which prevailed in a number of so-called post-Arab Spring countries was the shift from healthy pluralization to unhealthy polarization, from unity to division, and from solidarity to fragmentation. Of course, this took several forms and was exhibited to varying degrees in a number of Arab Spring countries, ranging from a full-blown civil war in Syria, to sectarian strife and fighting in Libya and Yemen, to the hijacking of the revolution by two non-revolutionary forces—namely the Muslim Brotherhood and the military—in Egypt. In every case, however, one of the main reasons behind this shift from solidarity and unity to division and polarization was the power vacuum which was created in many of these post-Arab Spring countries owing to the absence of a strong, vibrant, and well-organized civil society (El Nawawy and Khamis 2013).

In light of this last point, one of the most important lessons that can be learned is the need for Arab women's movements to be part and parcel of civil society organizations and other grassroots movements, and to foster better solidarity and coordination across the board. Simply put, women's movements, just like any other grassroots movements, cannot just grow and develop in a vacuum, or in isolation from other societal organizations or social causes. Rather, they need to build networks of solidarity and support, which can contribute to enhancing civic engagement, without which no political campaign or social cause can thrive. In other words, the success of Arab women's gender equity movements depends very much on the ability of Arab women to unite and collaborate with other women, across ideological differences and party lines, as well as with other political and activist groups, to achieve common goals and objectives.

Overall, it could be said that there is a need to exhibit more evidence of coordination, unity, organization, and solidarity within, and across, gender equity movements in the Arab world in order to provide more effective results and more productive and sustainable outcomes in the long run.

Another important point to consider is that although some of the literature on gender and the Arab Spring has documented the role of female activists in the uprisings and analyzed the implications of Islamists' electoral successes for Arab women and their activism, little is known about how ordinary Arab women have experienced the changes that accompanied the uprisings and how this compares with men's experiences (Salem 2015, p. 1).

This necessitates expanding our analytical lens, moving forward, to account for the views and assessments of not only women who are part of organized gendered movements and grassroots organizations, or women who are members of the elite, but also ordinary women who may not be part of any particular movement or organization, in a sincere effort to listen to their voices and to acknowledge their needs, demands, suggestions, and expectations.

This is especially important since the gains which some women activists and elites reaped in the midst of the Arab Spring did not always necessarily trickle down to reach wider segments of Arab women, across different demographic categories, national borders, illiteracy barriers, and digital divides (Salem 2015; Dawoud 2012).

One important research undertaking in the future, therefore, could be analyzing the causes behind this lack of a sufficient trickledown effect from the elites to the masses, and from the established to the emerging activists, in the realm of gender equity movements in the Arab world, and its various manifestations and implications, as well as the possible remedies and cures for this phenomenon, moving forward.

Another possible explanation for this limited trickledown effect could be said to be the digital divide between the technological haves and have nots in a region which has one of the highest illiteracy rates in the world, especially among women, not to speak of digital illiteracy, and where technical, infrastructural, and economic barriers could limit internet accessibility and availability.

Other possible reasons which can explain why no sufficient trickledown effect has taken place to wider segments of the population, so far, beside the high illiteracy rates in the Arab world, especially among women, and the digital divide between the haves and have nots, when it comes to technological savviness, accessibility, and availability, is the lack of a sufficiently vibrant and active civil society, which can facilitate grassroots engagement, through structured channels and organizations. This could be explained in light of the absence of "real," rather than decorative or tokenistic, opposition parties and non-governmental organizations (El Nawawy and Khamis 2013). Another possible explanation could be the narrow focus on urbanization, or the so called "urban bias," which means that most of the communication efforts, media establishments, and different forms of political, social, and economic efforts and initiatives are centered on capitals and urban areas (Khamis 2016), thus neglecting whole segments of Arab populations in rural and remote areas.

These limitations necessitate a discussion of the effectiveness of "cyberactivism" (Howard 2011), or more specifically, in this case, "cyberfeminism" (Daniels 2009; Fernandez et al. 2003; Gajjala 2003; Khamis 2013), and the possibility of relying on it to enact change on various levels in the present, as well as moving forward into the future.

In assessing the pros and cons, as well as the potentials and limitations, of the phenomenon of cyberactivism, as well as its sister phenomenon of cyberfeminism, it would be wise to adopt the middle ground of "cyberrealism" which acknowledges that "the new capacities created by the Internet represent a potential that can be tapped under the right circumstance and that do empower more peripheral groups", while avoiding the two bipolar extremes of "cyberoptimism", which assumes that the internet "will appreciably reduce digital inequality, ignorance, and apathy," and "cyberpessimism", which suggests that the internet "will further increase the influence and knowledge of the advantaged, exclude the disadvantaged, and introduce new possibilities of social control and manipulation by the powerful" (Muhlberger 2004, p. 226).

Adopting such an approach necessitates an acknowledgment of the relevance and importance of new media in aiding the process of favorable sociopolitical change and helping women in their struggle to make it happen, while equally acknowledging some of the limitations of these new media in bringing about this change, since they can only act as catalysts for change, and cannot be magical tools that could make it happen. At the end of the day, it is the actors in real life who could bring about actual change. This was clearly evident in the Arab Spring, with millions of citizens risking their lives in their struggle for freedom and dignity. Likewise, it is only the Arab woman herself who can bring about real change, by bearing the full burden and facing the real risks of her struggle for her rights (Khamis 2013).

Although cyberactivism was "inherently bound by the limits of connectivity, technological literacy, and by extension age and often urbanity, this does not delegitimize the experiences of those women who found their voices and sense of empowerment through their use of these platforms" (Radsch and Khamis 2013, p. 883). This is especially important to acknowledge since "a subset of young, primarily urban, educated Middle Eastern women used networked media platforms to exercise their agency, amplify their voices, and participate in their countries' revolutions" (Radsch and Khamis 2013, p. 883). In doing so, they emerged as influential role models and public opinion leaders for others to follow and to emulate, whether they were other women, or even men, who looked up to them with awe and admiration, as a result of their leadership, activism, bravery, and courage.

Some of the other limitations and constraints of the phenomenon of cyberactivism were the processes of clicktivism or slacktivism, which refer to the fear of substituting clicking for doing, which could give people a false sense of gratification. This poses the potential risk of re-exploiting new media as "safety valves" rather than using them as effective mobilization tools, as was the case before the eruption of the Arab Spring (Khamis 2013).

However, these terms could only be accurately used if a certain person, or party, has the option of taking effective action, but willingly decides not to do so, by choosing to substitute words, or in this case clicks, for actions. However, this is certainly not applicable if the only action which could be taken is engaging in online activism. A good example to illustrate this point is the role of activists who were forced to go into exile, out of fear for their own safety and the safety of their families, and who, therefore, had no option but to exercise their activism in the diaspora. A good example would be the leaders of Syrian, Libyan, and Egyptian opposition movements and groups who were forced to flee their countries out of fear and intimidation. For many members of such groups, their only vehicle of activism, or at least their primary one, became online activism. In this case, it would be unfair and misleading to describe them as engaging in clicktivism or slacktivism. Therefore, one of the blind spots which needs to be addressed in future research on the topic of women's activism is the role of women activists in the diaspora, as members of opposition movements, and the multiple forms of gendered activism(s) and resistance(s) they engage in on an ongoing basis (Khamis 2016).

The case studies in this volume grappled with the fluidity, dynamism, complexity, and intersectionality of various forms of activism, resistance, and struggle, which converged and diverged along the binary opposites of the online and the offline, the local and the global, the public and the private, the top-down and the bottom-up, and the secular and the religious.

In analyzing these multiple forms of activism and resistance, we have to explore a number of important issues, such as why and how can Arab women's movements have a broader popular outreach, as well as a more effective impact on decision-makers, when it comes to shaping policies and improving Arab women's lived realities simultaneously; what are some of the gaps that need to be filled in this regard; and what are some of the obstacles and barriers which need to be crossed. It is only through addressing all of these intertwined, intersecting, and evolving aspects that the effectiveness of gender equity movements in the Arab world in bringing about the desired changes in the legal, political, and social domains can be fully understood, properly interpreted, and adequately contextualized.

It is fair to conclude that Arab women have not just been engaging in a political revolution, as in the case of the Arab Spring movements; rather, they have also been engaging in personal, social, legal and communication revolutions in parallel to upend traditional norms of participation and visibility and to bring new issues into the public sphere (Radsch and Khamis 2013).

By so doing, they are writing a new chapter in the history of their region, in general, and the history of Arab women's feminism, in particular (Khamis 2010). However, in projecting the future of their leadership and activism, one must also consider the overall picture in their rapidly changing region, with all its political, economic, and social challenges and uncertainties (Radsch and Khamis 2013).

Undoubtedly, the mere fact that women in some of the most traditional and conservative Arab societies have broken out of their cocoons and rallied in huge numbers online and offline signals a new era in the history of their region and their evolving roles in it. That is not to say that the popular uprisings in these countries and the political transformations underway will automatically put an end to all forms of discrimination, inequality, and injustice against women in the Arab region. Rather, it means that Arab women today are much more willing to openly and bravely fight for their rights and are more capable of fighting back against stereotypes and barriers to participation, as the myriad online and offline activities that they have been engaging in, in this highly volatile region, clearly indicate (Radsch and Khamis 2013).

In conclusion, just as it is advisable to adopt a realistic and balanced approach when assessing the phenomenon of cyberactivism and the role of social media in enacting sociopolitical transformation, it would also be wise to adopt a realistic, and balanced, approach to predicting the future of Arab women's activism and assessing their continuous struggle for their rights in the aftermath of the Arab Spring uprisings, and their numerous political, economic, and social implications.

In doing so, it is especially important to acknowledge the many gains and victories which Arab women have been able to secure, so far, and the many opportunities they have for success in the future, but it is even more important to acknowledge the many serious struggles, threats, and challenges they are still facing, as well as the obstacles and uncertainties ahead of them.

By unpacking the multiple "unfinished revolutions" in this book, we have acknowledged the ongoing efforts of Arab women and their continuing gender struggles in this region to achieve equity, justice, recognition, and full participation in both the private and public spheres, as well as in the political, social, and legal domains simultaneously. We contend that by looking back at what has been done, and what hasn't been achieved, in the area of gender equity in the past, we can learn a great deal about how we should move forward, and in which direction, in the future. In doing so, we are gratified by what has been accomplished, but we are humbled by what remains to be achieved.

Bibliography

Alamm, W. 2012. Reflections on Women in the Arab Spring: Women's Voices from Around the World. Middle East Program: Woodrow Wilson International Center for Scholars. http://www.wilsoncenter.org/sites/default/files/International%20Women%27s%20Day%202012 _4.pdf

Daniels, J. 2009. Rethinking Cyberfeminism(s): Race, Gender and Embodiment. *Women's Studies Quarterly* 37 (1–2): 101–124.

Dawoud, A. 2012. Why Women are Losing Rights in Post-Revolutionary Egypt. *Journal of International Women's Studies* 13 (5): 160–169.

El Nawawy, M., and S. Khamis. 2013. *Egyptian Revolution 2.0: Political Blogging, Civic Engagement, and Citizen Journalism.* New York: Palgrave Macmillan.

Fernandez, M., F. Wilding, and M. Wright, eds. 2003. *Domain Errors! Cyberfeminist Practices.* Brooklyn: Autonomedia.

Fraser, N. 1992. Rethinking the Public Sphere. In *Habermas and the Public Sphere*, ed. C. Calhoun, 109–142. Cambridge: MIT Press.

Gajjala, R. 2003. South Asian Digital Diasporas and Cyberfeminist Webs: Negotiating Globalization, Nation, Gender, and Information Technology Design. *Contemporary South Asia* 12 (1): 41–56.

Howard, P.N. 2011. *The Digital Origins of Dictatorship and Democracy: Information Technology and Political Islam.* New York: Oxford University Press.

Khamis, S. 2010. Islamic Feminism in New Arab Media: Platforms for Self-Expression and Sites for Multiple Resistances. *Journal of Arab and Muslim Media Research* 3 (3): 237–255.

———. 2013. Gendering the Arab Spring: Arab Women Journalists/activists, 'Cyberfeminism,' and the Socio-political Revolution. In *The Routledge Companion to Media and Gender*, ed. C. Carter, L. Steiner, and L. McLaughlin, 565–575. London: Routledge.

———. 2016. Five Questions About Arab Women's Activism Five Years After the Arab Spring. *CyberOrient*, 10 (1). Available at: http://www.cyberorient.net/article.do?articleId=9772

Muhlberger, P. 2004. Access, Skill, and Motivation in Online Political Discussion: Testing Cyberrealism. In *Democracy Online: The Prospects for Political Renewal Through the Internet*, ed. P. Shane, 225–237. New York: Routledge.

Radsch, C.C., and S. Khamis. 2013. In Their Own Voice: Technologically Mediated Empowerment and Transformation Among Young Arab Women. *Feminist Media Studies* 13 (5): 881–890.

Salem, R. 2015. Gendering the Costs and Benefits of the Arab Uprisings in Tunisia and Egypt Using the Gallup Surveys, Working Paper 913, May 2015. Giza: The Economic Research Forum (ERF).

Index[1]

A

Activisms, viii–xii, 5, 7, 8, 14, 16–21, 54–56, 58–61, 67, 74, 75, 78, 84–86, 90, 119, 132, 138, 145, 146, 168, 170–172, 175, 176, 178, 180, 185, 197–199, 203, 204, 222–226, 228, 229, 241–247, 249–251
and gender, viii, 20, 128, 242, 245
Agencies, 2, 18, 94, 149, 155, 161, 227, 244, 249
Al jameyat al khayrieh (charitable organizations), 75
Al jameyat al matlabiyeh (advocacy women's organizations), 76
Arab Social Media Survey, 57
Arab Spring, viii, ix, 1–6, 14, 17, 18, 21, 27, 30, 53, 54, 59, 62, 66, 74, 79, 84–86, 89–105, 120, 128, 132, 138, 149–152, 154, 167–171, 173–175, 197, 199, 209, 241–247, 249–251
Arab uprisings, 89, 104, 219, 220, 226–228

Arab women, vii–x, xii, xiii, 2, 3, 5–8, 14, 15, 17–21, 55, 59, 83, 111, 128, 178, 241–247, 250, 251
Article 522, 81

B

Bahrain, ix, x, xii, 6, 53–57, 62, 64–67, 90, 96
Bahraini women, 53–68
Batoul, Lalla, 221, 222, 235n4, 235n8, 235n12
Beijing Conference for Women, 77
Beit el-Hanane (Home of Tenderness), 81
Ben Ali, Zinelabidine, 27, 28, 34–39, 50, 51
Bouazizi, Mohamed, 37
Bourguiba, Habib, 12, 14, 27, 30–35, 37, 39, 41, 49, 51, 115, 116, 122, 172
Bouzid, Sidi, 50

---

[1]Note: Page number followed by 'n' refers to notes.

© The Author(s) 2018
S. Khamis, A. Mili (eds.), *Arab Women's Activism and Socio-Political Transformation*, DOI 10.1007/978-3-319-60735-1

C

Cedar Revolution, xii, 73–86, 244
Citizen journalism, 53, 55, 57, 178, 243, 244
Citizenship, 18, 27, 63, 83, 85, 119, 122, 124, 186, 198, 219–234
Civic engagement, 55, 66, 83, 247
Civil rights, 6, 36, 50, 175
Clicktivism, 249
Code of Personal Status (CPS), 31–33, 41, 46, 47, 115–117, 119, 122, 172, 183, 188n10
Colonial period, 103, 235n6
Constitution, x, 2, 3, 6, 11, 28–30, 32, 34, 37, 40, 42, 45–51, 65, 89, 91, 113, 115, 118–124, 128, 134, 146n1, 169, 197, 220, 230–233, 235n2
Constitutional assembly, 40, 118, 121, 122, 127
Constitution-building, 4, 119
Constitution 2012, 119, 199, 201, 203–206, 208
Constitution 2014, 121, 129, 169, 170, 198, 201, 206, 209, 211n16
Consultative Council, 152, 154–156, 160, 161
Convention on the Elimination of all forms of Discrimination Against Women (CEDAW), 34, 41, 45, 63–65, 124, 125, 129, 200, 209
Culture, 10, 14, 18, 30, 37, 49, 81, 85, 114, 133, 137, 141, 146, 198
Culture jamming, 131–133, 145
Cyberactivism, viii, xii, 18, 19, 53, 55–62, 244, 248, 249, 251
Cyberfeminism, xii, 248
Cyberrealism, 248
Cyber world, 59–62

D

Deep Morocco, 220–230, 233
Democratic standards, 3, 17, 28, 51
Democratic transitions, viii, 13, 54, 60, 66, 113, 128, 171, 174
Domestic violence, 35, 73, 79–82, 120, 231, 233
Driving campaign, 150–153, 156, 157

E

Egypt, ix, x, xii, 5, 6, 9–12, 85, 89–98, 102, 103, 111, 120, 124, 126, 128, 131, 134–138, 142, 144, 145, 170, 171, 197–210, 246
Egyptian revolution, 55, 134, 138, 174
Egyptian women, 5, 83, 91, 97, 112, 113, 126, 197, 200, 207
Electoral quota(s), 36
Empowerment, 19, 60, 61, 77, 83, 131–133, 138, 145, 146, 153, 242, 244, 249
Ennahdha, 29, 38–42, 47, 171
Equal citizenship, 3, 75
Equity, viii, xii, 3, 5, 18, 220, 222, 231–233, 242, 246, 247, 250, 251

F

Facebook, 18, 54, 58, 59, 83, 92, 132, 137, 139, 140, 143, 145, 167–170, 173–188
Family law, 31, 32, 41, 46, 54, 62, 64–68, 85, 225
February 20, 219
February 20 movement, 219, 231, 233
Female activism, 53, 54, 61, 132, 138, 145, 210n7, 247

Feminism, xi, 8–21, 79, 80, 105, 173, 220–230, 233, 241, 246, 250
Feminist, 6, 7, 11, 12, 15–19, 21, 40, 51, 79, 80, 83, 95, 97, 103, 132, 153, 172, 198, 210, 221, 222, 224–226, 231, 233, 242
Feminist theory, 22
Freedom House, 69n17

G
Gender complementarity, 30
Gender Development Index (GDI), 28, 33
Gender discrimination, 111, 121, 122
Gender equality, ix, 3, 6, 15, 21, 22, 27–51, 77, 80, 111, 113, 114, 120, 121, 131, 158, 169, 173, 183, 198, 206, 243
vs. gender complementarity, 30
Gender law, 199–201, 209, 210
Gender norms, 197
Gender standards, 3, 11, 12, 17, 28, 35, 51, 112, 116, 117, 119, 128
Gendered movements, 245, 247
Graffiti, 98, 132, 141, 142, 146, 244

H
Hamza, Oum, 226–228, 233, 237n29
Hariri, Rafiq, 77, 78
Hariri, Saad, 78
Hezbollah, 78
Human Development Index (HDI), 28
Human rights, 10, 12, 14, 28, 51, 55, 58, 61, 74, 76, 80, 85, 95, 120, 122, 128, 135, 139, 173, 186, 187, 198, 200, 203, 205, 209, 223, 226, 230–232, 244

I
Independent, 12, 15, 38, 44, 48, 55, 84, 85, 101, 118, 142, 183, 200, 201, 203, 208, 233
Islam is the Answer, 115
Islam and politics, 8
Islamist gender agenda, 113
Islamists, 34, 89, 91, 95–98, 100, 103, 104, 113–118, 121, 126, 128, 168–173, 198, 203, 232, 236n26, 247
vs. modernists, 169, 171

J
Jasmine Revolution, 167–189
Jumblat, Nora, 77, 78
Jumblat, Walid, 77

K
KAFA, 80–82
Karman, Tawakkul, 59

L
Labor, 47, 93–96, 98, 123, 149, 154, 155, 163n28
Laws, 6, 30, 54, 73, 91, 112, 151, 172, 199, 220
Lebanese civil war, 83
Lebanese Council of Women, 75, 76
Lebanese Human Rights Association, 76
Lebanon, ix, xii, 6, 9, 11, 73–86, 244
Lebanon Spring Revolution, 74
Legal rights, 14, 77, 80, 105, 209
Libya, 11, 89, 90, 92, 113, 120, 121, 126, 128, 246
Libya's transitional council, 92

M

March 8th 2005, 78
March 14, 2005, 78
Media activism, 56
MENA region, 132, 168, 174
Middle East, 31, 56, 90, 94, 101, 141, 145
Moghaizel, Joseph, 76
Moghaizel, Laure, 76
Moroccan exceptionalism, 220
Moroccan women, 219–234, 236n25
Morocco, ix, xii, 6, 11, 13, 90, 100, 170, 220, 221, 224, 226, 229–234, 235n1, 235n2, 235n6, 235n7, 235n11, 236n18, 237n26, 238n43
Morsi, Mohamed, 91, 206
Mudawwana, 222, 223, 225, 226, 238n45
Muslim Brotherhood (MB), 4, 92, 102, 120, 134, 202, 203, 205, 206, 246
Mutaw'in (members of the Committee for the Promotion of Virtue and Prevention of Vice), 151

N

Nasawiya, 80, 81, 83
Normative legal chance, 209
North Africa, 90, 94, 100–103

O

Occupy Movements, 167, 180
Opposition, 14, 16, 34, 36, 42, 56, 60, 62, 65, 67, 103, 116, 119, 120, 122, 124, 157, 160, 161, 172, 248–250

P

Parity, 38–40, 42–45, 49, 91, 127, 128, 183, 220, 221, 231
Patriarchal bargaining, 149, 150, 159
Pearl Roundabout, 65, 96
Performativity, 150
Pioneers, 75, 112, 128, 173, 222
Political Islam, 15, 20, 115, 171, 173, 246
Political transitions, 2, 21, 28, 51, 62, 111, 112, 168, 170
Positive legal rights, 209
Post-colonial period, 222
Post-revolution, 40
Power vacuum, 37, 111, 246
Private public spaces, 93
Private sphere, xii, 16, 18, 20, 86, 201, 242, 244
Protests, 1, 2, 21, 27, 28, 37, 46, 50, 54, 55, 57, 59–62, 64, 65, 73, 74, 77–79, 81, 84, 85, 91, 96–98, 104, 105, 111, 113, 119, 122, 131, 132, 134, 140, 146n1, 150, 151, 156, 162n6, 167, 174, 175, 197, 219, 220, 227, 231
Public space, 15, 16, 44, 89, 90, 92–102, 104, 105n1, 114, 120, 125, 126, 144, 222–226, 246

Q

Qur'an, 32, 118

R

Reform, viii, ix, xiii, 1, 3, 8, 9, 11, 13, 17, 20, 27, 31, 32, 34, 53, 54, 60, 76, 77, 103, 105, 113, 116, 117, 149, 154, 171, 172, 182, 185, 203, 219, 220, 222, 223,

225, 231–234, 235n1, 237n27, 243, 246
Religious discourses, 111–129
Religious parties, 3, 4, 14, 27, 47, 111–113, 116, 117, 120, 121, 123–126, 128
Reporters without border, 56, 58, 68n3
Resistances, viii–xii, 3, 7, 8, 21, 27, 59, 66, 84, 86, 111, 141–144, 146, 171, 222, 225, 227, 241–244, 250

S
Al-Sissi, Abdel Fattah, 91
Saudi Arabia, ix, xii, 6, 37, 58, 149, 150, 152–155, 157, 159, 161, 205, 244
Saudi Arabian women, 150
Saudization, 154
Secular discourses, 104, 112, 119, 121
Secularists, 96, 102, 169, 185
Sexual harassment, 82, 83, 89, 91, 98, 131–146, 198, 242, 244
Sharia courts, 63, 64
Sharia law, 41, 45, 112, 115–119, 121, 129, 188n5
Shia/Sunni divide, 61
Slacktivism, 168, 174–176, 185, 249
Social media, 2, 18, 19, 53–58, 60, 62, 66, 67, 68n5, 80, 89, 132, 136, 138, 139, 143–145, 151, 167–189, 242, 244, 245, 251
State building and gender, 30–34, 50, 115
State feminism, xii, 12–15, 17, 20, 97, 101, 102, 104, 172, 241
State identity, 117
Stealth revolution, 149–161

Sulāliyāt, 229, 230, 233
Sunna, 118
Syrian occupation, 79, 86

T
Taef Peace Accord, 77
Tahrir Square, x, 96, 126, 135, 136, 141, 199
Tunisia, 1, 27, 89, 111, 168, 197, 251
Tunisian constitution, 30, 49, 119
Tunisian revolution, 29, 50, 51, 56, 186, 187
Tunisia's National Constitutional Assembly, 28–30, 37, 41–43, 45, 48
Tunisian women, 3, 35, 44, 97, 112, 120, 169–171, 173, 177, 183, 186, 187

U
United Nations Development Programme (UNDP), 28, 176
Universalist human rights discourses, 90

V
Virginity tests, x, 89, 146

W
Women's activism, x, xi, 35, 60–63, 67, 223, 243, 244, 247, 250
Women's movement, 75, 76, 84, 167, 168, 200
Women's organizations, 44, 75–77
Women's rights, 40, 41, 46, 49, 73–86, 90, 100, 101, 112, 113, 116, 117, 120–122, 128, 169,

Women's rights (*cont.*)
  170, 172, 198–200, 203–205,
  207, 211n10, 211n18
Women's role in society, 111

Y
Yacoub, Roula, 73, 81
Yemen, 11, 90, 96, 113, 120,
  246

Printed by Printforce, the Netherlands